AF748833

Religion, Spirituality, and Masculinity

Religion, Spirituality, and Masculinity provides concrete, practical suggestions for mental health professionals. Drawing from decades of clinical experience working with men and interdisciplinary insights from psychology, sociology, religion, and more, the authors explore some of the most salient aspects of men's mental and spiritual health.

Chapters focus on topics such as men's relationships to religion and to masculinity, shame, and forgiveness, and concerns such as pornography use and drifting between religious affiliations. In addition to relevant theory and research, each chapter includes a case study and clear, science-informed strategies that can be incorporated into everyday practice in ways that improve men's health and wellbeing.

Anthony Isacco, PhD, is a licensed psychologist and associate professor in the graduate psychology program at Chatham University in Pittsburgh, USA.

Jay C. Wade, PhD, is a licensed psychologist in private practice in Bali, Indonesia. He is a fellow and past president of APA Division 51, the Society for the Psychological Study of Men and Masculinities, and a former associate professor of psychology at Fordham University, USA.

The Routledge Series on Counseling and Psychotherapy with Boys and Men

The Routledge Series on Counseling and Psychotherapy with Boys and Men includes books devoted to the process of helping boys and men in counseling and psychotherapy. Topics addressed include: counseling gay boys and men; addictions counseling with boys and men; helping older men; couples counseling with men; counseling gifted boys; assisting men with the transition to fatherhood; helping men with emotional intimacy; counseling boys with attention deficit hyperactivity disorder; counseling boys and men from different racial and ethnic backgrounds; and counseling aggressive boys.

Series Editor: Mark S. Kiselica, The College of New Jersey, USA

Men, Addiction, and Intimacy
Strengthening Recovery by Fostering the Emotional Development of Boys and Men
Mark S. Woodford

Breaking Barriers in Counseling Men
Insights and Innovations
Edited by Aaron Rochlen and Fredric E. Rabinowitz

Counseling Widowers
Jason Troyer

Counseling Gay Men, Adolescents, and Boys
A Strengths-Based Guide for Helping Professionals and Educators
Edited by Michael M. Kocet

Religion, Spirituality, and Masculinity
New Insights for Counselors
Anthony Isacco and Jay C. Wade

For more information about this series, please visit: www.routledge.com/The-Routledge-Series-on-Counseling-and-Psychotherapy-with-Boys-and-Men/book-series/RSCPBM

Religion, Spirituality, and Masculinity

New Insights for Counselors

Anthony Isacco and Jay C. Wade

Routledge
Taylor & Francis Group
NEW YORK AND LONDON

First published 2019
by Routledge
52 Vanderbilt Avenue, New York, NY 10017

and by Routledge
2 Park Square, Milton Park, Abingdon, Oxon, OX14 4RN

Routledge is an imprint of the Taylor & Francis Group, an informa business

© 2019 Taylor & Francis

The right of Anthony Isacco and Jay C. Wade to be identified as authors of this work has been asserted by them in accordance with sections 77 and 78 of the Copyright, Designs and Patents Act 1988.

All rights reserved. No part of this book may be reprinted or reproduced or utilised in any form or by any electronic, mechanical, or other means, now known or hereafter invented, including photocopying and recording, or in any information storage or retrieval system, without permission in writing from the publishers.

Trademark notice: Product or corporate names may be trademarks or registered trademarks, and are used only for identification and explanation without intent to infringe.

Library of Congress Cataloging-in-Publication Data
Names: Isacco, Anthony, author. | Wade, Jay C., author.
Title: Religion, spirituality, and masculinity : new insights for counselors / Anthony Isacco and Jay C. Wade.
Description: New York : Routledge, 2019. | Series: The Routledge series on counseling and psychotherapy with boys and men | Includes bibliographical references and index.
Identifiers: LCCN 2018059780 (print) | LCCN 2019004100 (ebook) | ISBN 9781315231488 (eBook) | ISBN 9781138280762 (hardback) | ISBN 9781138280779 (pbk.)
Subjects: LCSH: Men—Psychology. | Masculinity—Religious aspects.
Classification: LCC BF692.5 (ebook) | LCC BF692.5 .I73 2019 (print) | DDC 155.3/32—dc23
LC record available at https://lccn.loc.gov/2018059780

ISBN: 978-1-138-28076-2 (hbk)
ISBN: 978-1-138-28077-9 (pbk)
ISBN: 978-1-315-23148-8 (ebk)

Typeset in Bembo
by Swales & Willis, Exeter, Devon, UK

I would like to dedicate this book to the women in my life that make me a better man, Celeste, Sophia, Claire, Gianna, and Monica.

– Anthony

I would like to dedicate this book to my parents, Jean and J.C.

– Jay

Contents

Figures

Tables

About the Authors

Anthony Isacco, PhD, is a licensed psychologist in Pennsylvania and associate professor in the Graduate Psychology Programs at Chatham University in Pittsburgh, USA. His clinical practice is focused on the psychological assessment of Catholic deacons, seminarians, and women religious.

He has published widely in academic journals in the area of the psychology of men's health and has conducted empirical studies focused on Catholic priests and their health and wellbeing. He is the co-author of *All In: Breaking Barriers to Discerning the Priesthood* (2018, Lambing Press). Dr. Isacco earned a PhD in counseling psychology from Loyola University Chicago, a master's degree in counseling psychology from Boston College, and bachelor's degrees in psychology and philosophy from Franciscan University of Steubenville, all USA. He is a member of the American Psychological Association, Catholic Psychotherapist Association (CPA), and the CPA Seminary Assessment Working Group.

Jay C. Wade, PhD, is a licensed psychologist in New York, and licensed occupational therapist in New York and Maryland, USA. After a 17-year career working in mental health as an occupational therapist he began a career as a professor in the clinical psychology doctoral program at Fordham University in New York. Dr. Wade received his bachelor's degree from Morehouse College in Atlanta, Georgia, his master's in occupational therapy from Columbia University College of Physicians and Surgeons in New York City, and his doctorate in counseling psychology from the University of Maryland in College Park, all USA. Dr. Wade is a Fellow and past president of APA Division 51, the Society of the Psychological Study of Men and Masculinities. He currently resides in Bali and maintains a private practice.

Series Editor's Foreword

Spirituality is considered to be an essential part of the human experience, a key dimension of wellness, and critical to overall life satisfaction (Moe, Perera-Diltz, & Rodriguez, 2012). In many cultures, spirituality is a source of strength that can buffer individuals from "the negative effects of stress, and/or as variables that promote optimal functioning" (Pedrotti, Edwards, & Lopez, 2009, p. 54). Because membership in a religious denomination can foster supportive communities and a profound sense of meaning, "people who describe themselves as 'spiritual' or 'religious' report higher levels of happiness than those who do not" (Watson & Naragon, 2009, p. 211).

Certain conceptions of spirituality can have detrimental effects, however. For example, "exclusively harsh and premature conceptions of God can interfere with the capacity to enjoy pleasures in life . . . [and] have been tied to higher levels of psychological distress" (Shapiro, 2009, p. 615). People may apply spiritual solutions in inappropriate ways, such as those who reject medical help for serious illnesses and instead defer to the will of God, often with dire – and sometimes fatal – consequences. And members of rigidly dogmatic faith traditions may be the victims of scorn and rejection if they fail to abide by the norms of their congregations (Shapiro, 2009).

Pertinent to this book series, which is focused on men and masculinity, it is important to note that spirituality and religion can influence how males define their conceptions of what it means to be a man, husband, partner, father, and citizen (Kiselica, 2008; Kiselica, Benton-Wright, & Englar-Carlson, 2016; Wong, Liu, & Klann, 2017). Notions of masculinity vary across and within religions, with some faith traditions emphasizing tender manhood and others exalting tougher masculinity (Hofstede, 2016). These notions can have an impact on a man's behavior, functioning, gender role conflicts, and mental health, and they can affect the degree to which men are accepted in their faith communities (Jurkovic & Walker, 2006; Mahalik & Lagan, 2001; Robertson, 2012).

Considering the many potential influences that religion and spirituality can have on people's self-concepts and their wellbeing, authorities of counseling recommend that mental health professionals explore the spiritual dimension of their clients' lives throughout the process of counseling and psychotherapy, starting with an assessment of the role of religion and spirituality in the lives of clients and how clients define themselves spiritually; continuing with an exploration of their clients' spiritual issues and search for meaning; and utilizing spirituality as a potential resource with clients (Corey, 2006; Young & Cashwell, 2014). Accordingly, when I developed the *Routledge Series on Counseling and Psychotherapy with Boys and Men*, I determined that a book addressing men's spiritual lives would have to be a volume featured in the series. To our good fortune, Dr. Anthony Isacco, Associate Professor of Psychology at Chatham University, and Dr. Jay Wade, a former Professor of Psychology at Fordham University and former President of the Society for the Psychological Study of Men and Masculinity, accepted my call for just such a book, producing *Religion, Spirituality and Masculinity: New Insights for Counselors.*

Drs. Isacco and Wade are two of our nation's most highly respected scholars of the psychology of men and masculinity. Their collective wisdom on understanding and helping men and their expertise about spirituality and counseling make them a most fitting pair of authorities to author this book for the series. Writing in an accessible manner and with a soothing tone, Drs. Isacco and Wade have made a strong case for the important, positive roles that religion, prayer, going to church, and forgiveness can play in men's lives and in men's conceptions of masculinity. They argue convincingly that even men who consider themselves not to be affiliated with any organized religion have spiritual beliefs and issues that can affect their lives, and these become important topics when those men seek help through counseling and psychotherapy. The authors offer excellent suggestions for the process of addressing religion with men during counseling, including the use of prayer in counseling with religious men, and how to address men's shame. The special spiritual issues and needs of gay men and men who are spiritual drifters are addressed, and the detrimental impact of pornography on men's spiritual lives and mental health are documented, as are strategies for helping men to lead sexually healthier lives. Drs. Wade and Isacco strike a nice balance of theoretical concepts, research findings, and practical recommendations, which are powerfully supplemented by valuable case examples and tables summarizing key concepts for each chapter.

Fittingly for this series on men, Drs. Isacco and Wade have weaved the literature on the psychology of men and masculinity throughout the book, helping us to view the spiritual lives and needs of men through a gender-sensitive lens. They conclude their book by proposing a timely conceptual model for relationships among religion/spirituality, masculinity, and men's health, explaining how to apply the model in counseling. In short, they have provided us with a definitive guide to the practice of spiritual counseling with men, thereby making an important contribution to the literatures on the psychology of men and masculinity, and spirituality and counseling.

I applaud Drs. Isacco and Wade for their fine work, and I am honored to have their book as a volume in this series.

Mark Kiselica, Series Editor
The Routledge Series on Counseling and Psychotherapy with Boys and Men
Cabrini University, USA
October 21, 2018

References

Corey, G. (2006). Integrating spirituality in counseling practice. *Vistas Online: Article 25.* Retrieved at www.counseling.org/docs/default-source/vistas/integrating-spirituality-in-counseling-practice.pdf?sfvrsn=7ddd7e2c_10.

Hofstede, G. (2016). Masculinity at the national, cultural level. In Y. J. Wong & S. R. Wester (Eds.), *APA handbook of men and masculinities* (pp. 173–186). Washington, DC: American Psychological Association.

Jurkovic, D., & Walker, G. A. (2006). Examining masculine gender-role conflict and stress in relation to religious orientation and spiritual well-being in Australian men. *Journal of Men's Studies, 14*, 27–46.

Kiselica, M. S. (2008). *When boys become parents: Adolescent fatherhood in America.* New Brunswick, NJ: Rutgers University Press.

Kiselica, M. S., Benton-Wright, S., & Englar-Carlson, M. (2016). Accentuating positive masculinity: A new foundation for the psychology of boys, men, and masculinity. In Y. J. Wong & S. R. Wester (Eds.), *APA Handbook of men and masculinities* (pp. 123–143). Washington, DC: American Psychological Association.

Mahalik, J. R., & Lagan, H. (2001). Examining masculine gender role and stress in relation to religious orientation and spiritual well-being. *Psychology of Men & Masculinity, 2*, 24–33.

Moe, J. L., Perera-Diltz, D. M., & Rodriguez, T. (2012). Counseling for wholeness: Integrating holistic wellness into case conceptualization and treatment planning. *Ideas and Research You Can Use: Vistas 2012, Volume 1.* Retrieved at www.counseling.org/docs/default-source/vistas/vistas_2012_article_31.

Pedrotti, J. T., Edwards, L. M., & Lopez, S. J. (2009). Positive psychology within a cultural context. In S. J. Lopez & C. R. Snyder (Eds.), *The Oxford handbook of positive psychology* (2nd ed., pp. 49–57). New York: Oxford University Press.

Robertson, J. M. (2012). *Tough guys and true believers: Managing authoritarian men in the psychotherapy room.* New York: Routledge.

Shapiro, S. L. (2009). Meditation and positive psychology. In S. J. Lopez & C. R. Snyder (Eds.), *The Oxford handbook of positive psychology* (2nd ed., pp. 601–619). New York: Oxford University Press.

Watson, D., & Naragon, K. (2009). Positive affectivity: The disposition to experience positive emotional states. In S. J. Lopez & C. R. Snyder (Eds.), *The Oxford handbook of positive psychology* (2nd ed., pp. 207–215). New York: Oxford University Press.

Wong, Y. J., Liu, T., & Klann, E. M. (2017). The intersection of race, ethnicity, and masculinities: Progress, problems and prospects. In R. F. Levant & Y. J. Wong (Eds.), *The psychology of men and masculinities* (pp. 261–288). Washington, DC: American Psychological Association.

Young, J. S., & Cashwell, C. S. (2014). Integrating spirituality and religion into counseling: An introduction. In C. S. Young & J. S. Young (Eds.), *Integrating spirituality and religion into counseling: A guide to competent practice* (2nd ed., pp. 1–24). Alexandria, VA: American Counseling Association.

Acknowledgments

There are many people to thank such as professional colleagues who have supported and contributed to our work (James O'Neill, Jon Davies, David Shen-Miller, Thomas Plante, Britney Brinkman, Deanna Hamilton, Mary Beth Mannarino, Christina Lynch, Matt Englar-Carlson, Craig Garfield, Ethan Sahker), Chatham University students who were tremendous research assistants (Kate Meade, Meredith Deal, Bree Romero, Michael Hakala, Katie Finn, Zamen Abo-Zebiba, Yumna Amir), and Domenick Tirabassi, MS from the Wisconsin School of Professional Psychology. In addition, we appreciate Mark Kisileca's support and mentoring through the publication process as we are happy to contribute to the Psychotherapy and Counseling of Boys and Men series. Last but not least, we appreciate all of our family and friends for their support of this book over the years.

Introduction

In my clinical practice, I (Anthony Isacco) conduct psychological evaluations with men applying to enter a religious and spiritual ministry. Specifically, these men are in the process of discerning a vocation to become ordained priests or deacons in Christian Churches. My first question during the clinical interview is, "Why are you pursuing this vocation?" and 100% respond by telling me that they "feel called by God." As you read that last sentence, some thoughts, reactions, feelings may have emerged. What do you think about God? Do you believe in God? Have you ever felt called by God to do anything? Perhaps you considered negative stereotypes about Catholic priests or recalled negative experiences associated with Christianity. Regardless, it would be perfectly normal and natural to have some reactions. In the parlance of clinical training and the mental health professions, such reactions would be categorized under our on-going self-reflection in our pursuit of self-awareness, which is a part of multicultural counseling competence.

The clinical interview does not end there. Based on my training, clinical experiences with men, and research agenda focused on the psychology of men and masculinity, I also know the value of asking men about their masculinity ideology, gender roles, and sense of manhood – all of which are directly related to their identity and psychological health. I pose the following question: "What have you learned about being a man that is important to you?" The plot thickens so to speak. Many of the men respond to that question by stating, "What have I learned about being a man? I have learned that everything that our society and culture has told me about what I need to do to be a man is wrong." The message is clear – these men have become aware of and rejected stereotypical and harmful images of manhood. Their awareness has led them to actively and consciously choose to exhibit a different model of masculinity.

Some men discuss the importance of being a strong leader, a provider, and achievement-oriented, which I consider to be traditional, positive roles and norms of Western masculinity. Other men break from the script and list less traditional masculine qualities such as compassion, love, selflessness, service, and altruism that are important to them as men. In both cases, their religious beliefs and affiliation inform their answers and influence their expression of masculinity. For example, for men speaking of the values of compassion and service, they discuss their desire to become "more like Christ" as they seek a formal ministerial role. For men valuing the provider and leader roles, they also want "to be good Catholic men," and their expression of providing and leading is motivated by a sense of responsibility to their family and faith community. I am a Catholic man with many of the same beliefs and practices, which helps me to understand and relate to these men. However, I am in an evaluative role and have to be careful not to over-identify and lose my objectivity. Continued self-reflection and awareness help in this regard as well as the clinical tools and skills that I have honed as a counseling psychologist. My job is to ask questions that facilitate a deeper understanding of my male clients. It has been clear in my clinical practice that men think about masculinity, religion, and spirituality in reflective, critical, and intersecting ways.

Historically, science and religion have been viewed as incompatible. According to Neil deGrasse Tyson (1999), the central difference between the nature of science and religion is that "the claims of science rely on experimental verification, while the claims of religions rely on faith. These are irreconcilable approaches to knowing" (para. 3). This perspective translates to psychology as a science, and thereby the practice of psychology. Before I (Jay Wade) returned to school to pursue a doctorate in psychology, I worked in the mental health field as a psychiatric occupational therapist in New York with diverse populations, but primarily Black and Latino patients. There were two observations I was glaringly aware of: men were not treated as men but as patients, as if their gender did not matter; and patients at one time or another always made reference to God, faith, or religious beliefs. Neither gender issues relative to men nor religious issues were addressed in treatment. Granted, I was working within psychiatry – the field of medicine – and the treatment paradigm does not recognize such issues as relevant to the treatment of mental disorders. When I decided to pursue a doctorate in psychology in the early 1990s, I chose counseling psychology because of the recognition of cultural factors as important in providing counseling services. One day in my first year while attending the class on personality, the professor (not a counseling psychologist) made a statement that I *had* to respond to. He stated that if you are a true scientist you cannot believe in God. I responded with incredulity, telling him that the two are not incompatible, depending on how one defines God, and explained how so from my perspective. I gave myself as an example, explaining that I believe in God and I believe in science. Science can provide a way to understand God, and God is the explanation behind the scientific one. For example, astrophysics can explain scientifically how the universe came into being in terms of the Big Bang theory, and God is the explanation behind how it came into being or is behind the Big Bang theory. Of course, my comments sparked a rich discussion in the class. These intellectual debates are great for academia, but as a psychologist practitioner there is no way I could accept that position and be effective in working with clients. Neither could I accept that men's notions of what it means to be a man has no relevance when it comes to working with clients. These clinical experiences, as well as my own personal experiences and belief system, informed my research interests, in particular research on the psychology of men.

My many years of conducting research on men did not delve into the religious and spiritual aspects of men's lives until I visited Bali, observed Balinese culture, and saw how Balinese men differed dramatically from American men. It prompted a research question that I wanted to answer, which I was fortunate to do through receiving a Fulbright Senior Research Scholar Award. The question I had was, how do Balinese men define masculinity? Balinese culture is a religious culture based on Hinduism. As such, I was curious about how definitions of manhood intersected with Balinese religious culture. Given that I would study this phenomenon in Bali, Indonesia, I decided to also study Muslim men in Java, Indonesia asking the same question. My research with Indonesian men clarified the intersectionality of religion and masculinity, both in my qualitative and quantitative findings. For example, for Balinese men, religiosity related to Balinese masculinity is important to their definitions of manhood and their life satisfaction (Wade, Suryani, & Lesmana, 2018). In Javanese Muslim men, religiosity related to Javanese masculinity as important to their definitions of manhood and thereby their marital satisfaction (Wade & Wiloso, 2016). I wondered then, is this not true as well for men in the United States who consider themselves religious and/or spiritual? Looking back on my clinical experiences with men, I realize I spent more time attending to the masculinity-related issues than the religious and spiritual issues of men or women. I believe this may be so for other counselors, who inadvertently neglect to address either or both the masculinity and religious issues that relate to their client's concerns. This book was written to increase counselors' awareness of these cultural factors and their intersectionality, so as to enhance your ability to address the issues that men bring to counseling.

Professional and Training Barriers

Despite a growing recognition that religion, spirituality, and gender are often salient aspects to clients' wellbeing, identity, and culture, there are barriers to integrating competences into clinical practice. For example, psychologists and counselors identify as less religious/spiritual than the general public (Delaney, Miller, & Bisonó, 2013). As a result, it is not surprising that many counselors have limited awareness of religious and spiritual issues, and few discuss such issues in clinical practice (Crook-Lyon et al., 2012; Vieten et al., 2013). Part of the problem is that the psychology of religion and spirituality is rarely addressed in graduate training programs, and counselors do not receive the training needed to develop the required competences to use in their practice (Hathaway, 2013; Saunders, Petrik, & Miller, 2014). Similarly, the psychology of men and masculinity has encountered barriers to entering the "mainstream" of clinical training and practice (Wade & Good, 2010). For instance, Liu (2005) identified initial opposition to the psychological study of men and masculinity because there is a historical need to focus on populations of less power and privilege (e.g., women and racial minorities). Opportunities for clinical training are also limited in the psychology of men and masculinity, as few doctoral programs in counseling psychology require or offer a course in the psychology of men and masculinity (Mellinger & Liu, 2006) – a training gap that is likely generalized to other helping professions such as clinical psychology, social work, and counselor education. Taken together, professional biases in mental health and medical fields have created a lack of attention to the cultural factors of religion, spirituality, and masculinity that are salient in the lives and health of many men in the United States as well as other countries.

The Importance of Overcoming Barriers to Improve Men's Health

There is growing recognition among researchers and practitioners in the psychological, counseling, and healthcare fields that men's health is in a state of crisis (e.g., Courtenay, 2011; Davies, Shen-Miller, & Isacco, 2010). Known health services are often underutilized by men (Courtenay, 2011). Thus, novel pathways and interventions are needed to improve men's health (Davies et al., 2010). On the surface, religion and spirituality may not be a viable solution to improve men's health because it is often found that men are less religious than women (Trzebiatowska & Bruce, 2012). Yet, when properly understood and competently addressed, counselors can attend to the intersection of religion, spirituality, and masculinity in order to create positive pathways to health for men (Bonhomme, 2013; Garfield, Isacco, & Sahker, 2013). For example, traditional male socialization is likely an underlying mechanism to men's lack of health service utilization as well as their lack of engagement in religion and spirituality.

The associations between masculinity and religiosity/spirituality are complex and nuanced (Ward & Cook, 2011). For example, the traditionally masculine norm of winning positively correlated with religiousness, while the masculine norm of emotional control negatively correlated with religiousness (Ward & Cook, 2011). Ward and Cook's findings are contextualized within maturing fields of study, as the conceptualization and measurement of constructs of masculinity, religiosity, and spirituality have become more refined, complex, and reflective of people's experiences. By remediating negative aspects of traditional male socialization and highlighting the positive characteristics of masculinity, counselors can better connect to men and open new opportunities to improve their health and wellbeing. The purpose of this book is to provide counselors with clinical strategies that they can translate into their everyday practice in ways that improve men's health through the integrated pathway of religion, spirituality, and masculinity.

The majority of people are affiliated with a major world religion (Christianity, Judaism, Muslim, Buddhist, and Hindu). Religious affiliation, religious beliefs and practices, and spirituality are often important cultural factors that provide meaning to people's lives and saliency to their identity. Many men, despite the gender disparity in statistics regarding their religious affiliation and practices, also exhibit religious and spiritual identities that often intersect with other cultural factors in significant ways. It is ill-advised to consider religion and spirituality unimportant to men's health and irrelevant to counseling. As concern about men's health continues to rise, it is important to utilize available tools and resources that the psychological sciences have found to be helpful. Religion and spirituality have such tools that can help men live healthier lives (Plante, 2009). For example, African-American men emphasized the importance of spirituality, forgiveness, redemption, and community service to their masculinity ideology and sense of manhood (Hammond et al., 2006; Hammond & Mattis, 2005). This is one example of the intersectionality between spirituality and masculinity that is important for counselors to be aware of, reflect upon, and integrate into their cultural competencies. For counselors, the importance of this integration is well stated by Robertson (2013): "Religiousness may be the most influential force in a man's life . . . If, as counselors, we are not interested in his religiosity or spirituality, he will find that we are not fully interested in him" (p. 417). This book will provide readers with similar examples from the extant literature to enhance awareness and knowledge and follow up those examples with cases steeped in clinical practice to strengthen skills and apply in one's own practice.

Tips on How to Read the Book

Appreciate the Individual Differences of Men

We reference general religious teachings and cite studies from the social sciences throughout this book. The book is well researched as we drew from hundreds of studies across various health disciplines. We caution against stereotyping men based on findings from the research studies. Rather, we believe that addressing religion, spirituality, and masculinity is an individual process with specific men that requires careful conceptualization and assessment with tailored counseling interventions. Each chapter includes three sections focused on Conceptualization, Assessment, and Counseling Interventions. Those sections are intended to provide counselors with several clinical tools and strategies that can be applied individually to a male client. There is certainly not a "one-size-fits-all" model that would work with all men. Is he affiliated with a religion? What beliefs and practices does he adhere to? What are the benefits and costs of his religious and spiritual beliefs and practices? How does he express his masculinity? Is his masculinity enhancing or impeding his health? Taking time to answer those questions help to drive and to enrich the counseling process with a man in a way that is specific to his identities and contexts.

Enhance Your Cultural Competence

Masculinity, religion, and spirituality are considered important cultural factors associated with client health, identity development, and counseling competences (APA, 2002). We drew from a prevailing multicultural counseling competence model by encouraging counselors to increase their self-awareness, knowledge, and skills related to masculinity, religion, and spirituality (Sue, Arredondo, & McDavis, 1992). Similar to avoiding stereotyping and unhelpful generalizations taken from research studies, we encourage counselors to understand their personal biases and expectations more deeply in order to develop healthy therapeutic alliances with men. It is important for counselors to be aware of how they react (internally and externally) to men's disclosures about their religion and spirituality, expressions of masculinity, and to know about their religious and spiritual experiences, and to use clinical skills that are congruent to such cultural factors. We readily acknowledge that demonstrating cultural competence in regard to religion, spirituality, and masculinity is a challenge. It is an on-going process of examining and applying general trends and knowledge, while concurrently working to understand the specific lived experience and context of the man sitting in your office. When applying content from this book while counseling men, we agree that "perhaps the most important clinical implication is that counselors should carefully assess the opinions and needs of their particular clients" (Saenz & Waldo, 2013, p. 327). Taken together, there is synergy between appreciating individual differences and enhancing cultural competence.

Understand the Ethical Considerations

Professional ethics are of obvious importance in any clinical situation, context, and professional relationship. Ethics are routinely discussed and represent a prevailing theme in scholarship about integrating religion and spirituality into counseling. We agree with the common-sense conclusion put forth in the scholarship: the integration of religion and spirituality into counseling should not violate any ethical standards (e.g., Henry, 2015). Appreciating individual differences between clients and exercising cultural competence is a good start to avoid any ethical violations. We encourage counselors to read this book with some ethical standards in mind from the American Counseling Association (2014) and American Psychological Association's (2017) ethical codes. First, all counseling interventions discussed in this book are aimed at doing good and avoiding harm. Counselors should not implement an intervention that causes harm to a client. Second, some of the clinical tools, assessment strategies, and suggested interventions may require additional training for counselors to implement with competence. Thus, we advise counselors to practice within their competence while always striving to enhance their competence with additional training, supervision, continuing education credits, reading, and consultation. Third, the counseling interventions are ideally utilized, most effective, and ethically sound when there is congruence with the client's values, beliefs, and practices. Counselors should avoid imposing their own values and beliefs onto clients in a way that violates client autonomy, rights, and dignity. We believe that when the proper ethical safeguards are in place, counselors can successfully integrate the counseling interventions in this book in ways that enhance men's health.

Roadmap of This Book

Chapter 1, *How Do Men Use Religion?*, describes men with regard to religious affiliation, beliefs, and practices. Men use religion in ways that can be harmful to self and others, and in ways that can be beneficial. The chapter suggests ways that counselors can assess their client's religious identity and spiritual beliefs, conceptualize how the client uses or not uses religion in their life in harmful and/or healthy ways, and provide counseling interventions that are related to their client's use of religion.

Chapter 2, *How Do Men Use Masculinity?*, describes men with regard to masculinity and gender socialization. Men differ in their masculinity ideologies and adherence to gender roles and norms, given cultural differences in definitions of manhood and individual differences in conformity to masculine norms. Research has identified the harmful aspects of traditional masculinity for men's health compared to positive aspects that have been associated with positive health outcomes. The chapter suggests ways to assess the client's masculinity ideology and its origin, conceptualize how the client's masculinity ideology is harmful and/or healthy, and counseling interventions to facilitate the client's development of positive masculinity characteristics.

Chapter 3, *Men and Their Relationship with God*, discusses the relationship that men have with God. Men may be socialized away from engaging in a relationship with God due to masculine norms of independence, self-reliance, and avoidance of intimacy. Yet, for some men their relationship with God is a source of strength, support, connection, and coping. The chapter discusses related issues such as men's images of God, God Attachment, and the psycho-social implications of a positive or negative God Image and Attachment. The chapter offers ways to assess the client's relationship with God and the degree to which masculinity ideology has influenced his relationship with God, conceptualize how positive aspects or conflicts in his relationship with God influences his health and wellbeing, and counseling interventions that may help men develop an enhanced relationship with God.

Chapter 4, *Pray and Go to Church?*, examines the role of prayer and church attendance in men's identity and psychological health. Prayer and attendance at church services often enhance resilience, personal coping, and social support among other health benefits. However, men are less likely to attend weekly religious services, pray, meditate, and read scripture on a daily or weekly basis. Masculine gender role socialization seems to be a factor, as praying and going to church can be seen as asking for help, reliance on others, and being vulnerable, which are contrary to masculine norms of self-reliance, independence, and strength. The chapter suggests ways that counselors can assess the client's beliefs and behaviors regarding prayer and church attendance, conceptualize how masculine socialization may be facilitating or impeding those beliefs and behaviors, and implement counseling interventions that facilitate the exploration of prayer and church attendance.

Chapter 5, *Men's Shame*, examines how religion, spirituality, and masculinity influence men's experience of shame. Some men experience shame if they perceive themselves as not living up to the prevailing norms, expectations, and ideals of manhood. Shame can also emerge from religious influences and experiences such as not living up to the moral code and guidelines of one's religion. Men may also experience guilt, which is the feeling of wrongdoing, when they break the rules. Yet, guilt may motivate men toward healthy changes in their behaviors, attitudes, and emotions. The chapter provides suggestions on ways to assess the client's experience of shame and guilt, to conceptualize shame from an integrative religious and masculinity perspective, and to implement counseling interventions that facilitate psychological healing from the experience of shame.

Chapter 6, *Men and Forgiveness*, describes a process of healing and change for men that includes self-forgiveness and forgiveness of others. Forgiveness has known health benefits, but men have a harder time forgiving than women because of traditional gender role socialization. The chapter offers ways to assess the client's need for forgiveness, to conceptualize how presenting concerns are related to forgiveness, and to implement empirically based counseling interventions that facilitate psychological and emotional healing through experiencing forgiveness.

Chapter 7, *Pornography Use and Spiritual Issues with Men*, examines the sexual concern of problematic pornography consumption (PPC) among men. PPC is associated with psychological and interpersonal problems with men. Men's religiosity, spirituality, and sense of morals may exacerbate their experience of distress while motivating them to seek help to decrease PPC. This chapter provides a comprehensive assessment approach to PPC, conceptualization strategies that integrate addiction models, gender socialization, and spirituality, and provides counseling interventions from acceptance and commitment therapy and cognitive behavioral therapy that help men to decrease PPC.

Chapter 8, *Gay Men and Religion*, describes the religious and spiritual practices and experiences of gay men. Although some religions have specific churches, synagogues, and mosques that are welcoming of gay men, many religions exhibit direct and/or indirect aggression and hostility toward homosexuality and gay men, which can affect gay men's involvement in places of worship as well as their psychological functioning. As a result, gay men may miss out on the positive benefits of religious and spiritual beliefs and practices as well as continue to experience the negative effects of oppressive systems (e.g., see gaychurch.org). The chapter offers counselors ways to assess their client's attitudes toward religion and spirituality as a gay man, explore their positive and negative experiences associated with religion, conceptualize any religion-based internalized homophobia or other negative health outcomes, and implement counseling interventions that explore possible ways the client can be positively involved in a religious community.

Chapter 9, *Religious Drifters*, describes the religious and spiritual practices and experiences of men who are not religiously affiliated. Compared to women, in the United States more men have identified as atheists and religiously unaffiliated. The chapter defines a religious drifter and differentiates drifters from atheists, agnostics, and the religiously unaffiliated. Religious drifters may lack meaning in their life and express disappointment, sadness, and discontent without a spiritual home. The chapter suggests ways to assess the client's religious and spiritual journey to identify their narrative about drifting, explore the positive and negative experiences associated with being a religious drifter, investigate possible connections between the client's masculinity ideology and religious non-affiliation, and implement counseling interventions that explore the various possible ways of being meaningfully involved in a religious community.

Chapter 10, *Creating More Positive Pathways That Improve Men's Health*, integrates the previous chapters on the relationships between religion, spirituality, masculinity, and men's health. In this final chapter we describe pathways that specifically draw upon religion/spirituality and masculinity as paths to positive outcomes for men's health and wellbeing. A conceptual model is presented followed by examples of how the model can be applied in your work with men by addressing the intersecting religious, spiritual, and masculinity issues.

References

American Counseling Association (2014). *ACA Code of Ethics*. Alexandria, VA: Author. Retrieved from www.counseling.org/resources/aca-code-of-ethics.pdf.

American Psychological Association (2002). *Guidelines on multicultural education, training, research, practice, and organizational change for psychologists*. Retrieved from www.apa.org/pi/oema/resources/policy/multicultural-guidelines.aspx.

American Psychological Association (2017). *APA Code of Ethics*. Washington, DC: Author. Retrieved from www.apa.org/ethics/code/.

Bonhomme, J.J. (2013). An opportunity to improve men's health and wellness. *American Journal of Lifestyle Medicine, 7*, 73–74.

Courtenay, W. (2011). *Dying to be men: Psychosocial, environmental, and biobehavioral directions in promoting the health of men and boys*. New York, NY: Routledge.

Crook-Lyon, R., O'Grady, K., Smith, T., Jensen, D., Golightly, T., & Potkar, K. (2012). Addressing religious and spiritual diversity in graduate training and multicultural education for professional psychologists. *Psychology of Religion and Spirituality, 4*(3), 169–181.

Davies, J.A., Shen-Miller, D.S., & Isacco, A. (2010). The men's center approach to addressing the health crisis of college men. *Professional Psychology: Research and Practice, 41*(4), 347–354.

Delaney, H.D., Miller, W.R., & Bisonó, A.M. (2013). Religiosity and spirituality among psychologists: A survey of clinician members of the American Psychological Association. *Spirituality in Clinical Practice, 1*, 95–106.

Garfield, C.F., Isacco, A.I., & Sahker, E. (2013). Religion and spirituality as important components of men's health and wellness: An analytic review. *American Journal of Lifestyle Medicine,* 7(1), 27–37.

Hammond, W.P., Banks, K.H., & Mattis, J.S. (2006). Masculinity ideology and forgiveness of racial discrimination among African American men: Direct and interactive relationships. *Sex Roles, 55*(9–10), 679–692.

Hammond, W., & Mattis, J. (2005). Being a man about it: Manhood meaning among African American men. *Psychology of Men & Masculinity, 6*(2), 114–126.

Hathaway, W. (2013). Pathways toward graduate training in the clinical psychology of religion and spirituality: A spiritual competencies model. In K.I. Pargament, A. Mahoney, & E.P. Shafranske (Eds.), *APA handbook of psychology, religion, and spirituality: vol. 2. An applied psychology of religion and spirituality*, (pp. 635–650). Washington, DC: American Psychological Association.

Henry, H. (2015). Spiritual energy of Islamic prayers as a catalyst for psychotherapy. *Journal of Religion and Health, 54*, 387–398.

Liu, W. (2005). The study of men and masculinity as an important multicultural competency consideration. *Journal of Clinical Psychology, 61*(6), 685–697.

Mellinger, T.N., & Liu, W.M. (2006). Men's issues in doctoral training: A survey of counseling psychology programs. *Professional Psychology: Research and Practice, 37*(2),196–204.

Plante, T. (2009). *Spiritual practices in psychotherapy: Thirteen tools for enhancing psychological health*. Washington, DC: American Psychological Association.

Robertson, J. (2013). Perceiving religious men through counselor eyes: Risks and tips. *Journal of Counseling and Development, 91*, 410–418.

Saenz, R., & Waldo, M. (2013). Clients' preferences regarding prayer during counseling. *Psychology of Religion and Spirituality, 5*(4), 325–334.

Saunders, S., Petrik, M., & Miller, M. (2014). Psychology doctoral students' perspectives on addressing spirituality and religion with clients: Associations with personal preferences and training. *Psychology of Religion and Spirituality, 6*(1), 1–8.

Sue, D.W., Arredondo, P., & McDavis, R.J. (1992). Multicultural counseling competencies and standards: A call to the profession. *Journal of Counseling & Development, 70*, 477–486.

Trzebiatowska, M., & Bruce, S. (2012). *Why are women more religious than men?* Oxford, UK: Oxford University Press.

Tyson, N.D. (1999, October). Holy wars. *Natural History*. Retrieved from www.haydenplanetarium.org/tyson/essays/1999-10-holy-wars.php.

Vieten, C., Scammell, S., Pilato, R., Ammondson, I., Pargament, K.I., & Lukoff, D. (2013). Spiritual and religious competencies for psychologists. *Psychology of Religion and Spirituality, 5*(3), 129–144.

Wade, J., & Good, G. (2010). Moving toward mainstream: Perspectives on enhancing therapy with men. *Psychotherapy: Theory, Research, Practice, Training, 47*(3), 273–275.

Wade, J.C., Suryani, L.K., & Lesmana, C.B.J. (2018). Religiosity, masculinity, and marital and life satisfaction among Balinese Hindu men. *International Journal of Research Studies in Psychology,* 7(1), 99–114.

Wade, J.C., & Wiloso, P.G. (2016). Religiosity, masculinity, and marital satisfaction among Javanese Muslim men. *International Journal of Research Studies in Psychology,* *5*(3), 37–52.

Ward, A.Z., & Cook, S.W. (2011). The complex associations between conforming to masculine norms and religiousness in men. *Psychology of Men & Masculinity,* *12*(1), 42–54.

1 How Do Men Use Religion?

Men seeking counseling enter your office with a variety of religious and spiritual affiliations, practices, and beliefs. This chapter provides an overview of those affiliations, practices, and beliefs that are important to their worldview and health. Religion and spirituality are cultural factors that need to be addressed in counseling through assessment, conceptualization, and intervention. Integration of such cultural factors helps to facilitate rapport building, client retention, and positive therapeutic outcomes (Ponterotto, 2008). Our prevailing beliefs that drive this chapter are (a) religion and spirituality are salient cultural factors for many men, (b) men use religion and spirituality in both positive and negative ways, and (c) as a result, we provide counselors with resources to assess, conceptualize, and intervene with male clients in a manner that is responsive to their religion and spirituality.

Religious Affiliations

There are thousands of religions practiced all over the world. It would be extremely difficult, if not impossible, to provide information on every religious affiliation. Most literature on the topic categorizes religious affiliations into five "major" world religions: Hinduism, Buddhism, Judaism, Christianity, and Islam. There are hundreds of denominations and sects that are categorized under the five major world religions, resulting in the diverse practice of the religions. Part of this chapter will focus on the five major world religions, the associated religious beliefs and practices exhibited by male clients, and the pathways to health outcomes.

According to a 2012 report, the PEW Research Center on Religion and Public Life estimated that eight out of ten people in the world identify with a religious group (Pew Research Center, 2012). A growing number of people (one in six) are religiously unaffiliated (e.g., agnostics, atheists); these individuals may reject all forms of religion and spirituality while some still adhere to spiritual values, beliefs, and behaviors (Pew Research Center, 2012). Chapter 9 focuses on religiously unaffiliated and religious drifters in more detail. The Pew-Templeton Global Religious Future Projects (Pew Research Center, 2017) estimates that by the year 2020, 31.1% of the world's population will be Christian, 24.9% Muslims, 15.6% unaffiliated, 15.2% Hindu, 6.6% Buddhist, 5.6% folk religions, <1% Jewish, and <1% other. The demographic statistics are different in the United States: 70.6% Christian, 22.8% are unaffiliated, 1.9% Jewish, <1% Hindu, <1% Muslim, and <1% Buddhist (Pew Research Center, 2015). The point of both sets of statistics is to understand that most people affiliate with a major religion. More specifically, the Pew statistics imply that many counseling clients will be affiliated with Christianity or unaffiliated with a major world religion.

The unaffiliated category includes atheists, agnostics, and those without an affiliation to a major world religion. The unaffiliated clients may not identify with a major world religion but are not necessarily non-religious or non-spiritual. In fact, unaffiliated clients are likely to have religious and spiritual experiences, beliefs, and practices that need to be assessed. Those who are not currently affiliated with a major world religion may have been at some point and present with experiences and emotions relevant to therapy (Plante, 2009). Thus, religion can still be a salient factor for men even if they do not affiliate with a major world religion.

Considering Gender with Religious Affiliation, Beliefs, and Practices

Internationally and within the United States, there are notable gender differences in religious affiliation, beliefs, and practices. In general, more women are religiously affiliated compared to men (Hvidtjørn, Hjelmborg, Skytthe, Christensen, & Hvidt, 2014; Trzebiatowska & Bruce, 2012). In the United States, less men compared to women attend weekly religious services, pray, meditate, and read scripture on a daily or weekly basis (Pew Research Center, 2016). Taken together, the general narrative from the known statistics is that women are more religious than men. This has been considered somewhat of a strange finding because most deity figures are male (e.g., Jesus in Christianity) and most religious leaders are male. When it comes down to counting who is in the pews, more women than men are showing up. Yes, there is some truth to those statistics, but it would be an inaccurate over-generalization of the statistics to conclude that all men are not as religious as all women. There are nuances in the statistics, and the lived experiences of diverse men indicate that men use religion in positive and negative ways. The statistics have prompted investigations into why there are gender differences in religious affiliations, beliefs, and practices between men and women (Trzebiatowska & Bruce, 2012). For example, earlier scholarship has reported that men adhering to traditional masculinity are more likely to be less religious (Miller & Hoffmann, 1995; Robbins, Francis, Haley, & Kay, 2001; Sullins, 2006; Thompson, 1991). To expand, some men may view religious activities as feminine, i.e., "unmasculine," and not participate in order to preserve their sense of manhood (Robertson, 2013). To that point, more men identified as atheists and religiously unaffiliated compared to women in the United States (Pew Research Center, 2016). That theoretical interpretation is indicative of the kind of confluence of masculinity and religiosity that men experience and will be discussed in greater depth in subsequent chapters of this book.

Research across disciplines has found that men use religion and spirituality in positive and negative ways. When considering the positive and negative ways that men use religion, we suggest a similar philosophy as Pargament (2002) by encouraging counselors to explore how helpful or harmful a particular form of religious expression is for their mental health, depending on their presenting concerns and contextual factors. This section helps counselors to understand how men use religion and spirituality based on the common constructs found consistently in the psychological science. These constructs are general enough to be found across the five major world religions, but are expressed differently depending on the religious affiliation, individual male client, and other contextual factors. We start with the positive ways such as religious coping, religious support, to find meaning in life, and to develop masculine roles. We categorized a construct as 'positive' if it is (a) readily apparent, (b) consistently associated with positive outcomes, and (c) generally considered adaptive and healthy.

Religious Coping

Religious/spiritual coping is defined as "efforts to understand and deal with life stressors in ways related to the sacred" (Pargament, Feuille, & Burdzy, 2011, p. 52). Some examples of religious coping include asking God for help and surrendering control to a higher power. Coping with stress and psychological distress through religious and spiritual means is a highly researched area and has been consistently associated with positive health outcomes (Pargament et al., 2011). As a result, prayer, meditation, mindfulness, and other similar spiritual practices are often found on popular websites listing "the best" stress management/relaxation techniques (e.g., Moninger, 2017).

The prevailing conceptualization of religious coping entails positive and negative components. In this section, we focus on the positive components and discuss negative coping later in the chapter. Men's view of God is an important factor when determining if religious coping is categorized as positive or negative. One's view of God is often referred to as *God Image*, which refers to "a psychological working internal model of the sort of person that the individual imagines God to be" (Lawrence, 1997, p. 214). Chapter 3 delves deeper into God Image. Positive religious coping is accompanied by a view of God (i.e., the sacred) as loving, supportive, and involved while negative religious coping stems from perceiving God as punitive, judging, and abandoning.

Men have typically come into my (Isacco) office only after exhausting all of their usual coping skills and reverting to maladaptive ways of coping. They have tried exercising and talking to a friend and have turned to alcohol, drugs, and violence in other cases. Nothing helped, and the distress worsened. The usual coping skills were not helping with the new problems. Counselors may not immediately suggest religious coping as a new skill to address the presenting concerns. However, some men may benefit from using religious coping to alleviate symptoms. For example, male clients affiliated with a world religion (e.g., Christianity) that emphasizes a relationship with God may benefit from increased intercessory prayer. Religious coping can also include the use of support from religion and spirituality.

Religious Support

Religious support is based on the broader understanding of social support. Social support is a well-known psychological construct and distinct from coping constructs despite similar effects on mental health. Religious support is defined as the "perception of available tangible and/or emotional support within a religious context" and may entail perceived support from God, fellow believers, and/or religious leaders (Lazar & Bjorck, 2016, p. 235). Thus, one can see that there are different sources of support that can be addressed in counseling with men. In addition, faith activities such as services (e.g., mass in the Catholic Church), prayer groups, volunteerism, faith classes (e.g., Bible studies), and social activities in religious settings all contribute to the development of a social network and perceptions of religious support. The social sciences have often measured the frequency of engagement in religious activities as a key factor to psychological health outcomes, but the support from those activities is a primary mechanism accounting for positive outcomes.

Men with religious affiliations have natural communities and structures in place to seek support from when experiencing distress. For example, men in London considered Buddhism to be helpful to alleviating distress through meditation and belonging to a supportive community that promoted positive health behaviors (Lomas, Cartwright, Edginton, & Ridge, 2014). In this example, the religious support derived from fellow believers rather than religious leaders and a relationship with God. That makes sense because Buddhism has less emphasis on formal religious structures and a relationship with a higher power/God while still having components of religious support (community) and religious coping (meditation) in place to enhance men's health. The importance of social support in the religious context to men's health is a shared mechanism among men of various religious affiliations. In an exhaustive review of over 100 studies of religion, spirituality, and men's health, social support from religion and spirituality was a basic mechanism that helped to explain positive health outcomes (Garfield, Isacco, & Sahker, 2013).

In a presentation about his clinical experiences with men at the National Psychotherapy with Men conference (2014), Dr. Fred Rabinowitz discussed the lack of friendships in men's lives and described the sense of loneliness and isolation that men feel who come into his office for counseling. Loneliness and isolation in a world full of people are existential issues, which often correlate to spirituality. Religion and spirituality are one way to find social connections, a place in the world, and avoid the loneliness that men may explore in counseling. In a study of over 1,000 men and women, participation in religious activities with other people (e.g., events, bible study, choir practice) at least once a week was correlated with lower psychological distress, greater sense of happiness, and better self-report health (Maselko & Kubzansky, 2006). The impact of participation in religious activities was greater for the men compared to the women in the study. Thus, the search for meaning for men is still as relevant today as it was in the past. Religion and spirituality are naturally 'places' to find meaning in life.

Meaning in Life

Meaning in life refers to one's sense of purpose, value, and importance with their life. Inherently, meaning in life is good and certainly better than a lack of meaning in life. Similar to religious coping and religious support, meaning in life is also a well-researched and clinically used construct. Meaning in life has roots in established psychological theories such as Victor Frankl's logotherapy and similar existential theories (Frankl, 1959). In addition, meaning in life is embedded within an established paradigm of religion that has three components: extrinsic, intrinsic, and quest. Intrinsic religiousness refers to using religion to understand life and provide a basis for meaning in life (Allport & Ross, 1967). Similarly, spirituality is predominantly measured through two components: religious wellbeing and existential wellbeing, with the latter referring to a sense of life purpose (Jurkovic & Walker, 2006). Thus, religion and spirituality are inherently defined by providing people with meaning in life.

Having meaning in life is part of psychological wellbeing and a protective factor from adverse experiences. For example, in a quantitative study of 226 men with HIV/AIDs, male patients that exhibited spiritual growth such as meaning attached to their suffering and spiritual acceptance, experienced higher health-related quality of life, better mental and emotional wellbeing, improved social functioning, more energy and positive affect (Wiggins-Frame, Uphold, Shehan, & Reid, 2005). Taken together, it is not surprising that many men find meaning in life within their religion and spirituality, which contributes to positive outcomes.

Just as having meaning in life is part of psychological wellbeing, a lack of meaning in life is typically a sign of life dissatisfaction, angst, and despair. In 2014, CNN published a photojournalism story entitled *America's lost boys* (Patterson, 2014). The pictures tell a story of a generation of young men in the United States who lack meaning in their lives and struggle with unemployment, low outcome expectations, and a missing sense of identity. The phrase 'lost boys' is a play on words in reference to Peter Pan, i.e., the group of males that never grew up while living in a fantasy world in Neverland. The CNN story did not explicitly address their religion/spirituality, but indirectly illustrates how young men have lost faith in something greater, bigger, and more powerful. That something just may be the sacred. Lacking meaning in life seems like a natural consequence without a connection to the sacred and/or religious community. Referring back to Frankel's logotherapy, meaning in life is possible during times of suffering and the solution to existential vacuums.

Masculine Roles

Men use religion and spirituality to learn about manhood and how to assume masculine roles. This makes a lot of sense since the world religions discussed earlier have some combination of a God, deity figure, moral code, beliefs, and practices that points followers of those religions to a better way of living life. For example, Hinduism identifies three paths to transformation and liberation, Buddhists often meditate in front of an image of Buddha for spiritual advancement, Judaism believes that their God (*Yahweh*) provided commandments and the Torah for the chosen people to use to live more closely to God's design, Christianity calls people to love God and their neighbor as Jesus Christ taught, and Muslims go to *Allah* to achieve a life of felicity (Ludwig, 1996). These are brief examples that highlight the broader point – the world religions are structured and intended to promote virtuous behavior, personal transformation, and common good among people. In a qualitative study of 33 African-American men from Black churches (i.e., Protestant churches that historically and/or currently serve African-Americans) in the United States, participants described how their Church promoted marriage commitment and family stability (Collins & Perry, 2015). To quote one participant from the study, "It [being married] sends a message to the community that you are a serious responsible man because you are taking care of a family" (p. 436).

That theme of using lessons from religion to develop into a better man is largely congruent with my clinical work with men. I (Isacco) have found that men I work with in my clinical practice use their religion and spirituality to identify with an aspirational model and to adopt virtuous behaviors. When I conduct evaluations on applicants to study to be priests and deacons in the Catholic Church, I ask men "What have you learned about being a man that is important to you?" Most of the men have responded to that question by first describing how society has taught them the wrong messages about manhood. Stories of workaholism, womanizing, absentee fatherhood, interpersonal conflict, and competition represent some of the themes discussed. They credited their Catholic faith with teaching them the importance of being a strong leader and achievement-oriented while also learning to exhibit qualities such as compassion, love, selflessness, service, and altruism (Isacco, 2016). Taken further, these men essentially were striving to emulate the God in their religion – Jesus. It is certainly a lofty, if not unattainable, aspiration. Yet, the important point is that men learn positive attitudes and behaviors from religious and spiritual sources. The psychology of men and masculinity scholarship has not always done well at capturing how men learn positive qualities (Hammer & Good, 2010). The literature base has broadened in recent years with new theories about 'positive masculinity,' which examine "prosocial attitudes, beliefs, and behaviors of boys and men that produce positive consequences for self and others" (Kiselica, Benton-Wright, & Englar-Carlson, 2016, p. 126). In the context of positive masculinity theory, the relationship between the religious beliefs, affiliation, and practices that prompt men to exhibit positive masculine norms and roles of masculinity is critical to identify and to promote in our clinical work with men.

We also detail the negative ways that men use religion such as negative religious coping, religious/spiritual struggle, and forms of extreme religious adherence. We categorized a construct as 'negative' if it is (a) readily apparent, (b) consistently associated with negative outcomes, and (c) generally considered maladaptive and unhealthy.

Negative Religious Coping

As mentioned earlier, religious coping entails both positive and negative components. The previous section detailed the positive components to religious coping while this section focuses on how men use *negative religious coping*. Pargament, Smith, Koenig, and Perez (1998) conceptualized negative religious coping as a reframing of events as God's punishment, feelings of abandonment by God, expressions of confusion about one's relationship with God, and reinterpretations of outcomes as acts of the devil. Not surprisingly, Pargament et al. emphasize that negative religious coping, with views of a punishing God, is often associated with psychological distress, increased alcohol/substance use, depressive and anxiety symptoms, and worsening of grief (Aldwin, Park, Jeong, & Nath, 2014; Lee, Roberts, & Gibbons, 2013; Pargament, Koenig, & Perez, 2000).

Negative religious coping is a little bit of a misnomer as coping implies an adaptive response to a stressful trigger. Negative religious coping is both a negative cognitive image of God and a maladaptive response to stress as evidenced by the associated outcomes. Those basic linkages: positive view of God – positive religious coping – positive outcomes; and negative view of God – negative religious coping – negative outcomes, is generally supported in US and international studies (e.g., Bjorck & Thurman, 2007). However, it is important to note that some components of negative religious coping, such as expressing confusion about God and feeling abandoned by God, are not inherently negative. Those experiences are likely normal and expected responses to life's challenges, stressors, and negative life events. US studies find that people are more likely to use positive than negative religious coping (Pargament et al., 1998). Yet, compared to women, male clients may be more prone to view God as punishing, controlling, and judging, and struggle to utilize positive religious coping skills while experiencing negative mood states. A negative God image can contribute to a more pervasive religious/spiritual struggle that negatively impacts a male client's mental health. We go into more detail about religious/spiritual struggles in the next section.

Religious/Spiritual Struggle (Referred to as Spiritual Struggle)

Negative religious coping is a precursor construct to Religious/Spiritual struggle. There are similarities between the two constructs in terms of definitions and associated outcomes. Pargament and colleagues introduced both constructs to the psychology of religion literature and appear to be using *spiritual struggle* in their more recent studies. Spiritual struggle is defined as tension, strain, and/or conflict about sacred, religious matters (Abu-Raiya, Pargament, & Krause, 2016). Clients have spiritual struggles about a belief, practice, or experience that becomes the focus of negative thoughts and contributes to negative mood states. There are three broad types of spiritual struggle: (a) within oneself (e.g., lack of meaning), (b) with other people (e.g., clergy, parishioners), and/or (c) with God (e.g., anger, frustration). Spiritual struggle has been associated with a worsening of grief feelings, increased depressive symptoms, decreased sense of happiness, and alcohol abuse (Abu-Raiya et al., 2016; Holt, Roth, Huang, & Clark, 2015; Lee et al., 2013). Such outcomes are worsened if the individual engages in negative religious coping during their spiritual struggle (Desai & Pargament, 2015).

Similar to negative religious coping, a spiritual struggle is not always a negative per se. Harold Kushner, a Jewish rabbi, captured a collective essence of spiritual struggle in his best-selling book *When bad things happen to good people* (2004). Many people struggle with deep, spiritual, existential questions when faced with death, adversity, and negative life events. Confusion and a corresponding search for reasons are normal responses. Even widely known religious figures have doubts and struggles. For example, letters and personal writings from Mother Teresa of Calcutta were released to the public and revealed a holy woman living with an internal, profound spiritual struggle, namely not feeling God's presence (Kolodiejchuk, 2007). The point is, men may experience a spiritual struggle for legitimate reasons and their struggle may be a normative response to a life experience. A spiritual struggle may exacerbate difficulties for men by closing off available support systems and expose a lack of core beliefs that guide decisions and provide grounding during stressful times. Therefore, part of counseling men who are experiencing a spiritual struggle is to help them identify and rely on the core religious beliefs and practices that can override the negative aspects of a deep spiritual struggle.

Extreme Religious Adherence

The next set of negative uses of religion/spirituality relate to extreme religious adherence. The core teachings of major world religions focus on tolerance, altruism, and helping people to live virtuous, meaningful lives. Of course, followers of the world religions often fail to live up to those teachings, but the aspirations remain oriented toward the good. Extreme religious adherence can take many forms such as religious fundamentalism and religious fanaticism, which distort core religious teachings in ways that justify unhealthy behavior. The unhealthy behavior is problematic for religious men as well as other people. There are familiar and unfortunate examples of men using religion in fanatical ways to justify war, mass suicides, occults, and terrorism (Pargament, 2002). Those examples generate a lot of media headlines and social science research. However, we are not likely to see those individuals in counseling; thus, we will not focus on such populations in this book. However, counselors may see men that exhibit extreme religious fanaticism to a lesser degree while still justifying unhealthy behavior (Robertson, 2013). Men with rigid adherence to their religious beliefs and practices often exhibit maladaptive masculine roles, avoid counseling, and exhibit an imbalanced external locus of control.

In the psychology of men and masculinity literature, a consistent link between rigid adherence to traditional masculinity norms and negative mental health outcomes has been found in various research studies (Levant & Richmond, 2008). The man who refuses to seek help because he thinks help-seeking is unmanly while turning to alcohol, drugs, or violence instead, is the classic example of this empirical finding. At times, that link found in several empirical studies and the lived experience of men has been misinterpreted as meaning that traditional masculinity per se is negative. The popular media has picked up on the research and have used the term 'toxic masculinity' as a catch-all to denounce traditional masculinities. The baby has been thrown out with the bath water so to speak. Other scholars (e.g., Isacco, Talovic, Chromik, & Yallum, 2013; Mahalik, Talmadge, Locke, & Scott, 2005) have been clear to note that traditional masculinity per se is not problematic, disordered, or associated with negative health outcomes. Traditional masculinity is a multidimensional construct, meaning there are many ways to express traditional masculinity norms and roles. Current research and practical efforts have advanced to identify specific problematic and adaptive components of traditional masculinity. For example, Hammer and Good (2010, p. 303) found that traditional norms of masculinity such as

> [r]isk-taking, dominance, primacy of work, and pursuit of status was associated with higher levels of personal courage, autonomy, endurance, and resilience . . . conformity to the norms of winning, emotional control, self-reliance, and pursuit of status was associated with lower levels of personal courage, grit, personal control, autonomy, and resilience.

Hammer and Good's (2010) study is one example of the specified approach to understanding the impact of traditional masculinity on men's health that can be applied to clinical practice.

The conversation about traditional masculinity is similar to religiosity. Religiosity is often considered negative and this line of thinking is summed up with the popular phrase, "I'm spiritual not religious." The implication is that spirituality is good and religiosity is bad. As we have detailed earlier, men use religion in positive ways that contribute to their health and wellbeing. Yet, similar to rigid, extreme traditional masculinity, rigid, extreme uses of religion contribute to negative pathways for men's health and the health of others. For example, religious fundamentalism is a strict adherence to religious doctrine at the expense of open-mindedness toward other faith beliefs and culminating in a defensive, rigid, and authoritarian adherence to traditional religious doctrine (Altemeyer & Hunsberger, 2004). The similarities between rigid masculinity and religion are strong enough to suggest a link, as McDermott, Schwartz, Lindley, and Proietti (2014) argued, that problematic approaches to religion and masculinity go hand-in-hand. Such a link is contrary to the positive pathway established earlier describing how men use religion/spirituality to develop prosocial masculine roles.

Avoid, Resist, Critique Counseling

The hand-in-hand problematic approach to religion and masculinity is manifested in how men avoid mental health help-seeking. Much of the help-seeking literature related to men focuses on how traditional norms of masculinity pose a barrier to men seeking counseling services (Addis & Mahalik, 2003). Similarly, we have encountered men with a strong resistance to psychological interventions due to their religious and spiritual beliefs. In my clinical practice, I (Isacco) conduct a feedback session with religious men after a psychological evaluation. The feedback session reviews the findings of the psychological testing and recommendations. I recommend counseling to many religious men for various problems (e.g., anxiety, marital conflict, depression, sexual issues). The majority of the religious men react to my recommendation that they engage in counseling with a combination of shock and denial, sometimes anger and rarely with open-minded acceptance. The men that agree to follow up on the recommendation usually do so only because of a significant stressor (e.g., divorce, loss of job, family death), having exhausted all their typical resources, and/or at the firm suggestion of a trusted friend, religious leader, spouse, or mandated by the admission board to the religious formation program. Some of the avoidance is based on three common scripts:

(1) a previous experience(s) with a mental health professional who was perceived as non-affirming of their religious beliefs – "I went to a counselor and they told me that I should divorce my wife. Don't they know that divorce is wrong in my religion?!"

(2) negative word-of-mouth about mental health professionals – "my [wife, mother, father, friend, girlfriend, roommate] went to a counselor once and they told me that psychology does not respect my religion."
(3) Negative stereotypes about counseling – "if I went to counseling, they would just tell me it is my parents' fault and I need to express my emotions more."

To be fair, psychologists and counselors identify as less religious/spiritual than the general public (Delaney, Miller, & Bisonó, 2007). As a result, it is not surprising that many counselors have limited awareness of religious and spiritual issues, and few discuss such issues in clinical practice, which can be invalidating to religious clients (Crook-Lyon et al., 2012; Vieten et al., 2013). Religious men want to seek help from someone who is sensitive to their religion and spirituality. They will ask for referrals to a "Christian counselor, Catholic therapist" and often seek help first through a religious leader/minister (priest, pastor, rabbi) before counseling. The avoidance of appropriate psychological services prolongs the problem, and religious men are likely to enter your clinical practice in heightened degrees of distress as a result.

Sense of control is defined as an individual's perceptions of their ability to enact change related to a given outcome (Jackson & Bergeman, 2011). Internal and external locus of control are two popular categories in this area. Internal locus of control refers to the belief that an individual can influence events and outcomes, while external locus of control attributes changes to external factors. For example, a student receives an A on a test. If s/he exhibited internal locus of control, s/he would conclude that they studied hard and were intelligent enough to receive the A. A sense of external locus of control would cause the student to conclude that they received the A because the test was easy, the effectiveness of the teacher, and tutoring help from classmates. Religiosity and spirituality impacts sense of control; for example, we often hear people say, "Everything happens for a reason," which implies that life events occur outside of our control, but those events have a purpose. Similarly, another popular saying is "I prayed about [fill in the blank problem] and it is in God's hands now," which indicates a turning over of the responsibility to solve the problem to God, a higher power. Some of those beliefs may be counter to the assumptions, goals, and change mechanisms of counseling.

All things being considered, counseling is an intervention that facilitates self-introspection and individual change that requires an internal locus of control. We have seen religious men downplay their internal locus of control in favor of an imbalanced sense of external locus of control focused on God. An imbalanced external locus of control contributes to avoidance of counseling and represents a form of religious fanaticism that leads to negative health pathways in men. This imbalance is summed up well with the popular parable of the flood:

> A terrible storm came into a town and local officials sent out an emergency warning that the riverbanks would soon overflow and flood the nearby homes. They ordered everyone in the town to evacuate immediately. A faithful Christian man heard the warning and decided to stay, saying to himself, "I will trust God and if I am in danger, then God will send a divine miracle to save me." The neighbors came by his house and said to him, "We're leaving and there is room for you in our car, please come with us!" But the man declined. "I have faith that God will save me." As the man stood on his porch watching the water rise up the steps, a man in a canoe paddled by and called to him, "Hurry and come into my canoe, the waters are rising quickly!" But the man again said, "No thanks, God will save me." The floodwaters rose higher pouring water into his living room and the man had to retreat to the second floor. A police motorboat came by and saw him at the window. "We will come up and rescue you!" they shouted. But the man refused, waving them off saying, "Use your time to save someone else! I have faith that God will save me!" The flood waters rose higher and higher and the man had to climb up to his rooftop. A helicopter spotted him and dropped a rope ladder. A rescue officer came down the ladder and pleaded with the man, "Grab my hand and I will pull you up!" But the man STILL refused, folding his arms tightly to his body. "No thank you! God will save me!" Shortly after, the house broke up and the floodwaters swept the man away and he drowned. When in Heaven, the man stood before God and asked, "I put all of my faith in You. Why didn't You come and save me?" And God said, "Son, I sent you a warning. I sent you a car. I sent you a canoe. I sent you a motorboat. I sent you a helicopter. What more were you looking for?" (http://epistle.us/inspiration/godwillsaveme.html)

Such extreme external locus of control puts the power of change completely in a divine entity. Although turning over such power may be emotionally and spiritually comforting, it also limits the individual's movement toward initiating the internal mechanisms needed for psychological change. In my (Isacco) clinical practice with religious men, I see this problem arise with sexual behaviors such as masturbation and pornography consumption (see more in Chapter 7). Masturbation and pornography are considered sinful in the Catholic Church (and other religions) and thus, men express a desire to stop both behaviors. When I ask men what they have already tried to do to stop the behaviors, the vast majority describe years of prayer asking for God's help and frequent trips to the sacrament of confession asking for God's forgiveness. Few have moved past the religious/spiritual elements of the behavior and exhibited the internal locus of control to engage in the necessary psychological processes to decrease the targeted behavior.

Conceptualization, Assessment, and Counseling Interventions

Conceptualization

Men may not readily discuss their religion and spirituality with a counselor. Counselors may have a blind spot with religious/spiritual issues due to lack of training or personal biases. Therefore, it is important to not rule out the possibility of a religious/spiritual issue being related to their psychological distress in an initial conceptualization. In this chapter, we have identified several religious/spiritual issues that can be considered in a clinical conceptualization. The assessment section will detail more specific ways to identity a relevant religious/spiritual issue.

Understanding how men are using their religion and spirituality is a good starting point for a clinical conceptualization. To simplify the conceptualization, counselors can categorize their uses of religion/spirituality as positive or negative. The positive uses of religion with men include religious coping, religious support, meaning in life, and the development of prosocial masculine roles. The negative uses of religion entail negative religious coping, religious/spiritual struggle, exhibiting maladaptive masculine roles, and forms of extreme religious adherence. A key question to consider in a conceptualization is how are those uses of religion/spirituality related to their presenting problem? Men using religion/spirituality in positive ways may have sources of strength and resilience to help alleviate the presenting concerns.

Men may not categorize their negative uses of religion/spirituality as presenting concerns to disclose to a counselor. In other words, we have not had a man come to our offices for an intake session and begin by saying, "I need counseling because I view God as punishing me for my sins and I want to change my image of God." Negative religious coping and spiritual struggle are two areas that may be related to the presenting problem. Both are sources of distress and correlated with other negative psychological outcomes, but often fester at an unconscious level. Men may be more vulnerable to exhibiting negative religious coping and experiencing a spiritual struggle. Gender socialization, attachment, and psychoanalytic theories tie together to suggest that men are socialized to focus on aggression and competition while using past relational dynamics with attachment figures to construct their image of a God that leads to negative religious coping (Hvidtjørn et al., 2014). A common psychoanalytic interpretation is that a man's negative relationship with his father contributes to a negative image of God and vice versa. For example, if a man recalls harsh punishment from his father during his childhood, he is more likely to view God as punishing. Implicit negative images of God are often connected to repressed negative emotions, self-esteem issues, and other maladaptive behavior. Therefore, it will be important to facilitate deeper, explicit insight into his image of God, appropriate emotional expression, and decreasing problematic behavior.

In addition to male gender socialization, the degree of religiosity can influence men's use of negative religious coping strategies. It is common for individuals to believe that God rewards or punishes them for good or bad behavior in a kind of quid pro quo relationship. Counselors are more likely to see highly religious men using negative religious strategies during times of crisis and stress (Hvidtjørn et al., 2014). For example, an unexpected termination from employment causes a man to think that God is punishing or abandoning him. Part of the problem with such thinking is that he shifts the blame and responsibility to God rather than looking inwards for possible causes of the termination and personal responsibility, which is part of the imbalanced external locus of control problem.

Along those lines, we describe how men might exhibit an unhealthy rigidity to their religion/spirituality, which contributes to avoidance of psychological services and an imbalanced external locus of control. Another component of a conceptualization is to understand his degree of adherence to his religious beliefs and practices. The degree of adherence may shed light on their openness or closedmindedness to therapeutic change and initiation of needed mechanisms for individual change. Men with a balanced adherence to their religion will likely be able to draw upon their religious/spiritual strengths and resources to enhance their change efforts. Men with an extreme religious adherence may be resistant to or have difficulty with looking inward for change initiatives because of an overreliance on their religious/spiritual resources. In such a situation, the religious/spiritual resources become liabilities rather than strengths. Religious fundamentalism may be an expression of the male client's extreme religious adherence and influence the presenting problem vis-a-vis intolerance, interpersonal conflict, and harsh judgments of others (Silberman, Higgins, & Dweck, 2005). Religious fundamentalism entails a strong identification with the religious affiliation's worldview, sense of superiority, and may be another source of therapeutic resistance if the counselor is not part of the "ingroup" and is viewed as an outsider who is immoral, evil, in need of saving (McDermott et al., 2014). Although the counseling process may not change religious beliefs, practices, and values, counselors can better understand what religious/spiritual factors may be contributing to and correlated with the presenting problem. Thus, integrating the religious/spiritual constructs into a clinical conceptualization is important and helpful.

Assessment

This chapter has highlighted several areas of assessment that can inform our conceptualization of therapeutic interventions with men. We present a combination of informal (e.g., exploratory, open-ended questions) and formal (e.g., self-report instruments) methods of assessment for counselors to use in their clinical practice. See Table 1.1 for an overview.

Assessing men's religious affiliation helps to identify his religious practices and to what degree of adherence, including beliefs, practices, and values.

There are good books that provide an overview of the beliefs and practices of the major world religions. We recommend that counselors read *World Religions: An Indispensable Introduction* (McDermott, 2011), *Living Religions* (Fisher & Rinehart, 2016), and *The Sacred Paths* (Ludwig, 2005) to gain a working knowledge of relevant religious affiliations. However, for clinical purposes of building rapport and understanding how religion/spirituality influences the client's worldview and identity, it is more important to assess the specific religious affiliation, beliefs, and practices of each individual client. Individuals practice their religions in diverse ways; counselors do not want to overgeneralize, assume, or stereotype clients based on limited knowledge of their religious affiliation or a personal bias. Therefore, assessing specific areas used in the major Pew studies cited in this chapter, such as religious service attendance, belief in God, frequency of prayer, can help inform the degree of adherence to a client's religious affiliation. Religious affiliation, beliefs, and practices provide a baseline knowledge of a client's religiosity/spirituality. The other part of the assessment approach is to better understand if men are using religion/spirituality in healthy or unhealthy ways.

Related to the client's affiliations, beliefs, and practices is assessing the degree of religious adherence by the client. Religious adherence is not problematic per se. The assessment is geared toward identifying any extreme forms of religious adherence (avoidance, imbalanced external locus of control, and fundamentalism) that may interfere with the counseling process and be problematic to their mental health. The Religious Fundamentalism Scale (RFS) is a brief, self-report instrument that assesses four main beliefs: (a) there is one set of true religious teachings, (b) these teachings are under attack and must be protected, (c) there is only one right way to follow these teachings, and (d) adhering to these teachings leads to a special relationship with the deity (Altemeyer & Hunsberger, 1992). It is important for the counselor to keep in mind that religious fundamentalism may not be a problem. However, rigid, extreme adherence to religious teachings in a fundamental manner has created interpersonal conflict and a closed mindset for growth (Robertson, 2013).

It is common for a counselor to ask about a client's support systems. Therefore, counselors might find assessing his religious/spiritual supports as a natural point of integration by broadening their definition of supports. Specific questions may focus on religious/spiritual supports in three main areas – support from God, fellow believers, and religious leaders. The Religious Support Scale (RSS) is a brief self-report instrument that assesses those three areas (Fiala, Bjorck, & Gorsuch, 2002). A lack of religious support has the potential to exacerbate the presenting problem for him, while available sources of religious support might represent resources to draw upon with him.

Next, assessing religious coping (positive or negative) can be done informally and formally. Informally, it is common to ask a client about their coping skills and strategies. Counselors can simply ask if the client's religion and/or spirituality are parts of his coping. Specific types of positive religious coping include meaning, control, comfort, intimacy, and life transformation. Two brief self-report instruments may help counselors in this assessment process. First, the Brief RCOPE (Pargament et al., 2011) scale assesses the frequency of engagement in positive and negative religious coping activities during times of stress. Second, the Negative Religious Coping Scale (NRCOPE) scale assesses various types of negative religious coping: spiritual discontent, demonic reappraisal, passive religious deferral, interpersonal religious discontent, reappraisal of God's powers, punishing God reappraisal, and pleading for direct intercession (Pargament et al., 2000). Religious/spiritual struggles may not be as readily assessed by counselors as religious coping. Spiritual struggle is a deeper experience that may be harder to articulate by clients. Moreover, men in my (Isacco) clinical practice tend to explicitly report positive images of God as all-loving, merciful, and forgiving. Yet, myself and other counselors who work with religious/spiritual men have found that beneath those explicit descriptions often lie implicit, negative images of God and a deeper spiritual struggle. Therefore, assessment of spiritual struggle and a client's God image may be a longer process situated within the course of counseling.

Negative religious coping and spiritual struggle have similar features (e.g., demonic reappraisal, alienation from God) (Exline, Pargament, Grubbs, & Yali, 2014). As a result, the assessment process may help to differentiate the two constructs. Counselors may benefit from using the Religious and Spiritual Struggles Scale (RSSS), which is a brief self-report assessment of six domains of spiritual struggle: divine, demonic, interpersonal, moral, doubt, and ultimate meaning (Exline et al., 2014). A key distinction between negative religious coping and spiritual struggle is that spiritual struggle implies a deeper, more existential state. It makes sense that spiritual struggle is comprised of ultimate meaning; there also may be overlap between a spiritual struggle and a lack of meaning in life. Therefore, further assessment of meaning in life may be warranted for conceptual clarity as well as to determine the specific factor related to the presenting problem. The Meaning in Life Questionnaire (MLQ) is a brief self-report instrument of the presence of and search for meaning in life (Steger, Frazier, Oishi, & Kaler, 2006). The Meaning in Life Index (MILI) measures the degree to which individuals believe they have meaning in their life (Francis & Hills, 2008). As noted earlier, religion and spirituality often provide meaning to individual's lives and are generally positive pathways to health. A lack of meaning in life would be a likely sign of distress and despair. Overall, a fine differentiation between the various constructs may not be necessary to understand the impact on the client's psychological functioning. Yet, the assessment process may clarify the constellation of interrelated factors impacting the client and shed light on the direction(s) to take in counseling.

Counseling Interventions

This chapter has identified several religious and spiritual constructs that men may use in positive or negative ways that impact their health. It is unlikely that a man with meaning in his life, strong religious supports, and exhibiting positive religious coping will be a client in your clinical practice. Rather, he will likely be experiencing a spiritual struggle, exhibit negative religious coping, and lack meaning in his life. Discussion of therapeutic interventions will focus on addressing those overlapping areas. Specifically, counselors can assist men to resolve spiritual struggles and reframe negative religious coping into positive religious coping.

Exploring the spiritual struggle in depth and providing him with opportunities to articulate his experience is a good therapeutic starting point. It should be noted that resolving spiritual struggles is a continual process, and resolution occurs on a continuum, ranging from unresolved to fully resolved. The exploratory process helps to clarify the spiritual struggle and enables him to explicitly articulate a difficult-to-describe issue.

Helping men to find meaning in their spiritual struggle is another salient therapeutic intervention. The goal of spiritual meaning-making is to help the client to take a wider and deeper perspective of the spiritual struggle that refocuses him on an adaptive meaning to the struggle. As a result, he is better able to cope with the spiritual struggle. The counselor facilitates this process by asking some probing, exploratory questions such as: "What lesson can you learn from this struggle?" "How might you grow as a result of this struggle?" "How would God want you to respond?" The questions are aimed at helping him see another side to the spiritual struggle beyond the pain it is causing him in the present. The counseling process is advanced by the counselor challenging him to attach meaning to the spiritual struggle, even if it feels artificial at first and integration of the new perspective takes time to stabilize.

Drawing on his religious and spiritual beliefs and practices may play an important role in this part of the counseling process. Religiosity/spirituality are inherently geared toward shifting perspective to something and someone more powerful, higher, and bigger than oneself. Counselors may utilize a spiritual tool such as prayer or encouraging the male client to attend a religious service (Plante, 2009) to jump start the protective factor quality of religiosity/spirituality vis-à-vis reconnecting with a spiritual community, interpersonal religious support, and sense of divinity – all of which lead to a greater sense of meaning with men (Jurkovic & Walker, 2006; Maselko & Kubzansky, 2006).

Summary and Conclusion

This chapter identified and discussed the positive (religious coping, religious support, meaning in life, and positive masculine roles) and negative (negative religious coping, spiritual struggle, forms of extreme religious adherence) ways that men use religion and spirituality. In the process, counselors were presented with a comprehensive list of religious/spiritual constructs that are relevant to clinical practice. Conceptualization of male clients emphasized the need to be aware of the relevant religious and spiritual constructs while

Table 1.1 Assessment Areas and Methods

Assessment Areas	*Description of Assessment Method*
Religious Affiliation	Informal, Open-Ended Questions: What religious affiliation are you? How are you involved in your religion? What religious teachings do you or do you not believe in? What religious practices do you or do you not engage in?
Religious Beliefs and Practices	Informal, Exploratory Questions: Do you believe in God or a higher power? Is religion important to your life? How often do you attend religious services? How often do you pray and/or meditate?
Religious Coping and Support	Informal, Exploratory Questions: Do your religious or spiritual beliefs provide comfort and support or do they cause stress? (Koenig, 2000) Are you a member of a religious or spiritual community and is it supportive? Formal, Self-Report Instrument: The Brief RCOPE – both positive and negative religious coping Negative Religious Coping Scale – various types of negative religious coping Religious Support Scale – religious leaders, community, and God
Religious/Spiritual Struggles	Informal, Exploratory Questions: What emotions do you feel about God? How are you struggling to live up to the moral code of your spirituality? Formal, Self-Report Instrument: The Religious and Spiritual Struggles Scale – divine, demonic, interpersonal, moral, doubt, and ultimate meaning
Meaning in Life	Informal, Exploratory Questions: What gives you meaning in your life? Do you lack meaning? What is your purpose? Formal, Self-Report Instrument: The Meaning in Life Questionnaire (MLQ) – presence and search Meaning in Life Index (MILI) – belief in meaning in life

(continued)

Table 1.1 (continued)

Assessment Areas	*Description of Assessment Method*
Religious Adherence	Informal, Exploratory Questions: Have you ever avoided counseling because of your religious/spiritual beliefs? Do you follow your religious practices and teachings very closely or more openly? How does your religion/spirituality influence your control over personal change? Formal, Self-Report Instrument: Religious Fundamentalism Scale – one set of teachings, teachings are under attack, one right way to follow the teachings, following the teachings creates a special relationship with the deity

assessment efforts can be guided by informal and formal methods that facilitate clear identification of salient factors impacting their presenting problems. Counseling interventions are likely to benefit men by focusing on resolving spiritual struggles, reframing God images, and making meaning out of spiritual struggles – all of which have been shown to improve positive religious coping and psychological functioning.

Case Example

I worked with Howard in individual counseling for over a year at an outpatient counseling center in Pittsburgh, PA. Howard was in his mid-twenties, clean-cut, and very smart. He had graduated from a prestigious university and was working in his chosen profession of organizational technology and big data project management. Truth be told, I really did not know what he did but it sounded techy and cool. He came to counseling because his father had died a few months ago due to the sudden onset of an aggressive form of cancer. Howard considered his father to be his best friend and a bedrock of support. Needless to say, he was full of grief. He looked downtrodden, his eyes were puffy and bloodshot. He clearly had been crying before the first session, but had wiped the tears away rather hastily.

Grief, of course, is an expected reaction to the death of a loved one. So, I began by affirming Howard for seeking help rather than brushing off his emotions. I asked him if it was his decision to come to counseling or was it suggested to him. Howard explained that he had been thinking about it but did not schedule an appointment for a while because he "thought it would just blow over." His boss took him aside at work a few days ago and gave Howard some constructive feedback about his recent job performance. Howard was told that his recent work was sloppy, missing important details, and late. His boss has known Howard since he started at the company four years ago and, thus, knew that this was atypical for Howard. He suggested that Howard take a few days off and seek counseling. Howard acknowledged that he had been struggling at work and was "just trying to get through the day." Clearly, the grief from his father's passing was interfering with his work performance. I asked Howard what he wanted to get out of counseling and his response was surprising to me. He simply said, "I want to grieve properly." I was surprised because I expected Howard to focus on his work performance, but he had already made the connection.

As we began to address his grief, I asked Howard if he was a religious or spiritual person because people tend to draw upon their faith and spirituality during times of grief. Howard identified as Jewish and in particular, what is commonly referred to as "cultural Jewish." To Howard, that meant that he did not really practice any of the religious aspects of Judaism but identified with some parts of Jewish history, culture, music, food, and events. He was vague and described his parents as "more Jewish" than him but that they did not pass the Judaic faith onto him or his siblings. He recalled going to the synagogue for some religious events (e.g., family weddings) during his childhood and adolescence on a rare occurrence each year, but not regularly. Although being Jewish was important to Howard, it was clear that he was not using his faith for religious coping or religious support during his time of grief. Thus, my initial conceptualization of Howard was that he was not a religious man and was not using spiritual tools to address his grief, which was likely exacerbating his presenting concerns.

Therefore, I asked Howard how he had been coping with his father's death and who was supportive to him. Howard acknowledged that he had not been coping well and could not identify any healthy coping skills. He identified his fiancée, Megan, as his primary source of support. Howard effusively praised Megan as "always there for me . . . she has been great . . . is a great listener." Unprompted, Howard returned to the topic of religion and described Megan as a devout Evangelical Christian from an active and practicing Christian family. He then said a statement that I will never forget: "Megan knows exactly what she believes in and what she doesn't. I have no idea." He expressed frustration with that statement. At that moment, I conceptualized that being culturally Jewish was frustrating to Howard because he was going through an internal spiritual struggle related to his father's death. He did not seem mad at God or upset with the Jewish faith. Rather, he seemed lost and confused about how to make spiritual meaning of his father's death. I expressed my openness to discussing religious and spiritual matters to Howard as it would be relevant to his father's passing. I asked him if he wanted to use our counseling to explore his faith beliefs in such a manner. Howard agreed.

I felt the counseling process change when Howard agreed to discuss his faith beliefs as the presenting concern of grief became situated within this larger spiritual context. I began this next phase of counseling with a simple question to Howard. I asked him what he believed in? Howard was stumped by the question and shocked that he was stumped. He acknowledged that he has spent most of his adolescence and adult life declaring what he did NOT believe in and that he never constructed his own beliefs. We agreed that answering that question would take some time. In regard to his father, Howard openly wondered where his father was now that he is not on earth. Howard was not sure that he believed in heaven but wanted to believe that his father was in a better place. He expressed concern and anxiety about his father's whereabouts. His anxiety emerged at work as he had a panic attack during the work day, which required him to retreat to a bathroom stall for an hour. He also reported difficulty falling asleep and sleep disturbances.

Conceptually, I understood his anxiety as having a spiritual context as he was unable to find meaning from a loved one's death. He was engaged in a spiritual struggle but without the language, background experience, or sense of spirituality to understand or address the struggle. Howard's increased anxiety raised my concern. I utilized an integrative approach and implemented several cognitive-behavioral therapy (CBT) techniques to help Howard with his acute anxiety such as deep breathing, guided imagery, and behavioral modifications (e.g., taking a walk in the middle of his work day and seeking more consultation from colleagues). We discussed the option of a psychiatric appointment to explore medications, but he declined. We continued to explore religious and spiritual themes along with the CBT. For example, I gave Howard a copy of *Heaven: Our Enduring Fascination with the Afterlife* by Lisa Miller, a popular book about heaven that people of various faiths and backgrounds find accessible. I encouraged Howard to journal about his reflections from the book as well as to put down on paper his fears, anxieties, and hopes about his father's afterlife. I specifically recommended that he journal for 10–15 minutes before bedtime to express his thoughts, emotions, and reactions as a way to facilitate sleep. After a few sessions, Howard began looking and feeling relieved. He reported less anxiety, more sleep, and improved work performance. He even smiled.

I asked him why he was smiling. Howard stated that he had something important to tell me. He was a good story-teller, paused for effect, left me on the edge of my seat. I asked him to continue. Howard told me that, after reading the book and journaling about his father, he was not 100% sure if there is a heaven but he was 100% sure that his father was in heaven. I decided to take a clinical risk with self-disclosure and told Howard that I both 100% believe in heaven and believe with 100% certainty that his father was there as well. He smiled again, teared up, and expressed appreciation. That seemed like a good moment of meaning-making to us both.

Over the next few sessions, Howard's grief dissipated, and he talked less about his father. His focus shifted to his fiancée Megan and her family. Megan and Howard had postponed the wedding once due to his father's death but were moving ahead with their reset wedding plans. Howard was now confronted with an interfaith marriage situation. He came to a session with a determined look in his eye. Howard started the session by asking me if I remembered when he said that he does not know what he believes in, which was about six or seven months ago in one of our early sessions. Although I did recall that moment, he rushed past my response and emphatically stated that he wanted to revisit exploring what he believes in. I asked him why identifying his faith beliefs was so important to him now. Howard's upcoming wedding to a woman with clear religious beliefs and her family's strict adherence to their religion shocked him to his core. Decisions about his marriage, the wedding day, and family relationships were being made based on religion. To Howard, he either needed to get caught up to speed or risk being left behind, so to speak. I re-emphasized to Howard that I am open to discussions about religious and spiritual themes but that I am not Jewish or Evangelical Christian (his wife's religion) and thus, will lack knowledge of those faiths. Howard indicated that he was not so much seeking my knowledge of those faiths as he was hoping that I could provide a space for him to explore and articulate his beliefs without judgment while providing some feedback and guidance. I agreed that I could do that. We started this phase of counseling by me re-asking Howard the question from earlier in the counseling process – what do you believe in? Howard smiled at the question but had trouble answering it in the moment. We decided that he needed to take some time to think about the question and to put his thoughts into writing. He enjoyed the journaling and wanted to continue. I gave Howard an extra week off between sessions for his exploration.

Howard returned to counseling two weeks later with a full notebook of his beliefs, which he readily disclosed to me. His beliefs were logical, thought-out, and personal. Howard was not struggling with spirituality anymore. He had embraced the search for meaning and the exploration of his spirituality in relation to his fiancée. They did not agree on several important theological beliefs and often agreed to disagree. Howard felt that their relationship deepened by his openness to discuss religious and spiritual topics that were important to her. When we wrapped up counseling over a year after we started, Howard told me that he still feels sad that his father had passed and that he was glad that he still had that feeling. Yet, Howard had clearly processed his grief and accepted his father's death. The lingering sadness was simply a sign of how much he loved his father, and we agreed that he should not try to get rid of that feeling.

Howard is a good example of a young man that did not know how to use his religion and spirituality to help with a significant loss in his life. He initially did not use religion in any meaningful way to cope with the death of his father although death involves spiritual and existential themes. As is typical for many men, he tried to quickly "move on" and return to work. His lack of knowledge and corresponding inability to use religion as well as masculine socialization all exacerbated his presenting concerns. His spiritual struggle focused on confusion rather than anger. Counseling provided a non-judgmental space for him to explore and to articulate his religious and spiritual beliefs in relation to his father's passing. As a result, his spiritual struggle was largely resolved because he gained much-needed clarity into his religiosity and spirituality.

References

Abu-Raiya, H., Pargament, K.I., & Krause, N. (2016). Religion as problem, religion as solution: Religious buffers of the links between religious/spiritual struggles and well-being/mental health. *Quality of Life Research, 25*(5), 1265–1274.

Addis, M.E., & Mahalik, J.R. (2003). Men, masculinity, and the contexts of help seeking. *American Psychologist, 58*(1), 5–14.

Aldwin, C.M., Park, C.L., Jeong, Y.J., & Nath, R. (2014). Differing pathways between religiousness, spirituality, and health: A self-regulation perspective. *Psychology of Religion and Spirituality, 6*(1), 9–21.

Allport, G.W., & Ross, J.M. (1967). Personal religious orientation and prejudice. *Journal of Personality and Social Psychology, 5*(4), 432–443.

Altemeyer, B., & Hunsberger, B. (1992). Authoritarianism, religious fundamentalism, quest, and prejudice. *The International Journal for the Psychology of Religion, 2*(2), 113–133.

Altemeyer, B., & Hunsberger, B. (2004). A revised religious fundamentalism scale: The short and sweet of it. *The International Journal for the Psychology of Religion, 14*(1), 47–54.

Bjorck, J.P., & Thurman, J.W. (2007). Negative life events, patterns of positive and negative religious coping, and psychological functioning. *Journal for the Scientific Study of Religion, 46*(2), 159–167.

Collins, W.L., & Perry, A.R. (2015). Black men's perspectives on the role of the Black church in healthy relationship promotion and family stability. *Social Work and Christianity, 42*(4), 430–448.

Crook-Lyon, R.E., O'Grady, K.A., Smith, T.B., Jensen, D.R., Golightly, T., & Potkar, K.A. (2012). Addressing religious and spiritual diversity in graduate training and multicultural education for professional psychologists. *Psychology of Religion and Spirituality, 4*(3), 169–181.

Delaney, H.D., Miller, W.R., & Bisonó, A.M. (2007). Religiosity and spirituality among psychologists: A survey of clinician members of the American Psychological Association. *Professional Psychology: Research and Practice, 38*(5), 538–546.

Desai, K.M., & Pargament, K.I. (2015). Predictors of growth and decline following spiritual struggles. *The International Journal for the Psychology of Religion, 25*(1), 42–56.

Exline, J.J., Pargament, K.I., Grubbs, J.B., & Yali, A.M. (2014). The Religious and Spiritual Struggles Scale: Development and initial validation. *Psychology of Religion and Spirituality, 6*(3), 208–222.

Francis, L.J., & Hills, P.R. (2008). The development of the Meaning in Life Index (MILI) and its relationship with personality and religious behaviours and beliefs among UK undergraduate students. *Mental Health, Religion and Culture, 11*(2), 211–220.

Fiala, W.E., Bjorck, J.P., & Gorsuch, R. (2002). The religious support scale: Construction, validation, and cross-validation. *American Journal of Community Psychology, 30*(6), 761–786.

Fisher, M.P., & Rinehart, R. (2016). *Living religions*. New York, NY: Pearson.

Frankl, V. (1959). *Man's search for meaning: An introduction to logotherapy*. New York, NY: Washington Square Press.

Garfield, C.F., Isacco, A., & Sahker, E. (2013). Religion and spirituality as important components of men's health and wellness: An analytic review. *American Journal of Lifestyle Medicine, 7*(1), 27–37.

Hammer, J.H., & Good, G.E. (2010). Positive psychology: An empirical examination of beneficial aspects of endorsement of masculine norms. *Psychology of Men & Masculinity, 11*(4), 303–318.

Holt, C.L., Roth, D.L., Huang, J., & Clark, E.M. (2015). Gender differences in the roles of religion and locus of control on alcohol use and smoking among African Americans. *Journal of Studies on Alcohol and Drugs, 76*(3), 482–492.

Hvidtjørn, D., Hjelmborg, J., Skytthe, A., Christensen, K., & Hvidt, N.C. (2014). Religiousness and religious coping in a secular society: The gender perspective. *Journal of Religion and Health, 53*(5), 1329–1341.

Isacco, A. (2016). Measuring masculinity: Developmental contexts, men's health, and qualitative research. *Psychology of Men and Masculinity, 16*, 141–144.

Isacco, A., Talovic, E., Chromik, L., & Yallum, N. (2013). Addressing men's mental health with a strength-based approach. In J.M. Rippe (Ed.), *Lifestyle medicine* (2nd ed.) (pp. 369–381). Boca Raton, FL: CRC Press.

Jackson, B.R., & Bergeman, C.S. (2011). How does religiosity enhance well-being? The role of perceived control. *Psychology of Religion and Spirituality, 3*(2), 149–161.

Jurkovic, D., & Walker, G.A. (2006). Examining masculine gender-role conflict and stress in relation to religious orientation and spiritual well-being in Australian men. *The Journal of Men's Studies, 14*, 27–46.

Kiselica, M.S., Benton-Wright, S., & Englar-Carlson, M. (2016). Accentuating positive masculinity: A new foundation for the psychology of boys, men, and masculinity. In Y.J. Wong & S.R. Wester (Eds.), *APA handbook of men and masculinities* (pp. 123–143). Washington, DC: American Psychological Association.

Koenig, H.G. (2000). Religion, spirituality, and medicine: Application to clinical practice. *Jama, 284*(13), 1708–1708.

Kolodiejchuk, B. (2007). *Mother Teresa: Come be my light.* New York, NY: Doubleday.

Kushner, H.S. (2004). *When bad things happen to good people.* New York, NY: Anchor Books.

Lawrence, R.T. (1997). Measuring the image of God: The God image inventory and the God image scales. *Journal of Psychology and Theology, 25*(2), 214–226.

Lazar, A., & Bjorck, J.P. (2016). Gender differences in the structure and perception of religious support in a religious Jewish sample. *Psychology of Religion and Spirituality, 8*(3), 235–243.

Lee, S.A., Roberts, L.B., & Gibbons, J.A. (2013). When religion makes grief worse: Negative religious coping as associated with maladaptive emotional responding patterns. *Mental Health, Religion & Culture, 16*(3), 291–305.

Levant, R.F., & Richmond, K. (2008). A review of research on masculinity ideologies using the Male Role Norms Inventory. *The Journal of Men's Studies, 15*(2), 130–146.

Lomas, T., Cartwright, T., Edginton, T., & Ridge, D. (2014). A religion of wellbeing? The appeal of Buddhism to men in London, United Kingdom. *Psychology of Religion and Spirituality, 6*(3), 198–207.

Ludwig, F. (1996). After Ujamaa. Is religious revivalism a threat to Tanzania's stability? In Westerlund, D. (Ed.), *Questioning the secular state: The worldwide resurgence of religion in politics* (pp. 216–236). London: C. Hurst & Co. Publishers.

Ludwig, T. (2005). *The sacred paths: Understanding the religions of the world (vol. 1).* New York, NY: Pearson.

Mahalik, J.R., Talmadge, W.T., Locke, B.D., & Scott, R.P. (2005). Using the Conformity to Masculine Norms Inventory to work with men in a clinical setting. *Journal of Clinical Psychology, 61*(6), 661–674.

Maselko, J., & Kubzansky, L.D. (2006). Gender differences in religious practices, spiritual experiences and health: Results from the US General Social Survey. *Social Science & Medicine, 62*(11), 2848–2860.

McDermott, G.R. (2011). *World religions: An indispensable introduction.* Nashville, TN: Thomas Nelson.

McDermott, R.C., Schwartz, J.P., Lindley, L.D., & Proietti, J.S. (2014). Exploring men's homophobia: Associations with religious fundamentalism and gender role conflict domains. *Psychology of Men & Masculinity, 15*(2), 191–200.

Miller, A.S., & Hoffmann, J.P. (1995). Risk and religion: An explanation of gender differences in religiosity. *Journal for the Scientific Study of Religion, 34*(1), 63–75.

Moninger, J. (2017). *10 relaxation techniques that zap stress fast.* Retrieved from www.webmd.com/balance/guide/blissing-out-10-relaxation-techniques-reduce-stress-spot#1.

Pargament, K.I. (2002). The bitter and the sweet: An evaluation of the costs and benefits of religiousness. *Psychological Inquiry, 13*(3), 168–181.

Pargament, K.I., Feuille, M., & Burdzy, D. (2011). The brief RCOPE: Current psychometric status of a short measure of religious coping. *Religions, 2*(1), 51–76.

Pargament, K.I., Koenig, H.G., & Perez, L.M. (2000). The many methods of religious coping: Development and initial validation of the RCOPE. *Journal of Clinical Psychology, 56*(4), 519–543.

Pargament, K.I., Smith, B.W., Koenig, H.G., & Perez, L. (1998). Patterns of positive and negative religious coping with major life stressors. *Journal for the Scientific Study of Religion, 37*(4), 710–724.

Patterson, T. (2014) CNN Photos. *America's 'lost boys' generation.* Retrieved from http://cnnphotos.blogs.cnn.com/2014/07/06/americas-lost-boys-generation/.

Pew Research Center. (2015). *Religious landscape study.* Retrieved from www.pewforum.org/religious-landscape-study.

Pew Research Center. (2016). *The gender gap in religion around the world.* Retrieved from http://assets.pewresearch.org/wp-content/uploads/sites/11/2016/03/Religion-and-Gender-Full-Report.pdf.

Pew Research Center: The Pew Forum on Religion & Public Life. (2012). *The global religious landscape: A report on the size and distribution of the world's major religious groups as of 2010.* Retrieved from http://assets.pewresearch.org/wp-content/uploads/sites/11/2014/01/global-religion-full.pdf.

Pew Research Center: The Pew Forum on Religion & Public Life. (2017). *The Pew-Templeton Global Religious Future Projects.* Retrieved from www.globalreligiousfutures.org/explorer/custom#/?subtopic=15&chartType=bar&data_type=percentage&destination=from&year=2020&religious_affiliation=all&countries=Worldwide&gender=all&age_group=all&pdfMode=false.

Plante, T.G. (2009). *Spiritual practices in psychotherapy: Thirteen tools for enhancing psychological health.* Washington, DC: American Psychological Association.

Ponterotto, J.G. (2008). Theoretical and empirical advances in multicultural counseling and psychology. In S.D. Brown & R.W. Lent (Eds.), *Handbook of counseling psychology* (pp. 121–140). Hoboken, NJ: John Wiley & Sons Inc.

Rabinowitz, F.E. (2014). *Deepening psychotherapy with men: Stories, metaphors, and road trips*. Presented at the National Psychotherapy with Men Conference in Fullerton, CA.

Robbins, M., Francis, L.J., Haley, J.M., & Kay, W.K. (2001). The personality characteristics of Methodist ministers: Feminine men and masculine women? *Journal for the Scientific Study of Religion, 40*(1), 123–128.

Robertson, J.M. (2013). Perceiving religious men through counselor eyes: Risks and tips. *Journal of Counseling & Development, 91*(4), 410–418.

Silberman, I., Higgins, E.T., & Dweck, C.S. (2005). Religion and world change: Violence and terrorism versus peace. *Journal of Social Issues, 61*(4), 761–784.

Steger, M.F., Frazier, P., Oishi, S., & Kaler, M. (2006). The meaning in life questionnaire: Assessing the presence of and search for meaning in life. *Journal of Counseling Psychology, 53*(1), 80–93.

Sullins, D.P. (2006). Gender and religion: Deconstructing universality, constructing complexity. *American Journal of Sociology, 112*(3), 838–880.

Thompson, E.H. (1991). Beneath the status characteristic: Gender variations in religiousness. *Journal for the Scientific Study of Religion, 30*(4), 381–394.

Trzebiatowska, M., & Bruce, S. (2012). *Why are women more religious than men?* New York, NY: Oxford University Press.

Vieten, C., Scammell, S., Pilato, R., Ammondson, I., Pargament, K.I., & Lukoff, D. (2013). Spiritual and religious competencies for psychologists. *Psychology of Religion and Spirituality, 5*(3), 129–144.

Wiggins-Frame, M., Uphold, C.R., Shehan, C.L., & Reid, K.J. (2005). Effects of spirituality on health-related quality of life in men with HIV/AIDS: Implications for counseling. *Counseling and Values, 50*(1), 5–19.

2 How Do Men Use Masculinity?

What is masculinity, and how do men determine what it means to be masculine, for themselves and for other men? How is masculinity something that can be used, and for what purposes? Chapter 2 describes men with regard to the psychological study of masculinity and gender socialization. First, masculinity is defined as a social and psychological construct. Masculinity research has been varied, but the predominant research paradigm currently examines masculinity as an ideology. We will explore differences among men in their masculinity ideologies and adherence to gender role norms. Moreover, this chapter will describe how culture contributes to definitions of manhood, such that there are cultural differences among individual men and groups of men that are important to know and understand. This overview of masculinity and cultural variations of manhood provides the backdrop to identify the harmful aspects of masculinity for men's health compared to positive aspects that have been associated with positive outcomes. Consequently, we suggest ways to assess the client's masculinity ideology and its origin, conceptualize how the client's masculinity ideology is harmful and/or healthy, and clinical techniques to facilitate the client's development of positive masculinity characteristics.

Masculinity Defined

In Western society, anatomical males are primarily associated with masculinity and females with femininity. Through social learning, boys and girls are taught by families and society how to think, act, and feel based on anatomical sex. Those characteristics and roles in society that a culture deems are primarily associated with being male are therefore considered masculine. If asked "what does it mean to be a man?" the answer would be considered a description of masculinity or manhood. However, what is considered masculine can be attributed to females as well, but the characteristics still would be considered masculine. Such characteristics are not only about how a man is supposed to think, act, and feel but what roles he takes on in society as well.

Theories about masculinity have been proposed from several different paradigms, but primarily masculinity has been viewed as a trait, gender role, or ideology. As a trait, masculinity is considered a personality characteristic or attribute. Bem's (1974) seminal theory and research on sex role identity (or gender role identity) in the 1970s showed that masculinity and femininity were two separate dimensions of personality, as opposed to a single dimension, such that a person can be high or low in both masculine and feminine characteristics. As such, a man's gender role identity could be sex-typed (high masculine/low feminine traits), cross-sex typed (high feminine, low masculine traits), androgynous (high masculine/high feminine traits), or undifferentiated (low masculine/low feminine traits). The androgynous identity was believed to be the psychologically healthiest identity, as it would allow for adaptability and flexibility, and research supported this contention. However, the masculine sex-type or masculine gender role orientation was also found to correlate with certain positive characteristics, such as self-esteem, perhaps due to the types of traits that are listed as masculine on the measures (Anthill & Cunningham, 1980; Lundy & Rosenberg, 1987). Examples of such traits include making decisions easily, assertive, self-reliant, willing to take a stand, ambitious, and leadership abilities. Thus, measurement of masculinity focused on those attributes that are considered socially desirable for men.

The gender role perspective considers masculinity as a behavior, in which actions or social roles are defined by a culture as masculine or feminine, or are viewed as typical of men and women (Pleck, 1981). Based on Pleck's (1981) model of gender-role strain, trying to live up to cultural standards of masculinity can have negative psychological, physical, and interpersonal consequences for men such as depression, anxiety, psychological distress, marital problems, health problems, substance abuse, and risky sexual behaviors. This perspective comes from a critique of masculinity and has a rather singular contextual focus on the hegemonic masculinity of US culture. However, Pleck acknowledged that gender role norms vary over time, within a culture, and between cultures. Nonetheless, there is value in considering that no matter what cultural context, trying to adhere or conform to gender roles can be problematic because gender roles are inconsistent and contradictory, or the norms themselves may be psychologically damaging. Alternatively, non-adherence or non-conformity can likewise be problematic, because of the condemnation that can occur as a consequence.

Masculinity as an ideology is an extension of the gender-role strain perspective, regarding masculinity as a belief system at both the individual and cultural levels. Masculinity is a sociocultural construction, and "masculinity ideology refers to beliefs about the importance of men adhering to culturally defined standards for male behavior" (Pleck, Sonenstein, & Ku, 1993, p. 85). Masculinity is therefore a cultural phenomenon that can be internalized by the individual within that culture. As such, there are masculinity *ideologies*, or many *masculinities*, in that masculinity beliefs and standards can vary within and across cultures. For the most part, research in this area has focused on characterizing and researching aspects of traditional masculinity in the United States and the Western world that are in line with the gender-role strain perspective; that is, those aspects of masculinity that are problematic. In this regard, research has examined attitudes about masculinity and gender roles (e.g., "men should be competitive"), gender role conflict (e.g., "hugging other men is difficult for me"), masculine gender role stress (e.g., "feeling as though you are not in good physical condition"), and conformity to masculinity norms (e.g., "In general, I will do anything to win").

Traditional Masculinity Ideology

Much of the research on masculinity ideology has focused on the negative aspects of what has been labelled "traditional" masculinity, which is the hegemonic masculinity of US men. Traditional masculinity, in these terms, not only restricts men from exhibiting signs of behavior or thought attributed to the female role but also entails a wide array of specific behaviors and self-perceptions that men closely adhere to. While most men do not embody all of these qualities, society supports hegemonic masculinity within all its institutions. Given the research has focused on problematic aspects of masculinity, there has been an abundance of research indicating the harmful effects of adhering or conforming to many of the norms of traditional masculinity or endorsement of traditional masculinity ideology (e.g., Arciniega, Anderson, Tovar-Blank, & Tracey, 2008; Brannon, 1976; Courtenay, 2011; Levant & Richmond, 2008; Mahalik et al., 2003; Pleck, 1995; Pleck, Sonenstein, & Ku, 1993; Wade, 2015).

Some of the traditional masculinity beliefs in the United States that have been identified by men and masculinity scholars are that men are, or should be, the following: successful at work, competitive, emotionally controlled, anti-gay, self-reliant, always ready for sex, physically tough, aggressive, dominant, and risk-taking. Men who have strong masculinity beliefs such as these, and who feel they must conform to such masculinity norms, are more likely to have both physical and mental health problems. Although it is not all men, or with regard to all of the aforementioned examples of traditional masculinity, there is a great deal of evidence to support the negative effects of traditional masculinity norms. For example, based on research using the Male Role Norms Inventory, *endorsement* of traditional masculinity ideology has been found to be related to reluctance to discuss condom use with partners, fear of intimacy, lower relationship satisfaction, more negative beliefs about the fathers' role and lower paternal participation in child care, negative attitudes toward racial diversity and women's equality, attitudes conducive to sexual harassment, self-reports of sexual aggression, alexithymia (difficulty accessing and expressing one's emotions), and reluctance to seek psychological help (see Levant & Richmond, 2008).

Based on research using the Conformity to Masculine Norms Inventory (Mahalik et al., 2003), *conforming* to traditional masculinity norms has been found to be related to negative attitudes toward seeking psychological help, psychological distress, the motivation and desire (drive) to be muscular, depression, low self-esteem, poor health behaviors, romantic relationship dissatisfaction, sexist attitudes, and unfavorable attitudes toward gay men (see Isacco & Wade, 2017). It should be noted that these findings are with respect to traditional masculinity generally (i.e., total scale) and not the individual masculinity norms. Additionally, Mahalik (2000) maintained there are benefits and costs to men for both conforming to, and not conforming to, the masculinity norms of the dominant culture. For example, conforming aids males in developing their identity as men and provides social and financial rewards. However, the costs can be the psychological and physical health problems that are associated with enacting certain traditional male role norms. Thus, a benefit of nonconformity is avoiding these problems. On the other hand, nonconformity to masculine gender norms may result in being negatively evaluated and rejected by others.

Positive Masculinity

An alternative perspective to the gender-role strain model of masculinity is the positive psychology-positive masculinity (PPPM) paradigm developed by Kiselica, Benton-Wright, and Englar-Carlson (2016). As opposed to traditional male role norms being problematic for men, there are aspects of masculinity that have positive consequences for men and others. Kiselica and colleagues (2016) identified 11 healthy characteristics: male relational styles; male ways of caring; generative fatherhood; male self-reliance; worker-provider tradition; men's respect for women; male courage, daring, risk-taking; group orientation of boys and men; male forms of service; men's use of humor; and male heroism. The 11 characteristics are considered to emerge from the male gender socialization process but are not considered exclusive only to men, and not all men exhibit all of the strengths. The model also suggests that as opposed to conformity and adherence to male role norms, adaptability and flexibility in one's sense of masculinity and enacting male role norms is what is psychologically healthy.

The PPPM model has implications for counseling and psychotherapy with regard to a strengths-based approach to interventions with male clients (Kiselica et al., 2016). In this way the therapist pays attention to the client's strengths with regard to his masculine self-concept or enacting of male gender roles, in addition to attending to the problems he is having. To do so could help in developing rapport, but it can also help the client to see positive aspects of who he is that he may not be aware of, thereby increasing his self-esteem.

Precarious Manhood

The notion that masculinity is something that is *performed* by boys and men is often referred to in the literature because of the saying "Act like a man!"

Paul Kivel (1992) came up with a popular metaphor – the Act-Like-A-Man Box – to represent the rigid set of expectations that boys must deal with while growing up in the United States. He refers to it as a box because it feels like one, in the sense that a boy must fit himself into this box 24 hours a day, 7 days a week. If a boy tries to step out of the box, he is pushed back in with ridicule and verbal abuse not just from other boys, but from girls, women, and men as well. Sometimes behind the ridicule is the threat of violence. So, boys and men need to perform masculinity in order to show others that they are in the box, or to *act* like they are, because they fear the consequences of stepping outside the box. Continuing with the metaphor, what is expected of men by US society are boundaries that keep men in the box despite any contrary feelings to not conform to those societal boundaries. As a result, men often cover their authentic feelings. Societal forces work to keep men inside the box by means of verbal and physical attacks; for example, being called a wimp, sissy, nerd, fag, punk, or bitch, and fear of (if not actually) being hit, beat up, rejected, or sexually assaulted. Kivel (2013) offered the box as a metaphor for the pressures all boys must deal with, although the extent to which a boy will have control over the conditions of his life will vary depending on his race, socioeconomic status, and culture.

Masculinity as performance is consistent with Vandello and Bosson's (2013) theory and research on precarious manhood. The theory has three main tenets: (1) manhood is a precarious social status, which is elusive and must be achieved or earned; (2) the status of manhood is tenuous and impermanent; and (3) manhood requires public demonstrations to achieve social status because manhood is primarily confirmed by others. Additionally, precarious manhood is in contrast to womanhood, because womanhood flows more naturally from biological changes and remains secure once achieved. The researchers conducted several experiments whose results supported the three tenets.

The third tenet, that manhood requires action (demonstrations) to achieve social status, is most relevant to the concept of masculinity as performance, as well as how men use masculinity. To test this tenet, the researchers (Weaver, Vandello, Bosson, & Burnaford, 2010) asked male and female participants to complete open-ended statements that began with, "A real man. . ." or "A real woman. . . ." The sentences were coded for action verbs, and male participants used more action verbs to describe a real man than they did when describing a real woman. Female participants did not vary in how they completed the two sets of sentences. To test the proposition that manhood requires public demonstrations for confirmation from others, the researchers asked male and female participants to read a fake police report about a bar fight between two people of the same sex over an opposite-sex romantic interest. The perpetrator was considered the person responsible for initiating the fight with a kick or punch after a public insult by the other person, who was considered the victim. Participants rated the perpetrator's behavior based on situational and/or dispositional causes. Female participants and those who rated a female victim provided more *dispositional* causes for the perpetrator's violent behavior. Male participants rated the perpetrator's violent behavior using more *situational* causes. Although their research is limited to US samples and speaks more so to industrialized societies, the researchers refer to Gilmore's (1990) research on masculinity in different cultures to argue that across cultures manhood is considered a status that has to be earned and can be easily lost.

Culture and Masculinities

Within each society or national culture there will be a predominant masculinity ideology, what has been referred to as "hegemonic masculinity" (Connell, 1987). It is the cultural standard to which men strive, and in this sense, it is a culture's version of the masculine ideal. The concept of hegemonic masculinity also includes how masculinity allows for men's dominance over women (patriarchy) and other men. Within a given culture, there are nondominant masculinities that are subordinate to hegemonic masculinity, such as the masculinities of racial/ethnic and sexual minority men. Hegemonic masculinity is supported by cultural norms and societal institutions, such that it privileges those men who are able to enact it and validates a man's masculine identity. To maintain that privilege and status, and one's masculine identity, women and other men, femininity and nondominant masculinities, are viewed as inferior. For example, this is done through the use of sexist, racist, classist, and homonegative language and behavior. However, for men whose masculinities are subordinated, in the construction of a masculine identity they may likewise view women (femininity) and other masculinities (hegemonic and other subordinated) as inferior, and use language and behavior to maintain their masculine identity and status. For example, gay men may use derogatory terms to refer to heterosexual men, and racial/ethnic minority men may use terms that disparage White men's masculinity. However, because the masculinities are subordinated, there is no privileged status with respect to other men.

Although hegemonic masculinity is the dominant masculinity, there will be other masculinities that are similar to it or that are in reaction to it. In a country as diverse as the United States, there will be many masculinities to which a boy will be exposed. However, factors such as race, ethnic culture, socioeconomic status, religious orientation, and social context influence the kind of masculinity ideology that boys learn and internalize through gender socialization. To investigate cultural differences, most of the scholarship on masculinity has focused on the traditional masculinity ideology of the dominant culture in US society and the extent to which diverse groups of men endorse it or conform to traditional masculine norms. However, there is some literature that has described or investigated how masculinity is constructed in diverse groups of men within the United States and in other countries, such as African-American, Latino, Jewish, Asian-American, Russian, Indonesian, and American gay men.

As opposed to describing the masculinity ideology of a culture or subculture, Wade (1998) developed a theory of male identity to provide a psychological explanation for differences among men in their masculinity ideology and other gender-related phenomena. Wade's theory, *male reference group identity dependence*, attempts to explain why men may internalize different conceptions of masculinity and vary in the extent to which they conform to gender role standards. As a theory of identity, masculinity is viewed as an aspect of male identity, and therefore is used as a means of self-definition for some men.

Based on reference group theory (Sherif, 1962), Wade (1998) conceptualized the *male* reference group as a psychological phenomenon – an internal psychological representation of males like oneself or like one aspires to be. The male reference group is the purveyor of masculine culture. It serves as a frame of reference and source of one's self-concept with regard to gender roles. The male reference group may include males in the environment, males who are admired, males who are rewarding to the individual, males whom the individual perceives as being rewarded by others, and/or male role models. Thus, the male reference group may be real or vicarious, and often manifests in the configuration of one's male peer group.

Adolescence is a stage in which exploration and integration of identity become salient (Erikson, 1968). In the process of formulating an identity, peer groups help adolescents develop identities. By choosing to associate with a particular group of friends, adolescents define themselves and create their own social style. Adolescent males will internalize those males and images of males portrayed in sports, film, and music videos, and imitate or try to become like cultural models in terms of dress, manner, language, attitudes, and values. Boys will internalize the masculinity they observe in boys and men because they identify with and want to be like those males – because of feelings of similarity to other males, and because such males are perceived as receiving valued social rewards. They will also define their maleness or masculinity based on other like males or their peer group, which would tend to be homogenous in character. Examples of this type of identity are a college male who is a member of a fraternity, who will only socialize and be friends with other men in his fraternity, and incorporates the fraternity's image of masculinity as his own; or a man who has sexist and prejudicial attitudes because this is what he has learned from other males in his environment with whom he identifies, and to have such attitudes is consistent with being a part of "the group." Wade refers to this type of identity as *reference group dependent*, because it is characterized by conformity to masculinity standards and dependence on a reference group for self-definitions of masculinity. Some males will continue to have this type of identity well into adulthood, whereas other males will develop a male identity that is not dependent on a male reference group.

The *reference group nondependent* identity is characterized by a gender role self-concept that is not dependent on a male reference group for self-definitions of masculinity. Consequently, a man will be relatively flexible, autonomous, and pluralistic in his gender-related attitudes, attributes, and behaviors. For example, a White heterosexual man would be comfortable around racial minority and gay men, and possibly have such men as friends. He would also likely have nontraditional attitudes about masculinity, such that he would be nonsexist, be relatively comfortable expressing feelings, value spending time with his family as much as he values his work, and be able to express views that may not be consistent with the majority of men. Most importantly, these attitudes and behaviors are not because of his dependence on a reference group to define for himself what it means to be characteristically male.

The above theories suggest that there is a dominant masculinity and subordinate masculinities within a society. The masculinity that is internalized is through identification with a male reference group, real and/or vicarious. For identification to occur, there must be feelings of similarity or a sense of connectedness to other males. For the reference group dependent identity, there will be feelings of similarity to some males but not others; there will be an ingroup-outgroup distinction (males like me, males not like me). Here, conformity is important and therefore displays of manhood or performance of masculinity would also be important to show others that you are part of the ingroup. It is a male identity that is rather "precarious."

Conceptualization, Assessment, and Counseling Interventions

Conceptualization

Men use masculinity as a means of self-definition – as an aspect of identity. However, men will vary in the extent to which masculinity is a salient aspect of their identity. When it is of high salience, conformity to the masculinity norms of his reference group will be important. Adhering to such norms, or his masculinity ideology, may be contributing to the problems that he is having and seeking help for. Many of the problems that men have can be directly or indirectly connected to the masculinity beliefs they hold and adhere to; for example, substance abuse, domestic abuse, anger issues, sexual identity concerns, romantic relationship difficulties, and self-esteem issues may be related to a man's conformity to masculinity norms (Mahalik, Talmadge, Locke, & Scott, 2005). Consequently, the client's problem may be conceptualized as his beliefs about masculinity and/or his adherence to masculinity standards that are problematic.

Assessment

The assessment process involves identifying how masculinity is related to the client's presenting concern or other problems in his life, as well as how masculinity might be a strength or potential resource. Initially, as well as in any future sessions, listen for any content that reflects masculinity beliefs or areas of gender role conflict when he talks about the problems he is having. Additionally, take time to discuss and explore with him his beliefs about masculinity in terms of what he feels is important to him as a man. Below are some questions for clinicians that can be used as a guide in the assessment of the client's masculinity ideology, gender role conflict, and conformity to masculine norms:

- To what extent has he been able to live up to or achieve the standards of masculinity he holds?
- In what ways does he feel that he has failed to do what is expected of him as a man (or as a husband/romantic partner, father, or son)?
- Does he believe that men are or should be a certain way, and that there is no other way? (For example, "men are promiscuous, it is natural, but women should not be"; and "men should never back down from a fight.")
- Is he having difficulty with being a husband/romantic partner, father, son, or worker because of what it means to him to be a man?
- Is he able to distinguish between those aspects of himself that are his personality versus his masculinity ideology? (For example, "I am just an aggressive person," versus "Men should be aggressive.")
- Are there aspects of his life in which he has a sense of masculine pride (e.g., provider, taking care of others, career success, fathering, self-reliance).

We find that many men will not be able to describe their masculinity ideology; so to ask them directly to describe their masculinity beliefs may result in very little knowledge that would be of use to the therapist. "Clients may simply be too close to the phenomenon to be able to stand back and identify how they enact gender or to be aware of the effects in their lives" (Mahalik et al., 2005, p. 664). Therefore, it is incumbent upon the therapist to be cognizant of masculinity ideology and strict conformity to it as a potential influence in what their male clients present as a problem or concern.

To aid in the assessment of a client's masculinity ideology, you can have him complete a questionnaire such as the Male Role Norms Inventory (MRNI-SF; Levant, Hall, & Rankin, 2012). The MRNI-SF has items that assess the extent to which the person endorses the Western cultural norms of negativity toward sexual minorities, importance of sex, restrictive emotionality, toughness, dominance, avoidance of femininity, and self-reliance through mechanical skills. He can complete the questionnaire online and get an interpretation of his results (https://akron.qualtrics.com/jfe/form/SV_2oBbBFGeFFAETOJ). Another measure that can be used is the Conformity to Masculine Norms Inventory (CMNI; Mahalik et al., 2003), which assesses the extent to which the person conforms, or does not conform, to masculinity norms found in the dominant culture in the United States. The measure asks about 11 norms including winning, emotional control, risk-taking, violence, dominance, playboy, self-reliance, primacy of work, power over women, disdain for homosexuality, and pursuit of status. Mahalik and colleagues (2005) provide guidance on how to use the CMNI with men in a clinical setting.

When taking into consideration the masculinity ideology of your client, it is important to consider the reference group and cultural influences. Your client's gender role socialization would be influenced by his culture of origin. However, his male reference group could differ from men of his culture of origin. For example, an African-American male may not feel similar or connected to other African-American men, so African-American men would not comprise his reference group. Another example is a gay male who rejects traditional masculinity and whose male reference group is gay men. What would be important to assess is (1) the extent to which he feels he is like other men, and (2) whether he defines his masculinity based on a particular male reference group. You can assess his male identity by asking questions about ethnocultural aspects of identity (e.g., does he feel he is like other Chinese men?) or sexual identity (does he feel he is like other gay men? other heterosexual men?). If he does not feel he is like any other men, he may be experiencing conflict about his masculine identity or identity confusion. If he identifies with a particular male reference group (e.g., athletes, Mormons, Christians, Latinos, a fraternity, a gang), it is likely that conformity to the norms of the reference group is important and should be evaluated for how such norms may be healthy or unhealthy, or contribute to the presenting problem. To do a more formal assessment of his male identity status, you can ask him to complete the Reference Group Identity Dependence Scale (Wade & Gelso, 1998).

Counseling Interventions

In an initial session, it would be important to acknowledge the strength it took for your client to seek help for the problem he has. This would be an accurate statement for many clients despite their gender; however, seeking help is contrary to the masculine norm of self-reliance. He may see himself as having failed in being able to "fix" his own problem, which would have a negative effect on his masculine self-esteem. When doing so, it should be stated within the context of it being something that is understood as being difficult for some men, because of masculinity norms. A discussion about how he feels about being in counseling would give you the opportunity to address his concerns about the process, but also to introduce the topic of men and masculinity within the context of help-seeking. It will set the stage for future interventions that involve addressing masculinity where indicated

Sometimes, if not often, men are not aware of how their attitudes, beliefs, and behavior are a result of their culture; in particular, their gender role socialization. When your client describes how he *should* act, feel, or behave, listen for the masculinity messages that are likely behind these "shoulds." Inquire of him where or how he learned that he should be that way. Take this as an opportunity to provide an explanation of male gender role socialization. The goal would be for him to gain knowledge about how some of his thoughts, feelings, and behavior are a product of his culture's standards of masculinity, and that what may be problematic is that he has internalized certain notions about what it means to be a man and his strict adherence to male role norms. Acknowledge and reinforce where he has been able to live up to his standards, but if they are harmful then point that out as well. For example, he may be a very good provider for his family but at the cost of being unavailable to his children and experiencing health problems due to work-related stress.

A client's masculinity beliefs can be challenged as a cognitive intervention. His beliefs may be "irrational" in the sense that he may consider himself a failure if he does not live up to certain male role norms. For example, having the belief that a man should be self-reliant is a masculine norm that would not need to be challenged. It is not irrational within a cultural context that has such a norm. However, what should be challenged is the belief that a man should *never* rely on others, or that when a man has to rely on others that he is somehow *less than* a man. In our experience, we have often found men who feel they can no longer be a father to their children if they are not able to financially provide for them. To some of them it means they are a failure as a father and as a man, even as a person. In such instances it has been helpful to challenge these beliefs and also to work with them on figuring out other ways they can provide for their children.

Sometimes the client will need to be educated about the costs and benefits of masculinity. In this way, he becomes aware of how what he does is not only something that is a cultural standard but one that he can choose to adhere to or choose to work at being more flexible with. For example, men who are highly invested and successful in their career, consistent with traditional male role norms, typically have used masculinity in a way that has benefited them in the world of work: aggressive, independent, objective, authoritative, risk-taking, task-oriented, decisive. However, the behaviors that are useful in the world of work may not be as useful in his romantic or marital relationship and relationships with his children. Often men are not aware of this, and once it is pointed out to them they can begin to work on becoming more flexible in their style of relating as well as cultivate more closeness in their relationships with others. The intervention is one that helps the client to understand more about how and why he relates to others in the way that he does while recognizing the costs and benefits of a masculine style of relating to others.

Wade (1998) argued that instead of, or in addition to, focusing on the client's masculinity beliefs as an intervention, therapists should focus on *the client's adherence or conformity* to those norms that are problematic. For example, if the client believes that a man should always be ready for sex, and this belief is causing him distress because he cannot live up to it, the therapist can address the belief as well as his strict adherence to it. In other words, addressing his masculinity ideology could mean challenging his beliefs about what it means to be a man, sexually. However, if the therapist were to focus on adherence and conformity, the intervention would focus on "should always," promoting a less rigid and more realistic perspective on male sexuality, and developing his own, personal standards for his sexual behavior. Generally, interventions with a man whose male identity is reference group dependent would involve developing his personal identity or a change in reference group. The counseling would involve helping the client examine the source of his feelings, attitudes, and beliefs, and the extent to which he owns them, or to be like others and accepted by others (especially for the adolescent and young adult male).

Case Example

Prior to becoming an academic, I (Wade) was the director of the social rehabilitation program at Harlem Rehabilitation Center (HRC), a psychiatric continuing treatment program at Harlem Hospital in New York, where the overwhelming majority of patients and staff were African-American. I rarely took on individual clients, but there was one young man who was referred to our program and to me specifically. As the young man approached my office, I had an initial impression. He looked like a character from a 1970s "Blaxploitation" film; in particular, a pimp. He wore an afro, and Black men had long since stopped wearing afros, and a fedora cocked to the side. He walked with a cane and had a limp; it was evident he had some hemi-paralysis. He sat down in the chair next to my desk and says "Whaz up, brother?" with a slight lisp.

William was 28 years old, tall and slender, had dark brown skin, and wore eyeglasses. He was clean and well groomed. He graduated college with a bachelor's degree when he was 24, and had never been gainfully employed. He was mildly depressed because he could not find a job, and he had been abusing cocaine and alcohol. He told me his problem was that he needed a job, could I help him get one? During the initial interview I found out the following information. He was an only child originally from New York and had received his degree from a university in Texas. He was not close with his family. He had hemi-paralysis as the result of a head injury sustained in a motor vehicle accident three years prior when he was 25 living in Texas. He had no friends. He lived alone in a room he rented in what was called an SRO (single room occupancy hotel). He received social security disability benefits. He was not romantically involved and had no children. There was no history of having a mental disorder or psychiatric treatment. He had come to the psychiatric outpatient clinic at Harlem Hospital saying he was depressed because he could not find work, so they referred him to HRC where in addition to the social rehabilitation program there was a vocational rehabilitation program. However, because of his substance abuse he was not eligible for the vocational rehabilitation program. Besides, the vocational program did not help people get jobs, rather it taught work skills through prevocational training and activities.

In our initial sessions I explored what William had been doing with regard to finding a job and what he thought were the reasons for his unemployment. I purposefully did not take the position that is the standard in the mental health field; that is, "first you must stop using substances, then after a period of abstinence, we can work on your vocational goals." In other words, treatment should focus on what is causing the substance abuse or at least treat the substance abuse behavior. I felt that if I took that approach I would lose him, because he certainly did not see his problem as his use of substances. It would be better to wait and see, further assess his use before making it the focus of treatment. However, I did a rather cursory assessment of his usage, and his response was "I only drink because I am bored. I got nothin' to do. Cocaine is only when I get my check, once a month, I do a little." I therefore went along with William's plan, and I told him I would work with him to help him get a job.

William attended the social rehab program three or four times a week and tended to be isolative, sitting among others reading a book or listening to music with headphones on. He sometimes would interact with others and rarely attended any groups; for the most part he did not see himself as a psychiatric patient. We met each time he came to the program, for about 30 minutes to an hour. We would discuss issues related to employment. According to William, he was not able to get a job because he is Black – White racism works against the Black man getting ahead. Another reason he was not getting hired is because he is physically handicapped. My response was that although that may or may not be true, I could not do anything about White racism and there was nothing that could be done about him being a Black man with a handicap. However, there are some things that we could work on that might better his chances for getting hired.

I started with giving William some homework assignments related to job seeking (e.g., reviewing the classifieds, working on a resumé) and he would come prepared to sessions to talk about his homework and any progress with job-seeking. I also monitored his use of alcohol, which was basically several cans of beer daily. Whenever we talked about his drinking too much or his low mood, William would return to the same place in which he firmly stood: his drinking and his low mood are because he is not working: "Help me get a job, man, then I will stop drinking." William looked forward to our sessions, and once I felt that rapport had been established I took a more confrontational approach with William. I asked him had he ever thought that maybe how he dresses, his appearance, might be something that got in the way of his being considered desirable as an employee. Did he think it made him more or less hirable? He took offense by my insinuating there was anything wrong with his appearance, though he was not angry with me. He responded with, "What's wrong with the way I look? I am a Black man, I want to look like a Black man, not some honky." "What? You want me to look like you? Like some White boy?" He said these things in a teasing way, not with any anger. This led to several discussions about "being a Black man" that took place over several sessions.

William was not unattractive, but his presentation or the overall package, so to speak, would not be attractive to an employer. In order for me to get him to present himself differently, I needed to address his racial identity and male identity, or the intersection of these identities. William had a reference group dependent identity, which is characterized by identification with an image or group of males perceived as similar to oneself, while not so with males perceived as dissimilar to oneself (Wade, 1998). There is rigid adherence to gender roles of the reference group, stereotyped attitudes, and limited or restricted gender role experiences and behaviors. In William's case, his reference group was a certain image of Black men as tough, gangster-like, fearless, cool, and controlled. Majors and Billson (1992) referred to this type of masculinity as "cool pose." Cool pose is *performed* to project a certain image and style of being "cool," and it manifests in how one dresses, walks, and talks. With such an identity, even though I was a Black man as well, I was not a part of his reference group because my masculinity was different from his; I was perceived as dissimilar.

In order for William to become hirable, he needed to present himself differently. Some of the cool pose performance of masculinity had to go, and needed to be replaced with a more "mainstream" presentation of himself as a man. Therefore, the counseling focused on changing his reference group or getting him to be more flexible with regard to his beliefs about masculinity. Given that there are costs and benefits to conforming to masculine norms (Mahalik, 2000), we had discussions about how his "style" as a Black man had its benefits but yet had its costs as well. For example, he felt that he was showing people he was a strong Black man, and he got respect from others and the attention of women as a result. It gave him a sense of identity as a Black man. On the other hand, with much reluctance, he was able to agree that it limited his possibilities in the world of legitimate work. He had no aspirations to be involved in illegal activities to make money, where we both jokingly agreed that his type of masculinity was better suited. He wanted mainstream employment. We used me as an alternative version of masculinity and had discussions about why he thought how I presented myself was that of a White man, and the costs and benefits of my style of masculinity or presentation.

William viewed me as a "sell-out," someone who gave up being authentically Black in order for financial gain and to gain status in the White world. I did not take offense to this characterization, rather we talked about how he feels about having to sell out in order to get a job. He believed that to sell out would mean he would have to change who he was in order to fit in. So in a sense, William would have a change in his self-concept, which was a fearful prospect. He thought he would be viewed as a "chump." I asked for his opinion about different famous Black men, such as Martin Luther

King, and whether he considered the man to be a chump? He would say yes sometimes and other times no, and we would explore why he held that opinion. Through this exercise he was able to see there are many masculinities of Black men, but also he became aware of the fallacy of his ideas about Black manhood. I was also able to show him that just as his masculinity was performance, so was the masculinity of many others, although for different reasons. He was able to understand how men who wear a shirt and tie to work are performing masculinity just as he is with his style of dress. In a way he would be changing his self-concept but only with regard to masculinity; who he was as a person would be unchanged.

After about three months of working with William, one day he walked into HRC looking totally different. Indeed, the entire staff and patients were stunned. Gone were the pimp style clothing and fedora. He had a haircut, no more afro. He wore a plain white dress shirt and dark slacks. I was also stunned. He sat down in the chair next to my desk and said, "Whaz up, brother?"

I convinced William that to get some work experience and build up his resumé, he should work as a volunteer for a while. I was aware of a volunteer program in another hospital and I sent William there to be interviewed. They accepted him into their program right away to do clerical work at the hospital. I continued to see William a few more times once a week just to see how things were going with him. William had stopped abusing alcohol and said he no longer wanted to buy cocaine when he got his monthly check. We stopped the sessions when it was clear he no longer needed help with finding a job. He was happy with the volunteer work.

There would likely be different dynamics at play in the counseling if William's therapist was of a different race and/or gender. However, there are certain aspects of this case that illustrate how to conceptualize, assess, and apply counseling interventions when the client's problem is related to his masculinity ideology. A therapeutic alliance would be essential in order to confront the client about what might be problematic about his masculinity ideology. William's masculinity was a subordinate masculinity, and it provided him with a sense of pride and status in reaction to hegemonic masculinity. It needed to be considered within the cultural context and understood as benefiting him in some way. However, his adherence to it and rejection of any other ways of expressing his masculinity limited his possibilities, interfering with his being able to gain any self-esteem from work, which is essential for many men in enacting their masculine identity. The concept of male reference group identity was used to understand his gender role self-concept, and the interventions focused on a change in his reference group to be able to change his masculinity ideology.

References

Anthill, J.K., & Cunningham, J.D. (1980). The relationship of masculinity, femininity, and androgyny to self-esteem. *Australian Journal of Psychology, 32*(3), 195–207.

Arciniega, G.M., Anderson, T.C., Tovar-Blank, Z.G., & Tracey, T.J.G. (2008). Toward a fuller conception of machismo: Development of a traditional machismo and caballerismo scale. *Journal of Counseling Psychology, 55*(1), 19–33.
Bem, S.L. (1974). The measurement of psychological androgyny. *Journal of Consulting and Clinical Psychology, 42*(2), 155–162.
Brannon, R. (1976). The male sex role: Our culture's blueprint for manhood and what it's done for us lately. In D. David & R. Brannon (Eds.), *The forty-nine percent majority: The male sex role* (pp. 1–49). Reading, MA: Addison-Wesley.
Connell, R.W. (1987). *Gender and power.* Sydney: Allen and Unwin.
Courtenay, W. (2011). *Dying to be men: Psychosocial, environmental, and biobehavioral directions in promoting the health of men and boys.* New York, NY: Routledge.
Erikson, E.H. (1968). *Identity, youth and crisis.* New York, NY: W.W. Norton.
Gilmore, D.D. (1990). *Manhood in the making.* New Haven, CT: Yale University Press.
Isacco, A.J., & Wade, J.C. (2017). A review of selected theoretical perspectives and research in the psychology of men and masculinities. In R.F. Levant & Y.J. Wong (Eds.), *The psychology of men and masculinities* (pp. 139–168). Washington, DC: American Psychological Association.
Kiselica, M.S., Benton-Wright, S., & Englar-Carlson, M. (2016). Accentuating positive masculinity: A new foundation for the psychology of boys, men, and masculinity. In Y.J. Wong & S.R. Wester (Eds.), *APA handbook of men and masculinities* (pp. 123–143). Washington, DC: American Psychological Association.
Kivel, P. (1992). *Men's work: How to stop the violence that tears our lives apart.* New York, NY: Random House Publishing Group.
Kivel, P. (2013). The act-like-a-man box. In M.S. Kimmel & M.A. Messner (Eds.), *Men's lives* (9th ed.) (pp. 14–16). Upper Saddle River, NJ: Pearson.
Levant, R.F., Hall, R.J., & Rankin. T.J. (2012). Male Role Norms Inventory-Short Form (MRNI-SF): Development, confirmatory factor analytic investigation of structure, and measurement invariance across gender. *Journal of Counseling Psychology, 60*(2), 228–238.
Levant, R.F., & Richmond, K. (2008). A review of research on masculinity ideologies using the Male Role Norms Inventory. *Journal of Men's Studies, 15*(2), 130–146.
Lundy, A., & Rosenberg, J. (1987). Androgyny, masculinity, and self-esteem. *Social Behavior and Personality: An International Journal, 15*(1), 91–96.
Mahalik, J.R. (2000, August). *A model of masculine gender role conformity. Symposium: Masculine gender role conformity – Examining theory, research, and practice.* Paper presented at the 108th Annual Convention of the American Psychological Association, Washington, DC.
Mahalik, J.R., Locke, B.D., Ludlow, L.H., Diemer, M.A., Scott, R.P.J., Gottfried, M., & Freitas, G. (2003). Development of the Conformity to Masculine Norms Inventory. *Psychology of Men & Masculinity, 4*(1), 3–25.
Mahalik, J.R., Talmadge, W.T., Locke, B.D., & Scott, R.P.J. (2005). Using the Conformity to Masculine Norms Inventory to work with men in a clinical setting. *Journal of Clinical Psychology, 61*(6), 661–674.
Majors, R., & Billson, J.M. (1992). *Cool pose: The dilemmas of Black manhood in America.* New York: Lexington Books.
Pleck, J.H. (1981). *The myth of masculinity.* Cambridge, MA: MIT.
Pleck, J.H. (1995). The gender role strain paradigm: An update. In R.F. Levant & W.S. Pollack (Eds.), *A new psychology of men* (pp. 11–32). New York, NY: Basic Books.

Pleck, J.H., Sonenstein, F.L., & Ku, L.C. (1993). Masculinity ideology and its correlates. In S. Oskamp & M. Costanzo (Eds.), *Gender and social psychology* (pp. 85–110). Newbury Park, CA: Sage.

Sherif, M. (1962). The self and reference groups: Meeting ground of individual and group approaches. *Annals New York Academy of Sciences, 96*(3), 797–813.

Vandello, J.A., & Bosson, J.K. (2013). Hard won and easily lost: A review and synthesis of theory and research on precarious manhood. *Psychology of Men & Masculinity, 14*(2), 101–113.

Wade, J.C. (1998). Male reference group identity dependence: A theory of male identity. *The Counseling Psychologist, 26*(3), 349–383.

Wade, J.C. (2015). Measurement of masculinity ideologies: A commentary. *Psychology of Men & Masculinity, 16*(2), 137–140.

Wade, J.C., & Gelso, C.J. (1998). Reference Group Identity Dependence Scale: A measure of male identity. *The Counseling Psychologist, 26*(3), 384–412.

Weaver, J., Vandello, J.A., Bosson, J.K., & Burnaford, R. (2010). The proof is in the punch: Gender differences in perceptions of action and aggression as components of manhood. *Sex Roles, 62*(3–4), 241–251.

3 Men and Their Relationship with God

In my clinical practice, I (Isacco) have asked hundreds of men over the years to describe their relationship with God. The question is one of the most powerful questions that I ask in my assessments and elicits a wide range of reactions from men. Below are just a few examples:

- John's eyes welled up and then he began to cry.
- Tom stuttered, stammered, and failed to articulate a coherent sentence. Seemingly exhausted, he finally said, "I don't know. It's so much."
- Henry stared at me and expressed appreciation for the question.
- Nathan became animated, his eyes widened, he raised his hands above his head, and responded emphatically "That's impossible to describe!"
- Domenick and many others started their responses with "Great question!" and spent time in deep thought before discussing God as "my best friend . . . a Father . . . someone who is always with me and loves me."

One thing has been certain – nobody has ever been bored by the question about their relationship with God. The range of reactions from men illustrates the benefit and the challenge with this chapter. For many men, their relationship with God is significant and will be relevant to discuss in the counseling process. Yet, the challenge is using counseling tools to address a relationship that men have with their God that is so deep, meaningful, and impactful. We have embraced the challenge in this chapter and welcome the opportunity to examine the divine relationship that encompasses men's lives in diverse ways.

Men's difficulty with putting words to their relationship with the divine mirrors the challenge of measuring the construct in scientific studies with typical psychological tools. Indeed, exploring and understanding an individual's relationship with God is complex but worthwhile because of the association to health outcomes among male populations (Abu-Raiya & Pargament, 2015; Isacco, Sahker, Krinock, Sim, & Hamilton, 2016). For some men, their relationship with God is a source of strength, support, connection, and coping (Isacco et al., 2016), while other men may develop a conflict with God and experience spiritual struggle, anger, and distress – the latter of which is associated with negative health outcomes (Abu-Raiya & Pargament, 2015). Moreover, men may exhibit problematic God images that are associated with poor mental health. The health outcomes and specific nature of their relationship with the divine are experienced uniquely by men and can depend on their masculinity ideology and gender role socialization. Thus, important points of integration in this chapter will be to describe the association between masculinity ideology and relationship with the divine. Understanding the points of integration provide a therapeutic target to offer more tailored interventions.

How would a counselor conceptualize, assess, and intervene with a man when his relationship with God is a salient factor? That is a primary question that we address in this chapter. We answer the question by focusing on two pathways that counselors are likely to utilize with men. The first pathway is referred to as the strength and coping approach. Men experience various life struggles, stressors, and challenges. Counseling entails helping these men to identify and use adaptive coping skills. It might sound reductionist to equate an individual's relationship with their God as a psychological "coping skill." There is some validity to such an assertion based on the prevailing ways that people describe the power and significance of their divine relationship. Yet, their relationship with God may be an underdeveloped and underutilized source of strength and resiliency during struggles and distress. Men may not readily seek help from their God in such instances due to gender socialization that suppresses help-seeking while valuing self-reliance in problem-solving (Addis & Mahalik, 2003). Even men that have engaged in counseling and other forms of help-seeking will need assistance to utilize additional resources and supports during times of distress.

The second pathway entails assisting men who are in a spiritual struggle, and their relationship with God is part of the struggle. A spiritual struggle is a broad term which involves a network of distressing emotions and negative thoughts related to an individual's spirituality. Under the spiritual struggle umbrella, they may also experience problematic God images and a divine struggle. Wilt and colleagues referred to a divine struggle as negative emotions and conflict centered on one's beliefs about God and perceived relationship with God (Wilt, Exline, Grubbs, Park, & Pargament, 2016). Men are prone to have negative beliefs about God and develop fractured relationships with the divine, which impacts their presenting concerns and mental health. Counseling helps them to work through their divine struggle as part of the therapeutic process to alleviate distress, anger, and emotional pain.

In summary, counseling men about their relationship with God can focus on activating an established but underused coping resource or resolving a divine struggle. We describe ways for counselors to assess their relationship with God (i.e., source of strength or struggle), conceptualize the integration with the client's masculinity ideology, and clinical techniques that may help men develop a positive relationship with God.

Defining and Differentiating Related Terms

The literature includes various terms about God across various fields and disciplines. We review the terms that are most closely associated with a relationship with God and can be clinically relevant with men. Counselors assess these terms in slightly different ways. In subsequent sections in this chapter, we provide direction on how these terms may be assessed and integrated into a clinical conceptualization.

God Concept

God concept is defined as an individual's definition of God, which includes an organizing schema of implicit and explicit feelings, images, and representations of God (Foster & Babcock, 2001). In short, a God concept is how he thinks about the divine. For example, considering God as a paternal figure is a God concept that is popular in Judeo-Christian faith beliefs. The example illustrates that a God concept is situated within an individual's theological set of beliefs about traits of the divine (Davis, Moriarty, & Mauch, 2013). Therefore, understanding his God concept requires an understanding of his religious affiliation and associated theological beliefs.

God Image

God image refers to an individual's perceptions about the nature of God (Bradshaw, Ellison, & Marcum, 2010). Individuals view God in different ways; for example, some men may see God as essentially loving, forgiving, caring, protective, benevolent, and personal, while other men view God as essentially remote, distant, uninterested, vindictive, punishing, and judging. Froese and Bader (2010) indicated that there are essentially four types of God images: (1) an authoritative God, (2) a benevolent God, (3) a critical God, and (4) a distant God. Such types are helpful for assessment and conceptualization purposes to categorize male clients' descriptions of their God image. A God image goes beyond an individual's view of God to an emotional and relational experience with the divine (Davis, Moriarty, & Mauch, 2013). For example, some Iranian Muslims may perceive God as a mixture of being closely involved in their lives, but scary (Ghorbani, Watson, Omidbeiki, & Chen, 2016).

Although distinct constructs, God concept and God image are considered two types of "God representations" (Olson et al., 2016). The two types of God representations share conceptual overlap and have often been used interchangeably as "God schemas" or "internal working models" of an individual's mental or neural experience with the divine (Davis, Moriarty, & Mauch, 2013). Both involve knowledge about God; the crucial distinction is that God concept is cognitive, theologically based "head knowledge" and God image is relational-emotional "heart knowledge" about the divine

(Currier et al., 2017). In this chapter, we focus more on God image because it aligns closer to the individual's *relational* experience with the divine.

God image has been studied in relation to psychological outcomes. Understanding how a client views God offers an important insight into his mental health and current psychological functioning. In samples of men and women, a positive God image (e.g., loving, caring, forgiving) has been associated with decreased psychiatric symptoms, lowered anxiety and depression, higher self-esteem, less feelings of shame, and increased ability to cope with stress, whereas a negative God image (e.g., cruel, judging) was associated with poor self-worth and increased psychiatric symptoms (Koohsar & Bonab, 2011; Nguyen & Zuckerman, 2016; Steenwyk, Atkins, Bedics, & Whitley, 2010). Those findings reinforce the importance of the assessment phase to inform how God image and mental health status are associated. Such information about whether the client has a positive or negative view of God informs subsequent clinical decision-making such as utilizing a more strength-based or remedial approach.

God Attachment

Both God concept and God image have been situated within attachment-based conceptualizations (Davis, Moriarty, & Mauch, 2013). God attachment is a stand-alone construct in the literature that is also based in classic attachment theory. Thus, there is conceptual similarity and distinction between God concept, God image, and God attachment. God attachment goes deeper into the man-divine relationship than God concept and God image. Specifically, God attachment is defined as how an individual appraises the relational dynamic with God in terms of secure, insecure, anxious, and/or avoidant styles (Ellison, Bradshaw, Kuyel, & Marcum, 2012). Rather than parents, individuals consider God as a primary attachment figure and seek safety and comfort within their divine relationship.

Several empirical studies have examined God attachment in relation to psychological wellbeing and mental health outcomes. Similar to associations reported earlier between God image and health outcomes, a secure attachment to God was associated with greater life satisfaction, lower levels of anxiety and depression, and increased sense of social support, while anxious attachment to God was associated with negative outcomes. Various kinds of socio-emotional-developmental problems may emerge if an individual has an insecure, anxious, or avoidant attachment relationship with their God, such as less self-directed coping and more alcohol use (Hernandez, Salerno, & Bottoms, 2010). In regard to both God image and God attachment, there may be a similar underlying mechanism that helps to explain the associations. Simply put, individuals turn to God during stressful times and are more likely to do so if they view God as loving, forgiving, and caring as well as having a secure attachment relationship with God. Thus, they activate and utilize an existing strength to overcome the distress and challenge. Conversely, viewing God as cruel, judging, and distant is likely to compound stress, while an insecure attachment with God is an absence of a possible support.

Relationship with God

Relationship with God and attachment to God are often used interchangeably. We acknowledge some overlap but emphasize that relationship with God and God attachment are distinct. God attachment refers to an individual's sense of security in relation to their God based on dimensions from classical attachment theory (Paine & Sandage, 2017). Relationship with God is defined by how individuals relate to a personal, divine being in terms of connection, interaction, mutual feelings of affection, intimacy, closeness, fulfillment of needs, and sense of belonging (Laurin, Schumann, & Holmes, 2014). Relationship with God is considered dynamic, real, and inclusive of positive and negative appraisals and emotions (Isacco et al., 2016). In short, a divine relationship is similar to the dynamics and experiences of interpersonal relationships for many people.

This is a book for clinical practice with men. However, a research project provides an important story that illustrates how a group of men describe their relationship with God. Please bear with us as we tell a brief research story.

A few years ago, my research team and I (Isacco) conducted a qualitative study with a small group of Catholic priests (see Isacco et al., 2016). We asked the priests a range of questions about their health and wellbeing, with one question being "What faith beliefs and/or spiritual practices most impact your mental and physical health?" Qualitative research is a lot like clinical practice. For example, as a qualitative researcher and counselor, you pose an open-ended question for exploration and wait to hear how the participant/client answers the question in their own words. Months into the data analysis process, the research team had a moment of unexpected insight. The priests had described a dynamic relationship with God as the most important faith belief to their mental health. They discussed the relationship as mutually beneficial, interactive, unitive, fluid, and central to their lives. Their relationship with God had clear psychological benefits such as providing a sense of connection and support, increasing positive emotions, empowering, enabling authenticity, and creating balance in their lives. They discussed God in a way that made God real, tangible, concrete even to members of the research team that identified as atheist. Our research participants were Catholic priests – men in spiritual and religious ministerial roles. It made sense that their mental health was closely connected to the source of their spirituality and faith, namely their belief in an intimate, dynamic relationship with God.

Yet, those relational characteristics and psychological benefits have been identified by other individuals and groups. Hodge and Horvath (2011) examined 11 studies regarding the spiritual needs of patients in health care settings. The participants across the 11 studies were from various regions across the United States as well as other countries (e.g., Finland, Taiwan); they identified with many of the world religions and some smaller religious communities: Catholic, Protestant, various Christian denominations, non-denominational Christian, Muslim, Bahai, Jewish, Mormon, Jehovah Witness, Buddhist, and Muslim. Relationship with God was one of the top six spiritual needs identified by patients across the various geographic regions and religious affiliations. Their relationship with God provided meaning and purpose, hope, comfort, reassurance as well as someone to question, blame, and "wrestle with" in the context of their current health situation (Hodge & Horvath, 2011, p. 311). Thus, an individual's relationship with God can serve multiple positive functions when under distress in a health context.

Although a relationship with God serves positive functions, for others, a relationship with God may be conflictual and strained (Wood et al., 2010). A conflictual relationship with God is associated with spiritual or divine struggle and typically includes feelings of disappointment and anger with God. The feelings of disappointment and anger with God stem from negative life events, past experiences of victimization, holding God responsible for personal harm, attributions of cruelty, feeling abandoned or punished, difficulty finding meaning in life, among other reasons (Exline, Park, Smyth, & Carey, 2011). Experiencing a divine struggle and the associated emotions toward God can be an expected reaction to negative life events and experiences. Yet, divine struggles have been associated with mental and physical health difficulties (Exline et al., 2011). One theoretical explanation for the association is that a divine struggle is usually a long-term stressor, and any chronic stressor contributes to poor health outcomes.

Relationship with God and Masculinity

Laurin and colleagues (2014) reported that a relationship with God is common for people of all walks of life. Several studies across various disciplines (e.g., psychology, sociology), going back to the 1960s (e.g., Vergote et al., 1969) have found that individuals exhibit a gendered God image. This section will describe some gender differences and how masculinity intersects with men's relationship with God.

It is common for individuals to make sense of God in familiar ways. The gendered God images are typically based in parenting models from their mothers and fathers (e.g., authoritarian, caring, loving) and corresponding theological beliefs (e.g., God as Father). People assign gender-socialized as well as family-of-origin-based masculine and/or feminine descriptors to God. Masculine descriptors entail adjectives, traits, and roles such as father, law, order, authority, justice, power, while feminine descriptors are focused on mother, caring, healing, loving, and nurturing (Shah, Bartkowski, & Xu, 2016). Along these lines, men and women have been found to have different gendered God images. For example, boys and men viewed God as more authoritarian, controlling, and purposeful as well as less loving, peaceful, and calming (Krejci, 1998; Steenwyk, et al., 2010). Such findings are largely congruent with literature reporting that men experience God as less forgiving and more vengeful than women (see Chapter 6).

Nguyen and Zuckerman (2016) examined gender differences in God images among 500 participants and found that women reported stronger beliefs in all four God images in the study compared to men (God as provider, God as ruler, God as creator, relational God). The statistical difference spanned all of the God image types and may be indicative of a prevailing notion that most people have male views of God because of dominant Judeo-Christian theological beliefs in a paternal God figure. Whitehead (2012), in a study with a national sample of 1,648 participants belonging to various world religions, reported that men and women with a masculine image of God also had a conservative gender ideology (e.g., men are better suited for politics; men should earn more than a woman). Such a finding may reflect larger patriarchal views in Western societies. Those traditional societal expectations of manhood may trickle down to individual men and contribute to their adherence to specific parts of a traditional masculinity ideology such as power over women, dominance, and primacy of work. Adherence to those certain masculinity norms may be a barrier for men to engaging in a trusting, dependent relationship with God. For example, men can be socialized away from engaging in a relationship due to masculine norms of independence, self-reliance, and avoidance of intimacy.

Conceptualization, Assessment, and Counseling Interventions

Conceptualization

In their relationship with God, men may describe connection, support, intimacy, closeness, a sense of belonging as well as frustration, anger, and struggle. They express a diversity of God images, ranging from problematic to very positive. There is not a one-size-fits-all model, which reinforces the need for an individualized conceptualization and assessment approach prior to implementing counseling interventions. For this chapter, we focus on counseling interventions that help men utilize their relationship with God as a strength to overcome challenges or to alleviate distress from a conflictual relationship with God. The conceptualization and assessment will help to determine what is the most appropriate approach.

The various constructs (God image, God attachment, relationship with God) and health outcomes are associated in a way that presents a straightforward way for a conceptualization. A positive God image, secure attachment to God, and a supportive-intimate relationship with God are all associated with positive health outcomes. A man that fits into this category is likely to describe God as loving, caring, forgiving, and someone he can trust to go to during times of stress, challenge, and distress. Men exhibiting indicators of such a positive connection are likely to fit well into a counseling approach that emphasizes God as a source of coping to overcome the presenting concerns. Simply put, their relationship with God is a strength that can be used in counseling. Conversely, a negative God image, insecure/anxious/avoidance attachment to God, and a conflictual relationship with God are associated with negative health outcomes. A man that fits into this category is likely to describe God as punishing, controlling, cruel, distant, and a source of distress, anger, and disappointment. Men exhibiting indicators of such a negative connection are likely to fit well into a counseling approach that involves some healing of the conflicted divine relationship. What are some contributing factors to help explain those two divergent paths?

Attachment theory is used to conceptualize a large part of a man's relationship with God. A basic, yet applicable, theoretical premise of attachment theory is that the nature of the bonding experience between infant and caregiver during early childhood influences subsequent intimate relationships in adulthood (Ellison et al., 2012). The premise has been applied to adults' relationship with God, with the belief that a secure and loving attachment with primary caregivers during childhood will lead to secure attachment styles with God as an adult. The opposite is also hypothesized; i.e., insecure, anxious, and avoidant attachment with primary caregivers during childhood will contribute to negative attachment styles with God as an adult. Thus, the clinical conceptualization involves an exploration of early parenting relationships to understand how they impact current interpersonal dynamics and the presenting concerns. In this context, the conceptualization extends to identifying how the early parenting attachment styles have influenced his attachment to and relationship with God. Evidence of trauma, abuse, harsh parental discipline, overly controlling conditions in the family of origin, traumatic events are all factors that may lead to a negative relationship with God as an adult. He may blame God for some of the childhood experiences and/or associate the negative behaviors of his parents with characteristics of God.

Given the prevailing masculine images of God and beliefs in God as a Father among many world religions, gaining specific insight into the attachment to his father will likely prove beneficial to understanding his relationship with God. For example, men may express a "father wound," resulting in unresolved feelings of loss and grief about their father, which they transfer into their divine relationship. Discovering how men were disciplined by their father as children is worthwhile to understanding cognitive and affective parts to their God image. An authoritative father during childhood, which is a balance of responsiveness and demanding, can contribute to an adult man perceiving God as loving, forgiving, and trustworthy (Chou & Uata, 2012). He is hypothesized to develop perceptions of God as cruel, judging, and punishing if he was raised by a strict disciplinarian father during childhood. These hypotheses, of course, do not generalize to all men, but provide a useful perspective for a conceptualization that can be brought to light through the counseling process. Men may tend to repress negative feelings from childhood (Rabinowitz & Cochran, 2002) and, thus, initially express positive thoughts and feelings about God. It is reasonable to conceptualize some initial positive expressions as masking some implicit negative feelings about God and contributing to intrapsychic conflicts. Masking of internal painful emotions is a common defense mechanism among men socialized in Western societies. Addis (2011) emphasized the theme of silence in his book about men; a primary takeaway is that men have very active inner lives but often suffer in silence to maintain their sense of manhood in relation to others.

Indeed, the degree of repression often relates to their gender role socialization and masculinity ideology. For example, men socialized in traditional forms of masculinity are more likely to be emotionally stoic or have difficulty expressing emotions, especially feelings of hurt, loss, grief, and woundedness (Rabinowitz & Cochran, 2002). A relationship with God mirrors dynamics with their interpersonal relationships. Similar to an interpersonal relationship, a divine relationship involves an array of emotions (positive and negative). While masculinity ideology may influence emotional expression and relatedness to God in several other ways, we focus on two in this conceptualization: (1) anger with God and (2) isolation from God.

Exline and colleagues have been at the forefront of studying anger with God as part of an individual's divine struggle. Becoming angry, disappointed, upset with God is a possibility. It is important to consider their masculinity ideology and gender socialization as a key contextual piece of information about their emotional reactions to God. Men adhering to traditional gender norms are more likely to become angry with God because anger is a safer emotion to express. Thus, to maintain their manhood status, he (unconsciously or consciously) concludes that it is safer to express anger than an emotion that may be deemed unmanly by others. Reacting with anger is a similar process for men to reacting with vengeance, as described in Chapter 6 ("Men and Forgiveness"). Integrating a "masculine depression" view into this conceptualization will help illustrate this point more clearly. Depression is marked by feelings of sadness, worthlessness, loneliness, and anhedonia. However, men adhering to a traditional masculinity ideology have been found to express depression in externalizing ways such as disruptive behaviors, arguments, anger, and aggression (Nadeau, Balsan, & Rochlen, 2016). Therefore, men adhering to a traditional masculinity ideology are more likely to express anger toward God to mask or to armor themselves from painful feelings and feelings considered too feminine for a man to express such as sadness.

Second, no matter the presenting concerns, counseling generally tries to help clients to approach and to utilize coping resources during times of stress. However, a spiritual struggle that involves anger and disappointment with God can lead to a disconnect with God during a time when connection would be helpful. Although not applicable for all men and women, some scholarship has indicated that men rely less on relationships to cope with stress and, thus, male clients may react similarly by isolating themselves from God (Reiner, Anderson, Hall, & Hall, 2010). Masculinity ideology plays a role in self-isolating behaviors, as they are adhering to such gender norms as independence and self-reliance in their attempt to solve problems. They often have difficulty seeking help from others for an array of problems and, thus, may not even consider seeking help from God to alleviate their presenting concerns. The presenting concerns may worsen if male clients attempt to turn to God for support and do not perceive reciprocal action from God. Men are likely to express such scripts as

> "God is not listening to me. I am alone with this problem."
> "I have prayed and God hasn't done anything."
> "God has abandoned me."

Those kinds of script are clear signals that they perceive unsuccessful attempts to seek help from God, contributing to his disengagement from the divine relationship and deepening his anger and disappointment with God.

Assessment

In Chapter 1, we identified differences in religious affiliations, beliefs, and practices between men and women. Belief in God is one specific difference, as the latest PEW Statistics (2015) indicate that 78% of men believe in God compared to 87% of women; conversely, 12% of men do not believe in God compared to 6% of women. Men who do not believe in God are not likely to have a personal relationship with God (see Chapter 9 "Religious Drifters"). A man's belief in God is typically contextualized within their religious affiliation. The world religions have different beliefs about the divine (e.g., monotheism, polytheism) and the relationship that humans have with the divine. For example, a Jewish man believes in a monotheistic God, often called Yahweh, while a Christian man believes in a monotheistic God while referring to him as Jesus. For assessment purposes, religious affiliation is not necessarily required for positive outcomes to occur, as Rosmarin and colleagues (2013) found that belief in God, separate from religious affiliation, was associated with higher response to treatment and reductions in depression and self-harm in a psychiatric sample. The primary point is that the type of belief(s) in God is the baseline for how individuals develop their God image, attachment, and relationship with God. Thus, it is worth asking if he believes in God or not prior to implementing additional assessments of their relationship with God. Some example questions include "Do you believe in God?" "What do you believe about God?" or you can use an inviting directive such as "Tell me about what you believe about God." Men may have an easier time disclosing what religious and spiritual beliefs they do not believe in; asking what they *do* believe in is a valuable therapeutic exercise that aids assessment efforts.

Table 3.1 has several self-report, paper/pencil assessment tools for God concept, God image, attachment to God, and relationship with God that can be used in counseling. The assessment tools have been used in various research studies and clinical settings, demonstrating versatile psychometric evidence and practical utility. The suggested assessment approach is to use a combination of the paper/pencil tools and exploratory questions. This section will provide examples of some open-ended questions that can be used in the assessment phases of counseling as well as deeper exploration of these complex experiences with the divine.

God Concept: How do you think about your God?

> What adjectives can you use to describe your God?

God Image: What kind of God is your God?

> How do you think and feel about your God?
>
> In what ways does your God impact your life?

Attachment to God:

> Assessing early childhood relationships is part of the Attachment to God assessment. Counselors invite him to describe his early childhood attachments with caregivers, solicit adjectives for those relationships, and inquire about emotions in specific events with caregivers (George, Kaplan, & Main, 1996). Information from this line of questioning will assist in shedding some light on his attachment to God. Next, counselors can ask some of the following sample questions:
>
> How do you feel about your relationship with God?
>
> Has your relationships with your parents influenced your relationship with God?

Relationship with God:

> How can you describe your relationship with God?
>
> Does your relationship with God provide you with support and strength to overcome challenges or stress and conflict?
>
> Is your relationship with God part of your current presenting concerns?

Finally, it is important to assess the degree of intersection between his masculinity ideology and his relationship with God. Using the masculinity ideology tools from Chapter 2 is a helpful way to assess his adherence to relevant norms such as self-reliance and aggression (from Levant's MRNI) and independence (from Mahalik's CMNI). In addition, masculine depression can be assessed using the Masculine Depression Scale (MDS; Magovcevic & Addis, 2008), which asks men whether and at what level they have experienced a number of externalizing symptoms (e.g., violence, irritability, avoiding others, alcohol consumption) during the past two weeks. To complement the use of the MDS, the counselor may pose some open-ended questions for exploration and insight. Some examples include the following:

- What feelings do you have towards God during this time of stress?
- Are you angry and disappointed with God?
- Have you approached God for help or avoided God?
- Is it possible that your feelings of anger and disappointment are masking more vulnerable feelings such as sadness with God?

Counseling Interventions

Counseling that addresses a client's relationship with God has been enacted in a variety of therapeutic modalities (individual and group), theoretical orientations (e.g., psychodynamic, existential, cognitive), formats (manualized or non-manualized), and settings (inpatient and outpatient) (Moriarty & Hoffman, 2007; Olson et al., 2016). Thus, counselors can incorporate his relationship with God into various counseling contexts. This section will primarily focus on individual counseling as it would be appropriate given relevant clinical and ethical issues (e.g., informed consent, client autonomy, and collaborative decision-making between client and counselor) (Moriarty & Hoffman, 2007). As discussed throughout the chapter, we will present two typical pathways in treatment: (1) strength-based and (2) remedial approaches.

A positive, healthy, supportive relationship with God is a reality for some men and can be used as a coping resource in counseling to alleviate the presenting distress and stress. For example, in a study of Latino men with prostate cancer, they considered God part of their "alliance of support" that buffered them from suicidal thoughts and provided hope for the future (Maliski, Husain, Connor, & Litwin, 2012). The strength-based approach described in this chapter draws from similar approaches with men (e.g., Englar-Carlson & Kiselica, 2013; Isacco, Talovic, Chromik, & Yallum, 2013) and is applied specifically to their relationship with God. Like all therapeutic approaches, a strength-based model is based on establishing a strong therapeutic relationship and understanding of his presenting concerns. Yet, a key theoretical assumption that guides the next steps is that identifying, accessing, and utilizing his strengths is a key mechanism toward facilitating healthy changes. Therefore, the counselor focuses the counseling process on exploring his relationship with God as a strength that can help him in the current time of difficulty.

Some men may readily identify their relationship with God as a strength and coping resource, while other men may need guided facilitation to arrive at the identification using the open-ended questions in the assessment section. After he has identified his relationship with God as a strength, counseling shifts to helping him utilize his divine relationship. The counselor facilitates an exploration of how he has perceived help from his God in past stressful situations. Lessons may be drawn from the past situations to the current situation. In addition, the counselor can work collaboratively with him to establish an action plan to direct his thoughts and behaviors toward utilizing his relationship with God in a more purposeful way. The action plan may include generalizable behaviors according to his religious beliefs, practices, and religious affiliation:

- Setting aside time each day to pray/communicate with his God and/or participate in a religious activity (see Chapter 4).
- Meeting with a spiritual leader for focused conversation(s) about God's role in his life.
- Reading suggested religious-spiritual literature for increased knowledge and understanding about God.

The strength-based approach encourages him to draw upon his relationship with God to cope with the current presenting concerns and as a resource for resiliency. In addition, the counselor prompts him to identify any potential barriers to enacting the action plan and how to overcome those barriers. The counselor and man proceed in counseling with the action plan in place and monitor how accessing his relationship with God impacts his mental health and psychological functioning.

The second counseling approach is used when his relationship with God is fractured and associated with negative emotions. His relationship with God can change, from positive to negative or negative to positive. For example, in older men, we have heard narratives about how they "used to" view God in a negative way earlier in their life but have learned to view God more positively. Like all relationships, his relationship with God is not static, but impressionable to changes over his life. Counseling can contribute to positive changes in a man's divine relationship. It is unlikely that he will begin counseling with an explicit treatment goal to improve his relationship with God. Rather, improving his relationship with God will be part of his corresponding psychological, emotional, and spiritual changes. Yet, it may arise to his explicit awareness that he has negative God images, an insecure God attachment, and/or a fractured relationship with God during the therapeutic process. He may express feelings of anger and disappointment toward God. The counselor and client need to collaboratively agree to integrate a remediation of his divine relationship into counseling. Upon agreement, the counselor may proceed with utilizing an integrative approach that has been put forth in scholarship and empirical studies by Moriarty and Davis (2012) as well as by Olson and colleagues (2016). It is worth noting that Moriarty and Davis were also part of Olson's research group. We appreciate Dr. Edward Davis for freely sharing the treatment manual with us for use in this scholarly project (Davis, 2018, personal communication).

The counseling approach to promote positive change in his relationship with God is based in narrative and attachment theories. A primary assumption from narrative theory is that he constructs a spiritual narrative of his life, which guides the counseling process by deconstructing negative narratives about God and reconstructing new, positive narratives about God. From attachment theory, a primary assumption is that the divine relationship narratives represent interpersonal experiences with his early childhood caregivers, which contributed to his schemas about relationships as an adult. Thus, counseling explores past experiences in his relationships with caregivers to increase insight into his present divine relationship. Counselors can use four core techniques that are based on those theoretical assumptions.

First, the counselor guides him through an expressive exercise to articulate his spiritual narrative. The expression of the spiritual narrative is suggested to be done in a combined writing and in-person format across counseling sessions. Some men may find expressive writing to be especially beneficial for identifying and expressing emotions about their divine relationship (Wong & Rochlen, 2009). The counselor poses some open-ended questions to facilitate the construction of the narratives; some examples are provided below (Pargament, 2007):

- When did you first learn about God?
- How did you foster your relationship with God when you were younger?
- Have you had periods in your life when you felt disconnected or lost from God?
- What feelings do you have about God? How have those feelings changed?
- How do you feel that your problems have affected your relationship with God?

Second, constructing such narratives are likely to elicit negative and painful emotions. Thus, incorporating soothing interventions is important. The counselor uses some mindful-awareness practices such as contemplation, mindfulness, guided reflection, and prayer to process and regulate painful emotions. Together, the counselor and client identify themes, plots, and characters within the narrative that are relevant to the negative emotions and presenting concerns. An imagery technique has been identified as particularly helpful because it addresses both the cognitive and affective components to the relationship with God (Moriarty & Davis, 2012). The counselor assists him in meditating on a spiritual passage (e.g., the Prodigal Son) by imagining himself in the scene and interacting with the characters. The interactions with the characters within the scene provide insight into current problematic relationship dynamics. The counselor encourages him to engage multiple senses and to recall as many details as possible. He discusses his feelings, thoughts, and interactions. The guided imagery technique is set in a safe therapeutic environment and accompanied by grounded breathing.

Third, the counselor engages him in a modified automatic thought-recording exercise. A cognitive approach may be welcomed by some more cognitively oriented men. The thought-recording exercise entails five categories.

(1) The situation, which asks him to briefly describe an actual event that he perceived God as contributing to his negative feelings.
(2) Feelings, which are the negative feelings identified as a result of the described situation. He rates the intensity of each feeling from 0 to 100 (with 100 being the most intense).
(3) Automatic thoughts, which are the corresponding thoughts about God to the situation and feelings.
(4) Real God Response is a category that implores him to consider a more realistic understanding of God in the situation based on religious teachings.
(5) Outcome is re-rating the feelings from category 2 after completing the Real God Response.

The goal of this cognitive tool is to help him experience positive emotions about his relationship with God, which counter his previously held negative representations and emotions.

The co-constructing of a new, more positive narrative about God in his life is the fourth and final core technique. The cognitive tool described above begins the process toward this reorientation. In this technique, the counselor works with him to review the problematic narratives about God discussed in the first narrative construction and then works to create healthier adaptations. For example, the counselor asks him to identify potential idealized endings to his stories about God. This technique calls for him to forecast how his narrative may end if he relates to God in a new, healthier way. As he wraps up his forecasting, the counselor inquires about what he may learn from such an ending and change in his life.

Summary and Conclusions

A relationship with God is real, complex, and important for many male clients. Men may treat their relationship with God like other relationships in their life, including a mixture of positive and negative emotions as well as challenging and supportive experiences. Counselors can conceptualize working with men according to two primary approaches: (1) a strength-based approach that helps them to identify and to utilize their relationship with God to cope with the presenting concerns, and (2) a remedial approach that focuses on shifting negative appraisals of God to new, healthier relationship dynamics with God. In the process of enacting such a therapeutic approach, the counselor utilizes an integrative theoretical conceptualization and multifaceted assessment methods in their clinical and ethical decision-making.

Case Example

Peter was a 50-year-old, white, married man with two teenage children when I met him in my private practice. He was applying for admittance into a training program for a clergy role in a Christian Church. My initial and primary role with Peter was to conduct a psychological assessment of his personality and psychological functioning, which would be part of his admission application that the Church's Admission Board considers when rendering decisions.

I review each applicant's resumé, intake paperwork, and accompanying documentation (e.g., letters of recommendation) prior to the clinical interview. On paper, Peter mostly looked like a wonderful applicant. He had an extensive volunteer service history within the Church, was a published author, had an advanced degree in theology, and a stable family life. He exhibited qualities of positive masculinity such as involvement in fraternal organizations within his church. In addition, his pastor relied on him to recruit other men for volunteer projects and service-oriented activities. Peter was always up for the task. One item caught my attention – a letter from his pastor noting an overall endorsement of his application but expressing a concern that Peter is sometimes abrasive with fellow congregants "about the rules." Without further context at that point, I made a note of that comment and wondered if the comment would be relevant in the clinical interview.

Peter arrived at the assessment in an obvious state of anxiety. He was sweating through his shirt, his hands were shaky and wet, he stuttered a bit in his speech, and he averted eye contact. He positioned his body and chair at a 45-degree angle opposite me and appeared to be looking out the window or at the wall and ceiling during the clinical interview. Peter denied being anxious or nervous when I inquired. I assured him that it is common for applicants to be a little nervous and that he seemed nervous to me. But again, he denied feeling nervous. Although Peter exhibited positive masculinity qualities in his service, his lack of emotional awareness and language was common among men adhering to traditional norms of masculinity such as stoicism. I conceptualized Peter's reluctance to admit his anxiety as his way of protecting his sense of manhood in relation to me.

The clinical interview entails questions about the applicant's family of origin, developmental history, and spiritual health among other functional domains. The theme of accomplishment emerged with Peter. He worked hard in school, earned straight As, and went to graduate school to accomplish his educational goals. He wrote a book, which he viewed as a "life time achievement." He brimmed with pride as he discussed how he followed all the rules of his faith. At that moment, I recalled the pastor's comment and asked Peter how he would minister to a diversity of people as a clergy in his Church, even people who do not follow the rules? Peter expressed frustration with such people and reported, "The Church is clear on what you can and can not do. I don't understand why people wouldn't just do what they are supposed to." I asked Peter why "the rules" were so important to him, and he stated that God made the rules for us to follow and he must respect God's rule, *or else*. Or else what? I asked. Peter looked at me very intently and directly for the first time in the interview and responded, "Or else, you go to hell." I conceptualized Peter's statements about God as reflective of negative God images focused on God as vindictive, judging, and punishing. His masculinity played a role in his God image as men are prone to harsher God images. He appeared to relate to God and others in a corresponding manner. He believed that he and others had to follow the rules to remain on good terms with God. This was a core belief of Peter.

His sense of accomplishment also emerged when he discussed his family of origin. Peter was the third of seven children in his family, and he described his father as distant and mother as "never satisfied" with any of the children. Peter expressed a constant desire for attention and praise from his parents and sought it through seeking accomplishments. As I do with all applicants, I asked him why he was applying to the clergy training program. Peter gave a stock answer, reporting that he felt called by God and that he wanted to serve others. I doubted the authenticity of his response. I concluded that he was seeking the clergy role out of an unconscious desire to achieve another accomplishment to gain his parents' approval and to abide by additional rules that would gain him God's love. He had developed an anxious attachment style with his parents that had transferred to his relationship with God. I communicated my conclusion to the Admission Board through a report and to Peter in a feedback session. He was very defensive to my conclusion and exclaimed how "offended" he was with such an interpretation. He denied applying to the training program for any other reason than to do God's will. I took his reaction as a sign that I had made an accurate interpretation and arrived at an appropriate conclusion.

The Admission Board admitted Peter on a conditional basis. The conditions were that he begin counseling to address his clear anxiety and to work through lingering family-of-origin issues that may be clouding his vocational decision-making. In addition, Peter was asked to sign a release of information form allowing me and his counselor to coordinate his treatment and to serve as mutual consultants. Peter would then undergo a follow-up psychological assessment when counseling was finished. Peter begrudgingly agreed to those conditions. I referred Peter to a colleague for counseling who has competence integrating religion and spirituality into his practice. I consulted on the initial case transfer, the counselor was given a copy of my psychological report, and I received regular updates about the counseling process.

After about a year of individual, outpatient counseling on a weekly basis, my colleague and Peter terminated counseling. I spoke with my colleague on the phone about the counseling process and received a treatment summary report from him. I conducted a follow-up psychological assessment, which the Admission Board considered when deciding if Peter had met the set conditions or not.

Peter reported that he went to counseling very angry at me, the Admission Board, and God. He felt unjustly persecuted and did not understand why God had not "rubber stamped" his application, since after all, God called him to a clergy role. Peter was more comfortable expressing anger due to his masculine socialization. There was hurt and feelings of rejection beneath the anger. The counselor empathized with Peter and invited him to pray to God in session. Peter accepted the invitation and prayer became part of how they structured their sessions. Peter prayed at the beginning and end of each session. After a few sessions, the counselor shared some observations about the way Peter prayed to God. The counselor noted that Peter kept asking God to change other people such as me and the Admission Board. He also conveyed to Peter that he felt Peter was "selling God short" by only asking God for assistance in avoiding wrong-doing. The counselor challenged Peter to think about how *he* could change (not other people) since the counseling was for him. In addition, the counselor provided Peter with a spiritual book entitled *This Tremendous Lover* for bibliotherapy homework. The counselor instructed Peter to read the book slowly and take notes on how the author describes God compared to how Peter thinks of God. They would discuss his notes on a periodic basis in session. Peter returned the next session having read through half of the 24 chapters. His eyes were wide, and he had a notebook in his hand. He quickly sat down and without so much as a normal greeting or prayer, started discussing his reactions to the book. The central thesis of the book is that God loves each person and invites humans into a mutually loving relationship. Peter admitted that he never thought of his relationship with God in such terms but wanted to learn more about how he could approach his relationship with God differently. Per the report of Peter and the counselor, Peter was able to connect his relationship with God to his relationship with his parents in meaningful ways. He gained insight into how his constant need for achievement and approval from his parents and God contributed to harsh interpersonal dynamics with people that would interfere with effective ministry.

My follow-up evaluation with Peter revealed a decrease in anxious symptoms and a man more at ease with others and himself. He continued to exhibit a mild level of anxiety although he was able to make eye contact with more regularity and sat across from me at less of an angle. I administered the16PF as part of the evaluation and he had a high score on the Anxiety global factor, indicating that he will likely always have an undercurrent of anxiety to his personality. However, he showed openness to change and feedback as well as concrete progress on relevant therapeutic goals through relatively long-term counseling.

In the follow-up evaluation, I asked Peter what was the most valuable lesson that he learned during the past year and how he is different because of that lesson. Peter immediately pointed to the book that he brought to the evaluation, *This Tremendous Lover*, and described in detail his initial defensiveness to understanding and relating to God in a more positive way. Part of accepting God as loving was Peter being more compassionate

Table 3.1 Assessments for God Concept, God Image, God Attachment, and Relationship with God

Construct	*Assessment*
God Concept	*The God Concept Adjective Checklist* (Schaefer & Gorsuch, 1992) is a 47-item checklist that assesses 11 schemas that collapse into 2 categories: (1) positive God concept includes benevolent, omni, guiding, stable, deistic, powerful, and caring; and (2) negative God concept includes false, worthless, wrathful, and condemning.
	The God-10 (Exline, Grubbs, & Homolka, 2015) is a 10-item checklist of adjectives about views of God as cruel (cruel, unkind, rejecting), distant (distant, remote, unavailable, uninvolved), and loving (loving, caring, forgiving).
God Image	*The God Image Inventory* (Lawrence, 1997) has 72 items and measures 3 categories: (1) belonging, which includes presence and challenge; (2) goodness, which includes acceptance and benevolence; and (3) control, which includes influence and providence.
	God Image Measure (Nguyen & Zuckerman, 2016) has 16 items and measures 4 types of God image: (1) provider, (2) relational, (3) ruler, and (4) creator.
God Attachment	*The Attachment to God Scale* (Rowatt & Kirkpatrick, 2002) has 9 items and assesses 2 attachment styles: (1) secure, and (2) anxious attachment to God.
	The Attachment to God Inventory (Beck & McDonald, 2004) has 28 items and measures 2 attachment styles: (1) avoidance of intimacy, and (2) anxiety and abandonment.
Relationship with God	*Attitudes Toward God Scale* (Wood et al., 2010) has 9 items and assesses 2 factors: (1) positive attitudes toward God, and (2) disappointment and anger with God.
	Divine Struggle Subscale (Exline, Pargament, Grubbs, & Yali, 2014) of the Religious and Spiritual Struggles Scale has 5 items and measures the degree of divine struggle (e.g., anger, doubts).

with himself, which was a model of masculinity that he was not previously taught. As a result, he learned that he was negatively constraining how he felt about other people and himself. He acknowledged that counseling was difficult as the counselor challenged his core beliefs about God, and they worked to establish new beliefs based on the teachings in the book and life experiences. Peter reported that God may have called him to apply to the training program to first come to such realizations, which would help him progress in his training as a minister.

In my follow-up report to the Admission Board, I noted that Peter seemed genuine in his progress and that there were other markers of his improved psycho-spiritual health such as successful engagement in counseling and decreased anxiety. Yet, I also conveyed that Peter seemed to have a track record and personality that would likely indicate continued struggles in these areas. I could not answer if he had a true calling to the ministerial role in the Church, but I concluded that he would likely be a "mixed bag" in ministry. Peter expressed more agreement with that conclusion. The Admission Board allowed Peter to continue in the training program, but true to form, I have heard that he has been a hand full!

References

Abu-Raiya, H., & Pargament, K.I. (2015). Religious coping among diverse religions: Commonalities and divergences. *Psychology of Religion and Spirituality, 7*(1), 24–33.

Addis, M. (2011). *Invisible men: Men's inner lives and the consequences of silence*. New York, NY: Macmillan.

Addis, M.E., & Mahalik, J.R. (2003). Men, masculinity, and the contexts of help seeking. *American Psychologist, 58*(1), 5–14.

Bradshaw, M., Ellison, C.G., & Marcum, J.P. (2010). Attachment to God, images of God, and psychological distress in a nationwide sample of Presbyterians. *The International Journal for the Psychology of Religion, 20*(2), 130–147.

Chou, H.T.G., & Uata, D. (2012). The impact of parental discipline on the image of God. *Mental Health, Religion & Culture, 15*(7), 677–688.

Currier, J.M., Foster, J.D., Abernethy, A.D., Witvliet, C.V., Root Luna, L.M., Putman, K.M., . . . & Carter, J. (2017). God imagery and affective outcomes in a spiritually integrative inpatient program. *Psychiatry Research, 2*(54), 317–322.

Davis, E.B., Moriarty, G.L., & Mauch, J.C. (2013). God images and god concepts: Definitions, development, and dynamics. *Psychology of Religion and Spirituality, 5*(1), 51–60.

Ellison, C.G., Bradshaw, M., Kuyel, N., & Marcum, J.P. (2012). Attachment to God, stressful life events, and changes in psychological distress. *Review of Religious Research, 53*(4), 493–511.

Englar-Carlson, M., & Kiselica, M.S. (2013). Affirming the strengths in men: A positive masculinity approach to assisting male clients. *Journal of Counseling & Development, 91*(4), 399–409.

Exline, J.J., Grubbs, J.B., & Homolka, S.J. (2015). Seeing God as cruel or distant: Links with divine struggles involving anger, doubt, and fear of God's disapproval. *The International Journal for the Psychology of Religion, 25*(1), 29–41.

Exline, J.J., Pargament, K.I., Grubbs, J.B., & Yali, A.M. (2014). The Religious and Spiritual Struggles Scale: Development and initial validation. *Psychology of Religion and Spirituality, 6*(3), 208–222.

Exline, J.J., Park, C.L., Smyth, J.M., & Carey, M.P. (2011). Anger toward God: Social-cognitive predictors, prevalence, and links with adjustment to bereavement and cancer. *Journal of Personality and Social Psychology, 100*(1), 129–148.

Foster, R.A., & Babcock, R.L. (2001). God as a man versus God as a woman: Perceiving God as a function of the gender of God and the gender of the participant. *The international Journal for the Psychology of Religion, 11*(2), 93–104.

Froese, P., & Bader, C. (2010). *America's four gods: What we say about God – And what that says about us*. New York, NY: Oxford University Press.

George, C., Kaplan, N., & Main, M. (1996). Adult attachment interview. Unpublished manuscript, Department of Psychology, University of California, Berkeley (third edition). Retrieved from http://library.allanschore.com/docs/AAIProtocol.pdf.

Ghorbani, N., Watson, P.J., Omidbeiki, M., & Chen, Z.J. (2016). Muslim attachments to God and the "perfect man" (Ensān-e Kāmel): Relationships with religious orientation and psychological adjustment in Iran. *Psychology of Religion and Spirituality, 8*(4), 318–329.

Hernandez, G., Salerno, J.M., & Bottoms, B.L. (2010). Attachment to God, spiritual coping, and alcohol use. *The International Journal for the Psychology of Religion, 20*(2), 97–108.

Hodge, D.R., & Horvath, V.E. (2011). Spiritual needs in health care settings: A qualitative meta-synthesis of clients' perspectives. *Social Work, 56*(4), 306–316.

Isacco, A., Sahker, E., Krinock, E., Sim, W., & Hamilton, D. (2016). How religious beliefs and practices influence the psychological health of Catholic priests. *American Journal of Men's Health, 10*(4), 325–337.

Isacco, A., Talovic, E., Chromik, L.C., & Yallum, N.K. (2013). Addressing men's mental health through a strength-based approach. In J.M. Rippe (Ed.), *Lifestyle medicine* (pp. 369–382). New York, NY: CRC Press.

Koohsar, A.A.H., & Bonab, B.G. (2011). Relation between quality of image of God and mental health in college students. *Procedia-Social and Behavioral Sciences, 29*, 247–251.

Krejci, M.J. (1998). Gender comparison of God schemas: A multidimensional scaling analysis. *The International Journal for the Psychology of Religion, 8*(1), 57–66.

Laurin, K., Schumann, K., & Holmes, J.G. (2014). A relationship with God? Connecting with the divine to assuage fears of interpersonal rejection. *Social Psychological and Personality Science, 5*(7), 777–785.

Lawrence, R.T. (1997). Measuring the image of God: The God image inventory and the God image scales. *Journal of Psychology and Theology, 25*(2), 214–226.

Magovcevic, M., & Addis, M.E. (2008). The Masculine Depression Scale: Development and psychometric evaluation. *Psychology of Men & Masculinity, 9*(3), 117–132.

Maliski, S.L., Husain, M., Connor, S.E., & Litwin, M.S. (2012). Alliance of support for low-income Latino men with prostate cancer: God, doctor, and self. *Journal of Religion and Health, 51*(3), 752–762.

Moriarty, G., & Hoffman, M. (Eds.). (2007). *God image handbook for spiritual counseling and psychotherapy: Research, theory, and practice*. Philadelphia, PA: Haworth Press.

Moriarty, G.L., & Davis, E.B. (2012). Client God images: Theory, research, and clinical practice. In J.D. Aten, K.A. O'Grady, & E.L. Worthington Jr. (Eds.), *The psychology of religion and spirituality for counselors: Using research in your practice* (pp. 131–160). New York, NY: Routledge.

Nadeau, M.M., Balsan, M.J., & Rochlen, A.B. (2016). Men's depression: Endorsed experiences and expressions. *Psychology of Men & Masculinity, 17*(4), 328–335.

Nguyen, T.-v.T., & Zuckerman, M. (2016). The links of God images to women's religiosity and coping with depression: A socialization explanation of gender difference in religiosity. *Psychology of Religion and Spirituality, 8*(4), 309–317.

Olson, T., Tisdale, T.C., Davis, E.B., Park, E.A., Nam, J., Moriarty, G.L., . . . & Hays, L.W. (2016). God image narrative therapy: A mixed-methods investigation of a controlled group-based spiritual intervention. *Spirituality in Clinical Practice, 3*(2), 77–91.

Paine, D.R., & Sandage, S.J. (2017). Religious involvement and depression: The mediating effect of relational spirituality. *Journal of Religion and Health, 56*(1), 269–283.

Pargament, K.I. (2007). *Spiritually integrated psychotherapy: Understanding and addressing the sacred.* New York, NY: Guilford Press.

Pew Research Center: The Pew Forum on Religion & Public Life. (2015). *Religious landscape study: Gender composition.* Retrieved from www.pewforum.org/religious-landscape-study/gender-composition/.

Rabinowitz, F.E., & Cochran, S.V. (2002). *Deepening psychotherapy with men.* Washington, DC: American Psychological Association.

Reiner, S.R., Anderson, T.L., Hall, M.E.L., & Hall, T.W. (2010). Adult attachment, God attachment and gender in relation to perceived stress. *Journal of Psychology and Theology, 38*(3), 175–185.

Rosmarin, D.H., Bigda-Peyton, J.S., Kertz, S.J., Smith, N., Rauch, S.L., & Björgvinsson, T. (2013). A test of faith in God and treatment: The relationship of belief in God to psychiatric treatment outcomes. *Journal of Affective Disorders, 146*(3), 441–446.

Rowatt, W. & Kirkpatrick, L. (2002). Two dimensions of attachment to God and their relation to affect, religiosity, and personality constructs. *Journal for the Scientific Study of Religion, 41*, 637–651.

Schaefer, C.A., & Gorsuch, R.L. (1992). Dimensionality of religion: Belief and motivation as predictors of behavior. *Journal of Psychology and Christianity, 11*, 244–254.

Shah, S., Bartkowski, J.P., & Xu, X. (2016). Gendered God imagery and attitudes toward mothers' labor force participation: Examining the transposable character of religious schemas. *Journal for the Scientific Study of Religion, 55*(3), 540–557.

Steenwyk, S.A., Atkins, D.C., Bedics, J.D., & Whitley Jr, B.E. (2010). Images of God as they relate to life satisfaction and hopelessness. *The International Journal for the Psychology of Religion, 20*(2), 85–96.

Vergote, A., Tamayo, A., Pasquali, L., Bonami, M., Pattyn, M.R., & Custers, A. (1969). Concept of God and parental images. *Journal for the Scientific Study of Religion, 8*(1), 79–87.

Whitehead, A.L. (2012). Gender ideology and religion: Does a masculine image of God matter? *Review of Religious Research, 54*(2), 139–156.

Wilt, J.A., Exline, J.J., Grubbs, J.B., Park, C.L., & Pargament, K.I. (2016). God's role in suffering: Theodicies, divine struggle, and mental health. *Psychology of Religion and Spirituality, 8*(4), 352–362.

Wong, Y.J., & Rochlen, A.B. (2009). Potential benefits of expressive writing for male college students with varying degrees of restrictive emotionality. *Psychology of Men & Masculinity, 10*(2), 149–159.

Wood, B.T., Worthington Jr, E.L., Exline, J.J., Yali, A.M., Aten, J.D., & McMinn, M.R. (2010). Development, refinement, and psychometric properties of the Attitudes Toward God Scale (ATGS-9). *Psychology of Religion and Spirituality, 2*(3), 148–167.

4 Pray and Go to Church?

I was at a psychology conference a few years ago and was engaged in a wide-ranging conversation with colleagues about various topics. By all accounts, the conversation was free flowing, intellectually stimulating, respectful, and insightful. The topic of religion and spirituality came up, and a colleague looked at me and said, "Anthony, you're interested in the psychology of religion and spirituality, right?" I responded simply, "yes." And another colleague asked, "How do you integrate religion and spirituality into your clinical work?" I took the question at face value and answered matter-of-factly, "I pray with some of my clients, encourage them to pray on their own, and to connect with their faith community by going to religious and spiritual activities." At that, the wonderful conversation came to a screeching halt. The free flow of ideas ended, and my colleagues shifted awkwardly in their seats and avoided eye contact with me. What did I say?

I have prayed hundreds of times with clients, often at their prompting. It has been my experience that prayer between counselor and client enhances the therapeutic alliance and contributes to healing for the client. Perhaps the conversation with colleagues reflected the historically tenuous relationship psychology has with religion and spirituality or their lack of training in this area of cultural competence. The reaction from my colleagues continued to bring to light how integrating specific religious and spiritual interventions in counseling is difficult and, thus, requires training, ethical decision-making, and cultural competence. We agree, which is why we focus on how counselors can properly integrate prayer and religious service attendance with men. We conceptualize prayer and religious service attendance as health behaviors that provide coping and supportive resources to men that contribute to their mental health (Weber & Pargament, 2014). As a result, we consider the religious and spiritual practices to be part of ongoing efforts to think of men's health from an interdisciplinary and comprehensive perspective (Courtenay, 2011; Courtenay & Keeling, 2000). Many men are reluctant to engage in health-promoting behaviors despite the known benefits due to rigid adherence to masculinity norms and roles (Garfield, Isacco, & Rogers, 2008). Counseling interventions may facilitate engagement in the health behaviors of prayer and religious service attendance, which leads to improved health.

The purpose of this chapter is to examine the role of prayer and church attendance in men's health. This chapter will suggest ways counselors can assess men's beliefs and behaviors regarding prayer and church attendance to conceptualize how masculine socialization may be facilitating or impeding those beliefs and behaviors, and to implement counseling interventions that facilitate the use of prayer and church attendance as ethical and health-promoting tools.

Spiritual Tools in Counseling: Prayer and Religious Services

Prayer and religious service attendance have been around for thousands of years and are applicable to clients across the major world religions (see Table 4.1). Although non-religious individuals, religious drifters, and atheists pray less and attend fewer religious services compared to religious individuals, many individuals in those groups engage in those behaviors nonetheless (Speed & Fowler, 2016). Thus, counselors may find that prayer and religious service attendance are applicable to a wide range of clients. According to Plante (2009), prayer and attending religious services represent two spiritual tools that counselors can integrate into counseling, which have the potential to enhance the psychological health of clients.

This section clarifies the conceptualization and definitions of prayer and religious service attendance. Prayer and religious service attendance have been used to study religiosity and spirituality in the social sciences. The two constructs were primary indicators of religiosity for a while prior to the development of more complex measures and theories. Although we understand religiosity in more complexity now, prayer and religious attendance continue to be important to people's lives and, thus, the focus of current research and practice in the health psychology and counseling fields (Abernethy, Houston, Mimms, & Boyd-Franklin, 2006). Prayer and religious service attendance are now considered two behavioral indicators of religious commitment and involvement (Nicholson, Rose, & Bobak, 2009). In addition, both entail a spiritual component as individuals can have spiritual experiences in their individual prayer or community settings such as a religious service (Kvande, Klöckner, & Nielsen, 2015). While prayer is primarily focused on an individual's internal faith practice, religious service attendance emphasizes the communal and external practice of the faith. Some individuals construct a religious identity and adopt certain spiritual practices in relation to their religious community. An individual may pray a specific type of prayer while at a religious service with their community. Engaging in sacred reading is a religious and spiritual behavior that can be part of praying and attending religious services. In addition, sacred reading can be easily integrated into counseling as a form of bibliotherapy. Table 4.1 provides the main sacred text as well as popular books for each world religion. Prayer and religious service attendance often interact with each other rather than represent compartmentalized behaviors.

There are many definitions of prayer. Some consider prayer to simply be talking to God or raising one's mind and heart to God (Catechism of the Catholic Church, 1994). Psychology continues to put forth a similar definition by William James (1963) as "every kind of inward communion or conversation with the power recognized as divine" (p. 464). Among the many definitions, a common thread is that an individual is connecting with the divine. Indeed, prayer is a vehicle that drives an individual's relationship with the divine. We discussed the importance of men's relationship with God in Chapter 3, and prayer is a primary tool to nurture and deepen the divine relationship. Prayer is complex as there is more to consider than if an individual prays (or not) and how frequently. There are many types of prayer across various faith traditions (Table 4.1). Although the word "prayer" is used broadly, not all types of prayer have the same impact on an individual's health and wellbeing. For example, prayer that expresses appreciation and fosters connection with God is more likely to have a positive effect such as coping with anxiety and depression (Darabinia, Gorji, & Afzali, 2017). Using the definition put forth in this chapter, prayer is directed at the divine. Therefore, an individual's beliefs about God, God image, and God attachment are significant considerations to understanding their prayer. For example, praying to an unloving, distant God has been associated with increased psychopathology, while praying to a loving God has been linked to decreased psychopathology (Bradshaw, Ellison, & Flannelly, 2008). Taken together, it is important to understand *how* an individual prays in addition to *if* they pray.

Meditation represents a form of prayer and warrants some specific attention because it is found in some form across the major world religions as well as practiced by non-religious individuals to deepen their spirituality. In addition, meditation is considered to fall under the mindfulness umbrella, which seems to be ever growing in popularity and used in counseling. Meditation is broadly considered a set of health-promoting practices that foster self-control, attention, and awareness, and attend to the body, mind, and spirit (Lomas, Ridge, Cartwright, & Edginton, 2014b). The diversity of meditation is seen among the major world religions (Table 4.1). For example, Buddhists practice meditation to foster patience, compassion, and enlightenment. Catholics and Christians may meditate on a scripture passage in their quest to understand God more deeply in their life. Muslims often recite the Qu'ran as a form of prayer that is similar to meditation as the purpose is to invoke healing power to both mental and physical health from teachings that focus on peace, attention, reflection, and self-control (Darabinia et al., 2017). Religious drifters may practice a brand of secular mindfulness meditation outside of a religious context, which is typically referred to as mindfulness-based stress reduction (MBSR). MBSR focuses one's attention on controlled breathing while maintaining a non-judgmental awareness of one's thoughts and feelings. MBSR is widely popular and well researched but has been largely decontextualized from the historical Buddhist roots and spirituality. Thus, we do not focus on MBSR in this chapter. Instead, we conceptualize prayer and meditation from established religious-spiritual contexts with similar underlying mechanisms that foster wellbeing.

Religious attendance is defined as attending a service, usually obligated to some degree, within one's religious affiliation. As seen in Table 4.1, there are different kinds of religious services among the major world religions. Most religions have a primary religious service intended for the believers of the religion to gather in a community to practice their faith. Our conceptualization in this chapter broadens the definition to many other types of religious gatherings and community events in addition to the primary religious services. Thus, "going to church" perhaps refers to attending a mass on Sunday, but it has a more dynamic and comprehensive meaning to us. For example, churches often host a vast variety of activities such as bible studies, support groups, lectures, workshops, and food pantries. Accounting for the variety of religious activities and events in conjunction with attending a religious service will provide a better understanding of the individual's religious involvement and commitment as well as the potential impact on men's health. Throughout the chapter, we use the terms church attendance and religious service attendance as interchangeable. The terms apply to men going to church, an activity at their church, a house of worship, participating in a religious and spiritual event or activity, as well as utilizing resources and support within their religious community.

Prayer and Religious Service Attendance: Masculinity and Men's Health

In the United States and internationally, there is a general trend indicating that women pray, meditate, and attend religious services more than men do (Pew, 2016). In the Pew study (2016) of individuals in 84 countries, women prayed more than men in 43 of the countries and less than men in only one country – Jewish adults in Israel. According to the Pew report (2016, p. 10), "the difference between women and men in self-reported rates of daily prayer is the biggest average gender gap found in this study." The data is a little more nuanced about gender differences in religious service attendance. Women attend religious services more than men among 30 countries with a Christian majority but less among 28 countries with a Muslim and Orthodox Jewish majority. That latter finding is attributed to the religious norms of the Muslim and Orthodox Jewish faiths, which prioritize men's participation in religious services (Pew, 2016). The priority placed on men's involvement in the various faiths is an important factor in understanding the gender differences. Yet, it does not fully explain such gender differences. For example, the Catholic Church has a male-only presbyterate, which many interpret as giving men more power and priority. However, lay Catholic men reportedly pray and go to church less than Catholic women and when compared to men of other religions. Priority and power may not translate into prayer and attendance for all religious men. Further explanations are needed to fully understand men's engagement in such health behaviors.

Masculine gender role socialization seems to be a factor in men praying and going to church. This section examines men's prayer and church attendance habits within three theories – conformity to masculine norms (Mahalik et al., 2003), Wade's (1998) theory of male reference group identity dependence, and the positive psychology-positive masculinity (PPPM) paradigm (Kiselica, Benton-Wright, & Englar-Carlson, 2016).

The conformity to masculine norms theory (Mahalik et al., 2003) posits that there are societal expectations placed on men and that men adhere or do not adhere to those expectations. Conforming or non-conformity to the dominant masculinity norms has advantages and disadvantages. For example, men are expected to be self-reliant; therefore, they do not ask for directions and are praised if they successfully arrive at their destination but are criticized if they become lost. Similarly, men are expected to be strong and be capable of handling difficult situations on their own. Not surprisingly, men adhering to such norms are less likely to seek psychological help and demonstrate worse health behaviors than men with more flexible conformity to masculinity norms. Many faith traditions consider prayer as a means to surrender to God and to be vulnerable with the divine. Prayer is also a means to ask for help during times of difficulty. Religious service attendance requires joining a community of people and being intimate and vulnerable with others in prayer, worship, and religious activities. Such men may see praying as asking God for help and going to church as too interdependent. Taken together, prayer and religious service attendance may be perceived as counter to such established masculine norms of self-reliance, independence, and strength (Walton & Sullivan, 2004). We have conceptualized prayer and religious service attendance as health behaviors; thus, men conforming to masculinity norms (self-reliance, independence, strength) are less likely to engage in health behaviors such as going to the doctor and are similarly less likely to pray and go to church.

Wade's (1998) theory of male reference group identity dependence also helps to explain men's engagement or lack thereof in religious health behaviors. We primarily focus on men whose male identity is characterized as "reference group dependent," which means that they define their male identity in relation to a particular group of men with whom they feel a sense of similarity or connection. Such men depend on other males for their self-definitions of masculinity and therefore conform to the norms of the reference group. We apply the theory to men whose reference group would be religious or spiritual men, and whose peer group therefore would likely be characterized as such. In regard to prayer and church attendance, self-definitions of masculinity would include these behaviors because that is what men do. For example, some religious men such as Orthodox Jews or Muslims define their manhood in part by going to the synagogue and mosque, respectively, to pray with other men. These kinds of men look to other men from within their religious community to construct their male identity. In order to be an authentic Orthodox Jewish man or Muslim man, one prays the prayers and attends the religious services of that group. In my clinical practice, I encounter Catholic men who often discuss being inspired and challenged to live a more devout lifestyle from being in a men's group at their parish. They identify more as a "Catholic man" and engage in specific religious behaviors to further solidify their Catholic manhood. In most instances, this identification with the group has led to positive changes in their lives. Such a religious/spiritual-based construction of manhood may be applicable for other men as well and intersect with other social identities. For example, in a sample of 152 African-American men, manhood meant being morally virtuous, religious, and spiritual (e.g., including prayer, seeking divine guidance) within multiple systems of relationships (family, community) (Hammond & Mattis, 2005). For some African-American men, race and spirituality play a role in their male identity and religious behaviors. Conversely, men whose reference group for self-definitions of masculinity does not include being religious or spiritual would be less inclined to engage in prayer and church services. Conforming to the norms of the male reference group would mean as a man I (you) do not pray and go to church, and this would most likely be the beliefs or attitudes of his friends or peer group.

Wade's (1998) theory can also be applied to men whose male identity is constructed outside of a male reference group. They are considered as having a "reference group nondependent identity" because they are not dependent on a male reference group for self-definitions of masculinity. Such men will pray or not pray, attend religious services or not do so, as a result of defining for themselves their religious practices as a man and not because of conformity to male role norms. A reference group nondependent identity is typically positive because the man has individuated from external social influences (e.g., parents, friends/peers) to arrive at an independent decision that he is taking ownership of and is indicative of maturity. He has likely undergone a developmental spiritual journey that entailed a great deal of internal thought, self-reflection, experiential learning, and study.

Finally, the PPPM paradigm also helps to explain men's engagement in religious behaviors (Kiselica, Benton-Wright, & Englar-Carlson, 2016). According to PPPM, there are 11 healthy characteristics of traditional masculinity, and of those 11, there are 4 that seem particularly relevant to men's engagement in religious behaviors – male relational style, male ways of caring, humanitarian service of fraternal organizations, and a team-group orientation. A male relational style and a group orientation are defined as men relating to each other through a shared project, with a common goal. Male ways of caring are more focused on action empathy. Humanitarian service of fraternal organizations is seen in groups of men joining together with a common goal of serving other people and doing good in their communities. Taken together, it seems likely that religious/spiritual men who enact those four healthy characteristics of masculinity may focus more on service-oriented activities within a religious community. In terms of church attendance, men may not attend the traditional Sunday services so to speak, but they are expressing their spirituality in group-based, service activities that have a positive impact in their communities. They may consider such activities as spiritually energizing and socially fulfilling. Thus, their activities are an example of how our broader conceptualization accounts for more group-based and goal-directed religious behaviors beyond typical religious service attendance.

Matthew Leonard, a popular Catholic author and speaker, wrote a book in 2014 entitled *Prayer Works!* The title summarizes the book's thesis very well – your life will be better if you pray. Psychological and medical studies have found that prayer and attendance at church services enhance resilience, personal coping, and social support among other health benefits (Garfield, Isacco, & Sahker, 2013). Why is prayer and church attendance associated with better mental health outcomes? This section identifies the mechanisms that explain how prayer and church attendance may improve men's health.

Most psychological research describes prayer as a coping tool. In other words, prayer helps stressed individuals to better cope with negative emotions and distressful experiences. As discussed in Chapter 1, individuals often use religious coping during difficult times, and prayer is one way to enact religious coping. That basic mechanism has been deepened with advanced theory and research about prayer. For example, Bade and Cook (2008) identified four functions of Christian prayer: assistance, calm and focus, deferring and avoiding, and acceptance, which they measured with the Prayer Functions Scale (see Assessment section). Assistance refers to using prayer to ask God for help to handle difficulties, requesting resources (e.g., guidance, grace), and seeking direction. Calm and focus includes using prayer to talk with God, express feelings, and experience connectedness to God. Deferring and avoiding is prayer that puts the problem and difficulty into God's hands, i.e., a transfer of control. Acceptance builds on deferring and avoiding by expressing trust in God to handle the problem. For Muslim men, prayer has been found to help wellbeing by buffering against stress, increasing experiences of intimacy and inspiration, enhancing one's efficacy to solve problems, acquiring humility and empathetic regard for others, and feeling forgiveness (Henry, 2015).

Breslin and Lewis (2008) broaden the view of prayer mechanisms that are applicable across religions. Their model contends that prayer has physiological, psychological, placebo, social support, and spiritual influences on an individual's health. The physiological pathway is based on research detailing how prayer positively impacts neurological and cardiovascular processes in the body as well as encouraging the individual to engage in more positive health behaviors (e.g., abstinence from alcohol and substances). The psychological pathway includes finding meaning, hope, experiencing positive emotions, and self-exploration. Connecting the neuro-psychological paths is research finding that prayer engenders positive emotions (peace, joy, hope, faith, and calm), which can lead to physiological changes that further improve wellbeing (Jantos & Kiat, 2007). Prayer may improve health simply because an individual expects it to, i.e., the placebo pathway. Individuals often pray together (e.g., community prayer) or for each other (i.e., intercessory prayer), which creates a social support pathway to improving health. A spiritual pathway may include enhancing an individual's relationship with God and/or having a spiritual experience that increases their sacred awareness and sense of divine connection. In the spiritual context, individuals may have a "supernatural" experience in prayer that is difficult to measure, define, and describe in language familiar to a counselor. Nevertheless, the supernatural prayer helps the individual to transcend their problem and feel less distress, pain, and suffering (Jantos & Kiat, 2007).

Lomas and colleagues (2014b) studied meditation in a couple of studies with men practicing Buddhism in England. Congruent with our conceptualization of prayer and church attendance, they conceptualized meditation as a health behavior that can be promoted through interventions with men. Lomas, Edginton, Cartwright, and Ridge (2014a) contended that men with restrictive emotionality and socialized from expressing emotions are at risk for depression and deficits in emotional intelligence. Men in the study reported that meditation was part of a spiritual journey entailing phases of progress, impasses, and failures but that, overall, they felt healthier and happier as a result (Lomas et al., 2014b). Thus, men may feel like prayer and meditation are part of a health trajectory that has the potential to transform their lives' past mistakes and difficulties. Similarly, Lomas et al. (2014a) deepened the understanding of how men use meditation to cope by facilitating increased attentional focus and emotional awareness, which in turn, improved emotional management. The potential for meditation to help men with their emotional management and intelligence is noteworthy given the problems associated with emotional restrictiveness as a masculine norm. Men can learn to become emotionally aware and expressive with meditation, which taps into their spiritual identity while not violating their masculinity ideology. The effects of meditation and increasing emotional expressiveness may have transferability to other health behaviors such as exercising and interpersonal connection.

As discussed in Chapter 1, many men experience a crisis in loneliness and social isolation, which negatively affects their health in other ways such as depression, suicide, and increased stress. Church attendance represents a spiritual tool that can be used to buffer against the harmful effects of loneliness. The psychological literature has consistently identified a link between church attendance and health outcomes because of how going to church activates social support and a sense of community for individuals. Church attendance is important to consider within and outside of the context of religious affiliation. Individuals typically go to a religious service that is associated with their religious affiliation; for example, Catholics go to mass on Sunday. Conversely, religious drifters may not go to a religious service associated with an organized religion but may still attend group spiritual events in their spiritual quest and journey. "Non-attendees" represent a similar but distinct group to the religious drifters and non-religious groups. Non-attendees may or may not have a religious affiliation, but their defining characteristic is that they do not attend church services and lack engagement in religious practices (Waters, Millard, & Doyle, 2015). In a large-scale national study of over 7,000 Australians, 4.5% identified as non-attendees, and they reported more negative mental health indicators (e.g., nervousness, sadness, restlessness, hopelessness) than those in the non-religious and religious attendee groups. Thus, we have known about the positive effects of religious attendance for a while, and we are now beginning to understand some negative effects associated with non-attendance. The concern is that men who do not engage in group-oriented spiritual activities may be losing out on the health benefits if they are not engaged in compensatory behaviors that foster social support and a sense of community belongingness.

Although religious attendance has proved to be a simple conceptualization of religiosity and spirituality, it remains very popular to study in health research and an important indicator of health (Nicholson, Rose, & Bobak, 2009). In a recent study of 23,353 individuals from four decades of data in the General Social Survey (Mukerjee & Venugopal, 2018), religious attendance was the primary variable of religiosity. The results showed a positive association between religious attendance and self-rated health. The association was stronger for men compared to women, meaning that men were now benefiting from church attendance more than women, which may reflect the high need that men have for social connection and support in today's culture of loneliness.

The pathways between church attendance and health outcomes, as facilitated by social support, have more specific components to identify in men. Attending places of worship may also entail an expansion of an individual's social network, which increases community prayer opportunities, friendships, and a sense of community belongingness (Mukerjee & Venugopal, 2018). Going to a place of worship also exposes the individual to helpful information and educational and values-based programming. Some churches have grief support groups, addiction groups, counseling services, job loss and career ministries, and other social service resources (e.g., clothes, food in emergency situations) that provide instrumental, emotional, and actual support. Thus, a fuller picture of church attendance has emerged in the everyday lives of our clients. Attending church goes beyond a once per week worship service, but may entail a community that is capable of meeting social, occupational, emotional, and spiritual needs.

The church as a central hub of activity and services within a community is not a new concept. For example, historically and currently, African-American men might consider the role of "the Black Church" as important to their lives. Robinson, Jones-Eversley, Moore, Ravenell, and Adedoyin (2018) contended that Black men encounter systemic barriers to seeking support. Cultural factors that may play a role in Black men accessing support in various forms include beliefs about manhood that are antithetical to help-seeking, historic and institutional racism, mistrust of hegemonic helping systems (e.g., healthcare), and a lack of culturally relevant health resources. Thus, "it is significant that Black males attend church because it is there that they can be mentored toward their potential for greatness, receive affirmation, and receive social support" that mitigate against mental health problems (Robinson et al., 2018, p. 6). Such mentoring contributes to their male identity by being within a group of other men aiming to make a positive impact. Some Black Churches are developing integrative and culturally sensitive mental health services tailored to Black men, making "going to church" an understatement for the level of support that Black men can receive within their religious community.

Men of other ethnicities and religious affiliations have also found their church to be a point of access to health programs and support. For example, in a study by Gast and Peak (2011), Episcopalian, Catholic, Presbyterian, and Mormon White men discussed how their church provides emotional support in the form of forgiveness and love. The researchers concluded that a religious environment may be an optimal setting for men to receive social support and express emotions while still preserving their masculinity ideology. In addition, men's masculinity ideology may be broadened in church settings to adopt more non-traditional attitudes and beliefs as well as positive aspects of traditional masculinity such as service and humanitarian efforts. The men in the study identified the influence of their religious community as positively impacting their health and wellbeing (e.g., less stress, less alcohol and tobacco use). Overall, prayer and religious service attendance are two powerful components to an individual's spiritual life and health. Counselors can integrate these two components as spiritual tools in the counseling process with men.

Conceptualization, Assessment, and Counseling Interventions

Conceptualization

Prayer and religious service attendance are considered spiritual tools that can be integrated into counseling with a wide range of clients (Plante, 2009). When might those tools be helpful and appropriate with men? Integrating prayer and religious service attendance may help men with an array of presenting concerns such as anxiety, depression, family-of-origin issues, lack of meaning, loneliness, and trauma by activating coping and supportive resources.

Men may find prayer helpful when they are lacking or experiencing a struggle in their relationship with God (see Chapter 3). Prayer is a primary means to communicate with God for individuals of many religions and those who consider themselves "spiritual." Thus, a divine struggle may be because of a lack of prayer, or the struggle has not been resolved because he has not been engaged in prayer. Men come to counseling having exhausted most of their typical coping skills and resources. Thus, they may not be praying or meditating anymore or are frustrated with a perceived ineffectiveness of their prayer to help them in their current problem. It is also likely that men are not engaging in prayer and meditation as much as they used to because of the effect of their presenting concerns. Anxiety, stress, and psychological distress stemming from any situational or chronic problem stifles effective problem-solving, self-soothing, and coping. It is hypothesized that some men, based on their religious affiliations and beliefs, would benefit from using prayer in such situations. The functional mechanisms (Bade & Cook, 1998; Breslin & Lewis, 2008) will contribute to decreasing the anxiety, stress, and distress.

Identifying the presence or absence of social support in a client's life is standard in counseling. Counselors can extend that line of thinking into the spiritual domain by hypothesizing about how religious service attendance plays a role in his support network. Going to church may mean more than simply attending a religious service. A man's place of worship may be a central hub of activity within his community. Thus, men would benefit from going to their church when they lack social support, friendships, community belongingness while experiencing loneliness. Connecting with their church may lead to social fellowship as well as accessing social service resources and other networks of support. Some men may be seeking a religious and spiritual community and do not feel like they fit anywhere; thus, they are not attending any church services or connected to a spiritual community. Gay men (Chapter 8) and/or religious drifters (Chapter 9) are likely to have had such experiences. Similarly, they may be feeling pain from an experience of being excluded from a religious support network or seeking support from their church but finding that search unfulfilling. Counselors can view a client's unfulfilling and perhaps painful search for a spiritual community as part of a spiritual struggle, which exacerbates presenting concerns. Attending religious services and connecting with a spiritual community that are congruent to him may contribute to resolving some of the spiritual struggle. Similarly, it is hypothesized that the functional mechanisms (e.g., increasing social network, sense of belonging) of religious support will benefit him.

Prayer and religious service attendance are conceptualized within a gendered health behavior perspective (e.g., Courtenay, 2011). Given the gendered perspective, counselors can integrate known theories of gender role socialization to shed light on the interaction of masculinity and engagement in prayer and religious attendance. Using gender role socialization theory, the basic conceptualization would posit that men with a traditional masculinity ideology are less likely to engage in prayer and religious attendance (e.g., Garfield, Isacco & Rogers, 2008; Garfield, Isacco, & Sahker, 2013). Yet, recent scholarship has added more nuance to the impact of traditional masculinity ideology on men's health. The basic conceptualization is a good starting point for consideration but only provides partial insight for counselors. To explore deeper hypotheses about how masculinity interacts with religious health behaviors, counselors can draw from the three theories used in this chapter – conformity to masculine norms (Mahalik et al., 2003), reference group identity (Wade, 1998), and PPPM (Kiselica, Englar-Carlson, & Benton, 2016).

Using the conformity to masculine norms theory, a counselor hypothesizes that strict adherence to such norms as self-reliance, independence, and strength lessens a man's likelihood of praying and going to church services. Conversely, the PPPM paradigm posits that men that adhere less strictly to those three norms and enact certain positive characteristics of masculinity such as humanitarian service and a team orientation, are likely to be involved in spiritual activities that serve others with others in a group. The group may play a more prominent role for some men as they define their male identity in relation to a peer group, i.e., the reference group dependent identity status. Men whose reference group is religious men look to other religious men to define their masculinity and engage in congruent behaviors such as praying and attending church activities, whereas men whose male reference group is non-religious will define their masculinity by not engaging in such behaviors as praying and attending church activities. Understanding if men's self-definitions of masculinity are in relation to a particular group of men provides insight into their engagement or lack thereof in religious and spiritual behaviors. Such hypotheses provide insights to counselors about how some men may be defensive, resistant, or open to the integration of spiritual tools in counseling.

Assessment

Asking men if they pray and go to church, or not, is the starting point of a more thorough assessment of those health behaviors. As we have described in this chapter, those two health behaviors entail more than frequency counts. Table 4.2 has a list of self-report measures that can be used in conjunction with an exploratory approach using open-ended questions.

When assessing prayer, a counselor can explore the sacred entity that he prays to, what types of prayer he engages in, and what function the prayer serves in his coping. While assessing the types of prayer, counselors can specifically ask him if he meditates and, if so, what kind of meditation. Men in counseling may not be praying at all, praying with less frequency than their normal level, and/or are experiencing discontent in their prayers to the divine. Relatedly, some men are likely to express frustration because of a perception that their prayers are not being answered and feeling angry or exasperated with the divine. As a result, they may be experiencing a divine struggle, a negative relational dynamic with God, and have developed associated negative God images. The Prayer Experience

Questionnaire (PEQ; Dein & Littlewood, 2008) is a comprehensive assessment guide of both closed and open-ended questions that ask about quantitative aspects of prayer such as frequency but also qualitative aspects such as the experience of God listening to prayers. Some sample questions from the PEQ that are likely to be clinically useful are the following:

- How do you feel when you pray?
- Could you make your prayer more effective? How?
- Do your prayers sometimes fail? If so, why?
- When you pray, do you experience God listening to you?
- When you pray, do you experience God as close to you?

It is important for counselors to identify the underlying functions of prayer. Identifying the underlying functions provides insight into how and why prayers are affecting men's psycho-social-emotional health, which deepens the assessment process and guides counseling interventions. The Prayer Functions Scale (Bade & Cook, 2008) may be specifically helpful for assessing the functional aspects of prayer with Christian men by examining the specific functions of assistance, calming, deferring, and acceptance. These four functions are not exhaustive as other men may find prayer to serve supernatural functions that are difficult to assess with conventional tools and to describe in language. Thus, counselors need to be prepared to explore hard-to-articulate spiritual experiences from men.

Similarly, assessing religious attendance goes beyond asking about the frequency of attending religious services. Asking about men's attendance and participation in other activities at the church such as service projects, prayer groups, and workshops will provide a more comprehensive assessment of their religious involvement. Some sample questions are as follows:

- Do you belong to a particular church, parish, synagogue, mosque?
- How often do you attend religious services?
- How about other activities – do you participate in prayer groups, service projects?
- Are you aware of other resources and supportive services at your church?

Next, counselors can utilize The How It Feels at Church Survey (Baard, 1994) to assess men's intrinsic motivation for church membership and involvement. An assessment of his intrinsic motivation provides insight into how he engages in behavioral efforts to be involved with a church community. Low intrinsic motivation might signal minimal behavioral efforts or difficulty overcoming barriers, and high intrinsic motivation would suggest a sincere or strong effort to be involved.

Counselors need to ask men about their sense of support and the degree to which they feel connected to their religious community, as those are primary functional elements that facilitate a decrease in various presenting concerns. Open-ended questions similar to assessing prayer can be tailored to church attendance. Some examples include the following:

- How do you feel when you go to your church?
- Do you feel supported by your church community? Why or why not?
- When you go to church, do you experience God?
- When you go to church, do you feel close to your community?
- Could you become more involved in your church?

Overall, men of different religious affiliations and cultural backgrounds pray differently, observe different rituals, and frequent different houses of worship. Counselors need to be aware of such differences and the specific beliefs and practices of individual men. A thorough assessment approach with culturally sensitive skills will help counselors understand the individual differences among diverse men.

Counseling Interventions

Prayer and religious service attendance can be important ways to improve men's health and helpful psychological tools in counseling (Plante, 2009). Counseling interventions are based on understanding how men engage or do not engage in those two religious-spiritual practices in ways that promote or hinder their health. It is likely that prayer and church attendance will be irrelevant to some men and thus, inappropriate and unhelpful to integrate into counseling interventions. We have counseled many men that fit into that category and provided effective counseling with non-religious techniques. Yet, other men have benefited greatly from the use of prayer and church attendance in the counseling process as additional means of healing. On-going conceptualization and assessment identifies which category men fit into and guides the counselor's interventions. Client preference is a key indicator to guide clinical integration of spiritual practices (Harris, Randolph, & Gordon, 2016; Saenz & Waldo, 2013) as some men will prefer spiritual tools from the counselor while others will not. This section outlines a counseling approach that is respectful of client preferences, but is primarily applicable to working with men who prefer prayer and church attendance to be part of counseling. The approach includes broaching, cultural skills of hypothesis testing and dynamic sizing, and behavioral interventions.

Broaching is defined as on-going, explicit efforts by the counselor to invite the client to explore issues of diversity (Day-Vines et al., 2016). Client's spirituality, religious practices, and beliefs represent examples of diversity issues that counselors need to remain open to broaching with men. Within that on-going therapeutic dialogue of religion and spirituality, the counselor initiates a specific discussion about the role of prayer and church attendance in a man's life. The discussion may start with some of the open-ended questions from the assessment section. Broaching behaviors are consistent with an explicit integration of prayer in counseling put forth by Henry (2015). Henry (2015) applied an explicit integration specifically to Muslims, but the approach is applicable with men of other religious affiliations when their spirituality is clearly important to their lives. Specifically, the counselor discusses the role of prayer and church attendance with him and how those two religious behaviors may be further discussed in counseling.

Next, the counselor employs the cultural skills of hypothesis testing and dynamic sizing. Hypothesis testing is defined as using cultural knowledge about the man's cultural group to generate further explorations in counseling (Abernethy et al., 2006). For example, a man presents to counseling indicating that he is Catholic. The counselor should avoid arriving at a conclusion about him based on that knowledge, which may risk stereotyping him (e.g., he prays to Jesus). Instead, the counselor generates hypotheses for exploration. He may or may not pray to Jesus, which could have various implications. The clinical value of hypothesis testing is allowing the client to articulate the relevance of the hypothesis and the counselor learning from the client with an open mind.

Dynamic sizing complements hypothesis testing by learning from the explorative dialogues and understanding the interplay between the general knowledge about his cultural group and his individual beliefs and practices (Abernethy et al., 2006). The counselor holds general cultural knowledge about the client and adjusts that cultural knowledge to the individual male. Using the same example, the counselor understands that Catholics generally believe in a monotheistic God but learns that this specific Catholic man prays to the Holy Spirit. Thus, the counselor adjusts questions about his prayer beliefs and practices to use the term Holy Spirit in order to be linguistically congruent with him.

In terms of the client's prayer and church attendance, the counseling interventions of understanding client preferences, broaching discussions, hypothesis testing, and dynamic sizing all help to build rapport, enhance the therapeutic alliance, and deepen the counselor's understanding of his unique beliefs and practices. Thus, those interventions establish a solid foundation for subsequent behavioral interventions that are culturally sensitive, specific to his individual context, and helpful for facilitating positive therapeutic change. We present three behavioral interventions to implement with men.

Praying with clients is the first behavioral intervention. Some men will expect and prefer to pray with their counselor (Harris et al., 2016; Saenz & Waldo, 2013). Praying with men in session facilitates rapport, healthy interpersonal communication, expression of emotions, clarifies thoughts and perspectives, and enhances spiritual health. Counselors or clients may lead the prayer, which can be discussed and agreed upon by both parties. Prayer in session may take the form of spontaneous, informal prayer or a formal prayer agreed upon between the counselor and client (e.g., the serenity prayer used in addictions treatment). Similarly, counselors can also teach men meditation in session and lead them through meditative exercises to decrease anxiety and stress as well as to increase emotional health in men (Surmitis, Fox, & Gutierrez, 2018). Meditation may be particularly helpful to foster emotional awareness and expression in emotionally stoic men.

We acknowledge that some counselors may be unfamiliar with praying with clients and may not feel comfortable initiating the behavioral intervention due to lack of training and/or personal beliefs about prayer. In such cases, counselors do not necessarily need to initiate praying with men. Yet, we encourage counselors to remain open to praying with men, especially when men initiate it and the prayer is considered a religious practice that is healthy and important to the client. Our concern is that denying the client the opportunity to pray in session runs the risk of harming the therapeutic alliance. Counselors can view praying with a client who initiates it within counseling as an opportunity to engage in a cross-cultural experience and to exercise their multicultural counseling competences. Self-reflection on personal biases, seeking additional supervision, and training are all important components to gaining comfort and competence to engage religious/spiritual men in prayer.

After praying or meditating with the client, the counselor may use the experience as a catalyst for follow-up exploratory and insight-oriented questioning. For example, asking him to disclose any insights gained from the prayer or how he feels after praying are two simple follow-up techniques to deepen the counseling. An in-session prayer may also be used as a ritual to structure and ground the counseling sessions, e.g., praying to begin and end each session. Prayer in session may also take the form of using sacred readings such as reflecting on scripture passages for insight and meaning or recitation of specific texts (e.g., the Qu'ran) to promote healing and religious coping (Darabinia et al., 2017). Prayer and meditation in session may naturally lead the counselor to encourage him to utilize those behaviors outside of session to deal with stressors and to reinforce positive habits established in counseling.

To focus the out-of-session prayer, counselors can easily adapt the positive psychology intervention of the gratitude journal (Emmons & Stern, 2013). The basic gratitude journal intervention entails the client calling to mind something or someone that he values and appreciates and recording the experience(s) and feelings in a journal before bedtime. The gratitude journal as a psychotherapeutic intervention has been rigorously examined in randomized-controlled trial studies and has been associated with an increase in positive emotions, protective against negative emotions, improved sleep, and improved ability to cope with stress (Emmons & Stern, 2013). The gratitude intervention can also take the form of writing a letter of appreciation to someone in his life (Seligman, Steen, Park, & Peterson, 2005). The letter may be read with the counselor in session, or after discussing the letter in counseling it could be delivered to the intended person.

Both interventions can be adapted in similar ways to help men in their prayer and church attendance behaviors. The first adaptation is intended to assist men struggling with prayer because of a divine struggle, negative God images, and negative feelings about the divine. Men in this category contend that God is punishing and controlling them, not answering their prayers, and feel angry and abandoned by God. As a result, they may not be praying at all or are praying with anger. In such situations, the counselor encourages him to spend time before bed thinking of blessings, gifts, benefits, pleasures in life that he can attribute to the divine. The counselor instructs him to write down his feelings of appreciation to the divine in his journal. Or, he may decide to write a letter to the divine expressing his gratitude. The counselor and client may review the journal or letter in session. Similarly, for a man experiencing disconnect from a religious community, the counselor suggests that he attend a religious activity (e.g., service, prayer group, service project). After the religious activity is over, he journals about his experience with a specific focus on what he appreciated about the activity and the people at the activity. He journals about his feelings of gratitude related to the religious activity. He may also write a letter of appreciation to a specific person that was at the activity and had a positive impact on him. For example, a male peer is appropriate when conceptualized from reference group identity dependence theory. Both adaptive interventions facilitate a shifting of thoughts and emotions from negative to positive in the context of prayer and religious attendance.

A behavioral activation exercise is the last counseling intervention discussed in this chapter. Behavioral activation is an intervention that was originally intended to decrease depressive feelings by guiding clients to engage in pleasurable activities. Although behavioral activation has been applied to other psychological concerns, it continues to be used to decrease depression. The underlying theory posits that depressive feelings contribute to avoidance behaviors that maintain the depressive feelings (Kanter et al., 2015). Within that theoretical framework, it is logical to conclude that men may avoid prayer and church attendance, which exacerbates their depressed mood and associated spiritual issues.

The intervention is action based and therefore may appeal to certain men that prefer an active counseling approach. Behavioral activation is flexible to the client's goals, values, and culture. Behavioral activation to initiate prayer and church attendance is relevant for men experiencing depressive symptoms, perhaps related to their spiritual struggle, lack of meaning in their life, and/or relationship with God. The basic intervention entails the counselor asking the client to identify a meaningful activity, scheduling the activity, and tracking their feelings after completing the activity by addressing avoidance and other obstacles to activation (Kanter et al., 2015). A worksheet is typically used for structure and accountability. He engages in prayer and religious activities outside of session and returns to counseling to discuss lingering barriers to accomplishment as well as the experiences of completing the meaningful activities. Counselors should avoid overly judgmental reactions to failed attempts, but provide empathy, explore the barriers, and identify new strategies to overcome the barriers. Counselors positively reinforce the completed activities and further explore how the client was able to complete the activities, drawing out personal attributes and resiliency from him. The sessions may also be used to track his feelings and monitor for a decrease in depressive feelings and an increase in sense of meaning, accomplishment, and connection to God and others in his religious community.

Summary and Conclusions

Prayer and church attendance are two religious behaviors that are important to the health of men from various religions as well as those men who may consider themselves non-religious but spiritual. Counselors can utilize a gendered conceptualization to understand the role and function of prayer and church attendance, or other houses of worship, in the lives of men. This chapter integrated three theories of gender role socialization – conformity to masculine norms, reference group identity, and positive masculinity – to deepen the understanding of men's engagement in prayer and church attendance. Counseling interventions are based on a culturally sensitive approach that is respectful of client preferences and entails broaching, hypothesis testing, dynamic sizing as well as behavioral techniques of praying with clients, adapted gratitude exercises, and behavioral activation. Use of such an approach will improve men's health vis-à-vis increasing their engagement in meaningful activities, enhancing positive emotions in their spirituality, improving coping skills, connecting to male peers in their religious community, broadening their access to social support, and contributing to the resolution of associated divine and spiritual struggles. Thus, prayer and religious service attendance create pathways to improve men's health.

Case Example

Sam was born in the African country of Zimbabwe. He came to the United States as a teenager to attend a mid-sized university in an urban setting. He studied political science and conflict resolution, a sort of self-designed major that was very personal for Sam. At the time, Zimbabwe was under the control of Robert Mugabe's dictatorship. Sam vehemently opposed Mugabe's ruling government and had written some essays as a high school student that led to him being arrested for a brief period. He experienced intense physical assault while detained. After his prison release, the United States accepted him into the country as a political refugee.

Sam graduated from college with honors and was accepted into a prestigious graduate program to further study political science. He was extremely intelligent, very passionate, and strong about his convictions but also soft-spoken, gentle, and unassuming. Sam was a gentleman. After his graduation, there was a sense that political tensions had lowered in Zimbabwe. Eager to see his family after four years in the United States, Sam returned to Zimbabwe for what he anticipated to be a brief summer visit with his family before starting graduate school in the fall.

Sam was back in Zimbabwe for about a month when he met a lovely young woman, Grace, who soon became his wife. He deferred admittance to the graduate program as he and Grace welcomed their first child. After a year back in Zimbabwe, Sam was now eager to return to the United States to resume his academic studies. He packed his family up and went to the airport. They flew to the United States and arrived in New York full of hope and optimism.

However, the young family was shocked and terrified when immigration officials allowed Sam and his 1-year-old son, Charlie, to progress through the immigration process but informed them that Grace could not enter the United States. She was forced to return to Zimbabwe due to "incomplete paperwork and documentation." Sam was devastated. He arrived at the agency that I worked for in a state of complete despair, turmoil, and confusion.

The agency where I worked at that time is a non-profit organization with several departments, including services to assist refugees and immigrants. Sam first accessed the agency through that department, but he was so emotionally dysregulated and hysterical that the staff were unable to accomplish much in their initial meetings. A staff member in the refugee and immigration department brought Sam to the counseling department for services.

Sam was in crisis when we first met. Therefore, I focused our first session on risk assessment and crisis management. He scored a 50 out of 63 on the Beck Depression Inventory (BDI), including endorsement of suicidal ideation. He acknowledged having thoughts of crashing his car into another car or a wall or off a bridge. He cried profusely, sobbing into his hands. I asked him how likely he was to follow through on such thoughts. He gathered himself, the tears letting up a bit, and said "I won't do it. I really won't." I asked him what was stopping him, and he explained that he is a devout Christian. As a devout Christian, he understood suffering as part of his spiritual journey and that suffering leads to an eventual joyous resurrection. Sam considered suicide to be antithetical to his religious and spiritual beliefs. He also stated a sincere desire to "be here" for his young son and to be a father.

I was very concerned about Sam and moved quickly to establish a plan with him to decrease his depression and minimize his risk. We agreed to meet two or three times a week and I assessed his coping and supportive resources. He first identified a female cousin in the area who was babysitting his son while we met. Sam also identified "uncles and aunts" that lived in the area. I learned that "uncles and aunts" were an inclusive term in Zimbabwe, which entailed close friends of the family. I asked Sam if he saw his uncles and aunts and he said that he did not. It was apparent that he felt a sense of shame, as if he had let down his extended family by being unable to solve this problem on his own. He perceived his manhood as compromised because he was not able to secure the safe passage of his entire family to the United States. He had an irrational fear that his community would shun him. It was clear that he was a very proud man and was engaged in overly harsh self-talk for "not being able to handle this" on his own. I challenged his irrational fears and explored the benefits of seeing his uncle and aunts. Sam reported that they all go to the same Christian church on a regular basis, but that he had been afraid to go. We set a therapeutic goal that he would go to the church and connect with his extended family there. To reinforce this therapeutic goal and to try to increase a commitment to engaging in positive behaviors, I used a behavioral activation worksheet. We wrote down a specific time and date that he would go to the church and take the worksheet with him.

In addition, I picked up on his identification with the Christian faith and broached the subject of prayer with him. He reported that he is unable to pray because of "distractions . . . there is so much to do and I can't keep up." His state of crisis had made it difficult to utilize his normal coping skills, including engagement in prayer. I informed Sam that I am open to religious conversations and respectful of his Christian faith. He nodded, signaling understanding. I asked him if he wanted to try praying with me in session; I suggested that it might help him concentrate and be more productive. Sam expressed appreciation for the invitation, but initially declined.

In the initial phase of counseling, we met about three times a week. I administered the BDI during every session and assessed his suicidal ideation. His BDI scores started to gradually decrease. After about two weeks, his suicidal ideation became more passive and existential in nature. Sam reported that he had established contact with his uncles and aunts at the church, which improved his mood. They offered to provide babysitting while he attended his various appointments with me, the immigration department, government agencies, and his academic institution. They were also helping him financially and to find a job. Thus, his family and church community provided immediate instrumental support, which positively contributed to his mental health. In addition, Sam discussed feeling at home in the church and enjoying the preaching of the pastor. He identified with figures in the Bible reading who were dramatically tested by God such as Job and St. Paul. He began to feel a renewed sense of spiritual support from God and resilience to adversity. Counseling began to focus less on crisis assessment and management. We identified other coping resources. For example, he was able to buy a phone and phone cards that allowed for international calls to his wife. They began talking three or four times per week. He was so happy to hear her voice and know that she was safe. Grace had to go into hiding at an undisclosed location due to increased political tensions and her connection to Sam.

After about a month or so of counseling, which included approximately 12 sessions, Sam came to a counseling session with a determined look on his face. I noted my observation to him and asked him what was going on? Sam averted eye contact and reluctantly continued, "Remember when you said that you would pray with me?" I replied, "Yes I do." Sam responded, "Will you? Will you pray with me?" I agreed to pray with Sam and we explored how we would pray together. I asked about his preferences for prayer type (formal or informal), to whom (God, Jesus, etc.), and structure. He preferred an informal prayer, led by me, addressed to God. He asked me to start the prayer and he would finish it. Therefore, I led an informal prayer, seeking guidance for Sam and his family, expressing appreciation for God's role in our lives, asking that God keep Grace safe, and that we remain patient for their eventual reunion. Sam initially prayed for a miracle, but then simply asked that "Your will be done." I felt a sense of relief, acceptance, and surrendering from Sam to God, which I conveyed to Sam after the prayer. Sam agreed with my interpretation and further explained that although this situation is unbelievably challenging for him, he has come to realize that there is little that he can control in it and that he will "do what I can and leave the rest to God."

Our sessions decreased to twice a week to once a week over the following months. Sam returned to our 20th session with a big smile on his face. It was the first time I had seen him smile and I asked him why he was smiling. Sam described going on a hike deep into the woods over the weekend. He recalled being alone and far from people and buildings. Upon realizing that he was alone and surrounded only by nature, he "began yelling and screaming at God! I let God have it! I threw rocks and sticks and broke tree limbs!" I explored his experience with open-ended questions, expressing sincere curiosity while sensing Sam's need to tell this story. Sam responded to my probing by describing his satisfying feeling of spiritual and physical exhaustion after what I conceptualized was a cathartic experience for him. Laying on the ground of the woods, exhausted, Sam was aware of the complete silence and "sat there with God" for an unknown period. I thanked Sam for telling me the story and affirmed him in his prayer to God. I conveyed to Sam that he truly "lifted his heart" to God, which is a definition of prayer that I know and understand. Sam laughed and agreed.

We began to wrap up our counseling after about six months of working together and he met more regularly with staff in the immigration department. Sam's BDI scores were consistently between 11 and 16, indicating a mild level of depression appropriate to his circumstances. There were no signs or disclosures of suicidal ideation. He began a part-time job and took a reduced course load. Sam was attending religious services at his church on a regular basis and felt connected to his religious community. Although Grace did not gain entrance into the United States during my time counseling Sam, I am aware that she eventually joined Sam and Charlie in the United States and they remain a unified family at this time.

Table 4.1 Overview of Prayer, Religious Attendance, and Sacred Reading in World Religions

World Religions	*Types of Prayer*	*Type of Church Attendance*	*Sacred Text*
Christianity	Intercessory Prayer: prayer on behalf of others and for one's own needs and desires Contemplative Prayer: centering and meditative prayer Blessing, Adoration, Praise God Prayer of Petition: ask for what is needed Prayer of Thanksgiving	Christians are not commanded to attend Sabbath services while fellowship is encouraged on any given day of the week, and not just Sunday. Sunday is a traditional day of worship and remembrance of the Lord. Involves prayers, readings, preaching, and hymns. Mass is a central and obligatory act of worship for Catholic Christians to spend time with God and receive his graces. Takes place on Sundays. Consists of four rites: Introductory Rite, Liturgy of the World, Eucharist, and Mass. Consists of hymns, sign of the cross, readings from the Bible, sermons, kneeling to Christ (present in appearance of bread and wine), standing for prayer, and blessings.	Bible
Islam	Salat: prayer performed five times a day Wudhu': performed before Salat Salat al-Fajr: dawn, before sunrise Salat al-Zuhr-midday, after sun passes its highest Salat al-Asr: the late part of the afternoon Salat-al-Maghrib: just after sunset Salat al-Isha: between sunset and midnight Obligatory Prayers: Fajr-2 (2 after Obli.) Zuhr-4 (4, 2, and 2 after Obli.) Asr-4 Maghrib-3 (2 after Obli.) Isha-4 (2 and 3 after Obli.)	Salaat ul-Jumma/Friday Prayer is offered as congregation. Offered in place of Zuhar. Presentable; spend period in remembrance of God. Imams deliver khutbah, two parts of sermon are delivered before prayer. Person who delivered sermon leads prayer.	Qu'ran

Judaism	Daily Prayer: By tradition there are three daily prayers Shacharit: Morning (Preliminary prayers, Shema/Blessings, Amidah, and Concluding prayers) Minchah: Afternoon (Preliminary prayers and Amidah; includes Torah reading only on Shabbat and Yom Kippur) Ma'ariv:Evening after sundown (Includes preliminary prayers, Shema and its Blessings, Amidah and Concluding Prayers Ma'ariv and Shacharit services: 1) Warm-up prayers 2) Shema and Blessing 3) Amidah 4) Concluding Prayers Shabbat Prayers: Day of Rest prayers. Weekly ritual (25 hrs), commandments to remember (zachor) and observe (shamor). Require worshippers to have siddur (prayer book)	Shabbat is weekly day of rest and spiritual enrichment that starts on Friday (sunset) and finishes Saturday (nightfall). Day of zakhor (remember) and shamar (observe). Candles are lit and blessings are recited, evening service attended, studying Torah, enjoyment of feasts, and ritual.	Torah
Hinduism	Sakam: with expectation of fulfillment of desire Nishkam: devoid of any expectations Vyashti: for individual gain, removal of unhappiness, spiritual progress. Samashti: for the sake of the society	Puja is a showing of reverence to the divine through songs, rituals, prayers, and invocations. Make spiritual connect to divine. Performed on the floor with at least another member honoring gods/goddesses that protect household and family. Commonly worship at home and present tray of flowers, fruits, and food.	The Vedas

(continued)

Table 4.1 (continued)

World Religions	*Types of Prayer*	*Type of Church Attendance*	*Sacred Text*
Buddhism	Buddhists practice meditation as best way to connect, consider enlightenment, and achieve Nirvana Generative meditation: assist to strengthen and cultivate love, patience, appreciation, compassion Metta Sutta: discourse with Pali Canon. Develop goodwill for everything Concentrative meditation: focusing mind on breath, image, sound. Achieve mind clarity and awareness. Aim to achieve Dhyana Receptive meditation: achieve calm, clear and non-reactive state of mind and being Reflective meditation: investigating an idea in a systematic way	Uposatha Day is a day of preparation involving special observances for the Soma ritual. Held on days of half-moon, full moon, and new moon –eighth, fourteenth or fifteenth days of lunar fortnight. (full/new moons) Bhikkus meet to recite their Patimokka, while weekly (quarter moon) listen and speak of the Dhamma.	Tripitaka

Table 4.2 Assessments Used for Prayer and Church Attendance

Scale	*Description*
Religious Experience Questionnaire (REQ; Edwards, 1976)	The REQ is a 12-item measure to assess a personal affective relationship with God, perceived influence of God in one's life, including feeling forgiven and referring to God to help guide decisions.
Prayer Experience Questionnaire (PEQ; Dein & Littlewood, 2008)	The PEQ is a 25-item measure to assess prayer frequency, context, form, and content, along with phenomenological descriptions of the prayer's encounter with the sacred.
Religious Commitment Inventory-10 (RCI; Worthington et al., 2003)	The RCI-10 is a 10-item measure to assess the degree to which a person adheres to his or her religious values, beliefs, and practices and uses them in daily living.
Multidimensional Prayer Inventory (MPI; Laird et al., 2004)	The MPI is a 21-item measure to assess both quantitative and qualitative aspects of prayer. The 5 distinct aspects of prayer that are measured are as follows: occurrence, weekly frequency, daily frequency, duration, type (adoration, confession, thanksgiving, supplication, reception), and level of faith in the effects of prayer.
Prayer Functions Scale (PFS; Bade & Cook, 2008)	The PFS is a 58-item measure to assess the frequency with which individuals use prayer for 4 specific coping functions: assistance, calm, deferring, and acceptance.
The Prayer Inventory (Bänziger, van Uden, & Janssen, 2008)	The Prayer Inventory is a 24-item measure to assess the extent to which participants engage in 4 types of prayer: religious prayer, petitionary prayer, meditative prayer, and psychological prayer.
Church Attendance, Faith Community Support, and Religiosity Measure (Olson, Goddard, & Marshall, 2013).	This 5-item measure is used to assess church attendance, support from one's faith community, and general religiosity.
The How It Feels at Church Survey (Baard, 1994)	This 23-item measure is used to assess intrinsic motivation for church membership and participation, including autonomy, competence, and relatedness.
The Church Involvement Measure (CIM; Mattis, Fontenot, & Hatcher-Kay, 2003)	The CIM is a 4-item measure used to assess church involvement in African-American adults.

References

Abernethy, A.D., Houston, T.R., Mimms, T., & Boyd-Franklin, N. (2006). Using prayer in psychotherapy: Applying Sue's differential to enhance culturally competent care. *Cultural Diversity and Ethnic Minority Psychology, 12*(1), 101–114.

Baard, P.P. (1994). A motivational model for consulting with not-for-profit organizations: A study of church growth and participation. *Consulting Psychology Journal: Practice and Research, 46*(3), 19–31.

Bade, M.K., & Cook, S.W. (2008). Functions of Christian prayer in the coping process. *Journal for the Scientific Study of Religion, 47*(1), 123–133.

Bänziger, S., van Uden, M., & Janssen, J. (2008). Praying and coping: The relation between varieties of praying and religious coping styles. *Mental Health, Religion & Culture, 11*, 101–118.

Bradshaw, M., Ellison, C.G., & Flannelly, K.J. (2008). Prayer, God imagery, and symptoms of psychopathology. *Journal for the Scientific Study of Religion, 47*(4), 644–659.

Breslin, M.J., & Lewis, C.A. (2008). Theoretical models of the nature of prayer and health: A review. *Mental Health, Religion, & Culture, 11*(1), 9–21.

Catholic Church. (1994). *Catechism of the Catholic Church*. Vatican City: Libreria Editrice Vaticana.

Courtenay, W. (2011). *Dying to be men: Psychosocial, environmental, and biobehavioral directions in promoting the health of men and boys*. New York, NY: Routledge.

Courtenay, W., & Keeling, R. (2000). Men, gender, and health: Toward an interdisciplinary approach. *Journal of American College Health, 48*(6), 243–246.

Darabinia, M., Gorji, A.M.H., & Afzali, M.A. (2017). The effect of the Quran recitation on mental health of the Iranian medical staff. *Journal of Nursing Education and Practice*, 7(11), 30–36.

Day-Vines, N.L., Wood, S.M., Grothaus, T., Craigen, L., Holman, A., Dotson-Blake, K., & Douglass, M.J. (2016). Broaching the subjects of race, ethnicity, and culture during the counseling process. *Journal of Counseling & Development, 85*(4), 401–409.

Dein, S., & Littlewood, R. (2008). The psychology of prayer and the development of the Prayer Experience Questionnaire. *Mental Health, Religion, & Culture, 11*(1), 39–52.

Edwards, K.J. (1976). Sex-role behavior and religious experience. In Donaldson, W. J. (Ed.), *Research in mental health and religious behavior: An introduction to research in the integration of Christianity and the behavioral sciences* (pp. 224–238). Atlanta, GA: Psychological Studies Institute.

Emmons, R.A. and Stern, R. (2013). Gratitude as a psychotherapeutic intervention. *Journal of Clinical Psychology, 69*(8), 846–855.

Garfield, C.F., Isacco, A., & Rogers, T.E. (2008). A review of men's health and masculinity. *American Journal of Lifestyle Medicine, 2*(6), 474–487.

Garfield, C.F., Isacco, A.I, & Sahker, E. (2013). Religion and spirituality as important components of men's health and wellness: An analytic review. *American Journal of Lifestyle Medicine*, 7(1), 27–37.

Gast, J., & Peak, T. (2011). "It used to be that if it weren't broken and bleeding profusely, I would never go to the doctor": Men, masculinity, and health. *American Journal of Men's Health, 5*(4), 318–331.

Hammond, W.P., & Mattis, J.S. (2005). Being a man about it: Manhood meaning among African American men. *Psychology of Men & Masculinity, 6*(2), 114–126.

Harris, K.A., Randolph, B.E., & Gordon, T.D. (2016). What do clients want? Assessing spiritual needs in counseling: A literature review. *Spirituality in Clinical Practice, 3*(4), 250–275.

Henry, H. (2015). Spiritual energy of Islamic prayers as a catalyst for psychotherapy. *Journal of Religion and Health, 54*(2), 387–398.

James, W. (1963). *The varieties of religious experience*. New York: University Books.

Jantos, M., & Kiat, H. (2007). Prayer as medicine: How much have we learned? *Medical Journal of Australia, 186*(10), S51–S53.

Kanter, J.W., Santiago-Rivera, A.L., Santos, M.M., Nagy, G., López, M., Hurtado, G. D., & West, P. (2015). A randomized hybrid efficacy and effectiveness trial of behavioral activation for Latinos with depression. *Behavior Therapy, 46*(2), 177–192.

Kiselica, M.S., Benton-Wright, S., & Englar-Carlson, M. (2016). Accentuating positive masculinity: A new foundation for the psychology of boys, men, and masculinity. In Y.J. Wong & S.R. Wester (Eds.), *APA handbook of men and masculinities* (pp. 123–143). Washington, DC: American Psychological Association.

Kvande, M.N., Klöckner, C.A., & Nielsen, M.E. (2015). Church attendance and religious experience: Differential associations to well-being for Norwegian women and men? *SAGE Open, 5*(4), 1–13.

Laird, S.P., Snyder, C.R., Rapoff, M.A., & Green, S. (2004). Measuring private prayer: Development, validation, and clinical application of the multidimensional prayer inventory. *The International Journal for the Psychology of Religion, 14*, 251–272.

Leonard, M. (2014). *Prayer works: Getting a grip on Catholic spirituality*. Steubenville, OH: Matthew Leonard.

Lomas, T., Edginton, T., Cartwright, T., & Ridge, D. (2014a). Men developing emotional intelligence through meditation? Integrating narrative, EEG, and cognitive evidence. *Psychology of Men & Masculinity, 15*(2), 213–224.

Lomas, T., Ridge, D., Cartwright, T., & Edginton, T. (2014b). Engagement with meditation as a positive health trajectory: Divergent narratives of progress in male meditators. *Psychology & Health, 29*(2), 218–236.

Mahalik, J.R., Good, G.E., & Englar-Carlson, M. (2003). Masculinity scripts, presenting concerns, and help seeking: Implications for practice and training. *Professional Psychology: Research and Practice, 34*(2), 123–131.

Mattis, J., Fontenot, D., & Hatcher-Kay, C. (2003). Religiosity, racism, and dispositional optimism among African Americans. *Personality and Individual Differences, 34*, 1025–1038.

Mukerjee, S., & Venugopal, A. (2018). Religiosity and health through the decades: Is there a gender difference? *American Journal of Health Promotion, 32*(4), 1028–1041.

Nicholson, A., Rose, R., & Bobak, M. (2009). Association between attendance at religious services and self-reported health in 22 European countries. *Social Science and Medicine, 69*(4), 519–528.

Olson, J.R., Goddard, H., & Marshall, J.P. (2013). Relations among risk, religiosity, and marital commitment. *Journal Of Couple & Relationship Therapy, 12*(3), 235–254.

Pew Research Center (2016). *The gender gap in religion around the world*. Retrieved from http://assets.pewresearch.org/wp-content/uploads/sites/11/2016/03/Religion-and-Gender-Full-Report.pdf.

Plante, T. (2009). *Spiritual practices in psychotherapy: Thirteen tools for enhancing psychological health*. Washington, DC: American Psychological Association.

Robinson, M.A., Jones-Eversley, S., Moore, S.E., Ravenell, J., & Adedoyin, A.C. (2018). Black male mental health and the Black church: Advancing a collaborative partnership and research agenda. *Journal of Religion & Health, 57*(3), 1095–1107.

Saenz, R., & Waldo, M. (2013). Clients' preferences regarding prayer during counseling. *Psychology of Religion and Spirituality, 5*(4), 325–334.

Seligman, M.E.P., Steen, T.A., Park, N., & Peterson, C. (2005). Positive psychology progress: Empirical validation of interventions. *American Psychologist, 60*(5), 410–421.

Speed, D., & Fowler, K. (2016). What's God got to do with it? How religiosity predicts atheists' health. *Journal of Religion and Health, 55*(1), 296–308.

Surmitis, K.A., Fox, J. and Gutierrez, D. (2018). Meditation and appropriation: Best practices for counselors who utilize meditation. *Counseling and Values, 63*(1), 4–16.

Wade, J.C. (1998). Male reference group identity dependence: A theory of male identity. *The Counseling Psychologist, 26*(3), 349–383.

Walton, J., & Sullivan, N. (2004). Men of prayer: Spirituality of men with prostate cancer – A grounded theory study. *Journal of Holistic Nursing, 22*(2), 133–151.

Waters, E.K., Millard, H.M., & Doyle, Z. (2015). Losing hope: Mental health and religious service non-attendance in Australia. *Mental Health, Religion and Culture, 18*(2), 114–122.

Weber, S.R., & Pargament, K.I. (2014). The role of religion and spirituality in mental health. *Current Opinion in Psychiatry, 27*(5), 358–363.

Worthington, E.L., Jr., Wade, N.G., Hight, T.L., Ripley, J.S., McCullough, M.E., Berry, J.W., . . . & O'Conner, L. (2003). The religious commitment inventory-10: Development, refinement, and validation of a brief scale for research and counseling. *Journal of Counseling Psychology, 50*, 84–96.

5 Men's Shame

Men are prone to experience shame in gender-specific ways because of male gender role socialization (Shepard & Rabinowitz, 2013). In this chapter, we define shame and the areas in which it is experienced by men. We will differentiate shame from guilt and explain why this differentiation is important. We review the literature on shame as it relates to gender, masculinity, religion, and culture. Given this significant body of literature, we offer ways that you can conceptualize, assess, and treat shame and its consequences when working with male clients.

Differentiating Shame from Guilt

Shame and guilt are variously considered or referred to as self-conscious emotions, moral emotions, social emotions, or higher-order emotions (Murray & Ciarrocchi, 2007; Tangney, Stuewig, & Mashek, 2007). Haidt (2003) defined moral emotions as those "that are linked to the interests or welfare either of society as a whole or at least of persons other than the judge or agent" (p. 276). They motivate us to do good or what is right, and to avoid doing bad or what is wrong. They are considered self-conscious emotions because the self reflects upon the self and evaluates the self.

Frequently the literature refers to the seminal work of H.B. Lewis (1971) and the research of Tangney and her colleagues (e.g., Tangney, 1991; Tangney, Burggraf, & Wagner, 1995; Tangney & Dearing, 2002) for definitions of shame and guilt and how these two emotions differ. Generally, shame refers to the whole self and feeling that you have not lived up to the desired image of yourself, whereas guilt is the feeling that you have done something wrong with regard to a particular event, and it is not about the whole self but an aspect of the self (Ng, 1981; Wright, 1987). Shame is about wishing you were not such a person, so to speak, while guilt is about wishing you had not done something (although feelings of guilt can be associated with thoughts as well as behaviors). As such, shame is a more painful emotional experience than guilt, because it affects the perception of the entire self as opposed to a specific behavior. Additionally, guilt will often produce feelings of shame, or when the behavior causing guilt becomes habitual it can merge into shame (M. Lewis, 2010; "Self-Conscious Emotions," n.d.). "If one constantly does bad things, one must consequently be bad or at least incompetent" (Lund, 2017, p. 359).

There are several distinctions that are made with regard to the type of shame being referred to in the literature. One distinction is that of internal or internalized shame, and external shame (Shepard & Rabinowitz, 2013). External shame is an emotion that is in response to what others say or do in an attempt to discourage behavior that is socially unacceptable; for example, when others ridicule, criticize, embarrass, or ostracize the person (Ng, 1981). However, internal shame does not need the actions or presence of others to evoke feelings of shame, because the "others" have been internalized. Internalized shame has also been referred to as trait shame signifying a stable personality characteristic, which differs from state shame that refers to shame related to a specific event (Cook, 1996; Del Rosario & White, 2006; Reilly, Rochlen, & Awad, 2014). Such an enduring aspect of shame in which it permeates one's personality and identity has been referred to as chronic shame and toxic shame (Park, 2016).

Research on the associations between shame, guilt, and psychopathology shows shame and guilt to be correlated; however, only shame is related to poorer mental health (Benetti-McQuoid & Bursik, 2005; Lynch, Hill, Nagoshi, & Nagoshi, 2012). To be more precise, researchers have made the distinction of "shame-free" guilt, which has been found to be unrelated to psychological problems (Tangney et al., 2007). Anger has been investigated as a particular emotion associated with feelings of shame. Wright, Gudjonsson, and Young (2008) summarized the research indicating that individuals who are more inclined to feel shame are also more likely to experience angry feelings and not deal with their feelings constructively, whereas individuals more inclined to feel guilt are less likely to experience angry feelings and deal with their feelings constructively. Additionally, they are more likely to blame others. It is possible that the intense feelings of anger that shame evokes is toward the self, but because this is so unpleasant to the self the feelings are directed outward as a means of coping (H.B. Lewis, 1971; M. Lewis, 1992; Tangney & Dearing, 2002). Alternatively, the shame-related intense feelings of anger toward the self can result in depression (M. Lewis, 1992).

Gender Differences

H.B. Lewis (1971) made the link between gender differences in guilt and shame and differences in gender role socialization. Generally, research shows that females experience more shame and guilt than males do (e.g., Ferguson & Crowley, 1997; Lutwak & Ferrari, 1996; Lutwak, Ferrari, & Cheek, 1998; Lynch et al., 2012). One possible explanation is that in US culture women are more likely than men to acknowledge negative emotions on self-report measures, with the possible exception of anger, because the culture is more permissive of women expressing such emotions (Zhang, 2011). Along these lines, men and women tend to experience different emotional responses to shame, whereby the tendency is for women to experience greater depression and men to experience greater rage (M. Lewis, 1992).

However, there are some conflicting results, and authors have speculated that one possible reason for the conflicting results is in how shame and guilt are operationalized and the measures used (see Benetti-McQuoid & Bursik, 2005). Additionally, as opposed to gender per se, some researchers have investigated gender role identity; that is, one's masculine and feminine attributes. For example, Benetti-McQuoid and Bursik (2005) found that although women were more shame-prone than men, men and women who ascribed to themselves more feminine than masculine characteristics were the most shame-prone. Additionally, having more masculine than feminine characteristics was related to lower shame-proneness for women, whereas more feminine than masculine characteristics was associated with higher shame-proneness for men.

Men, Masculinity, and Shame

Men may experience shame when they have not lived up to the desired image of their masculine self, or the masculine ideal. Culturally defined expectations of masculinity, or how boys and men are supposed to feel and act, become internalized. The more a man evaluates himself by masculine ideals and fails to meet those standards, the more prone he is to experience shame (Efthim, Kenny, & Mahalik, 2001). Boys and men are also shamed into complying with gender role norms, such that conforming to masculine norms may be a way that males avoid feelings of shame and being shamed by others (Reigeluth & Addis, 2016; Shepard & Rabinowitz, 2013).

The experience of shame is a painful emotion that contributes to men feeling depressed and angry. Equally, not being able to control one's feelings of depression and anger can contribute to feelings of shame. For example, a man can feel shame for not having lived up to the desired image of his masculine self as breadwinner of the family, which causes him to feel depressed, and equally feel shame about feeling depressed, because men should be emotionally strong. A study with Australian men showed that when a man feels he must conform to masculine norms, he is also more likely to feel shame, and the more shame he feels the more likely he will feel depressed (Rice et al., 2016).

Certain life events, behaviors, and feelings may be more likely to evoke feelings of shame in men, such as loss of a job or being unemployed, a failed marriage, uncontrolled use of drugs or alcohol, feelings of inadequacy related to intellectual and physical attributes, and expressing and responding to gentle feelings (e.g., love, sympathy, tenderness). For example, men who had undergone marital separation within the last 18 months experienced more shame than married and single men, and there was a significant correlation between shame in response to the separation and depression for the separated men, but not the separated women (Kolves, Ide, & De Leo, 2011). Dearing, Stuewig, and Tangney (2005) investigated the relationship between shame-proneness and problematic use of substances in a sample of inmates, of which 90% were men, and found shame-proneness was strongly associated with alcohol and drug dependence. They argued that problematic use of substances may be a way to cope with feelings of shame; however, problematic use as well as the problems that are a consequence of substance misuse can also result in feelings of shame.

The experience of shame for some men is intolerable such that they may externalize blame as a defensive maneuver (Efthim, Kenny, & Mahalik, 2001), and externalization of blame can result in feelings of anger and verbal and physical aggression (Stuewig, Tangney, Heigel, Harty, & McCloskey, 2010). Shame was related to traditional masculinity, hostility, and aggression in a sample of US men (Jakupcak, Tull, & Roemer, 2005), and to difficulties with anger in a sample of British men who were detained in forensic psychiatric units (Wright et al., 2008). In men who had directly experienced an interpersonal trauma (e.g., physical assault, assault with a weapon), trait shame accounted for the relationship between posttraumatic stress and aggressive behavior in their intimate relationships (Schoenleber, Sippel, Jakupcak, & Tull, 2015).

Self-compassion may be one way that men can neutralize feelings of shame. Self-compassion involves "extending kindness and understanding to oneself rather than harsh judgment and self-criticism" (Neff, 2003, p. 89). As such, self-compassion may counter feelings of shame because there is no harsh criticizing of the self for failing to meet ideal standards of masculinity. Indeed, self-compassion related negatively to trait shame and conformity to masculine norms in a study of university men and men from the community (Reilly et al., 2014). In other words, when men have self-compassion they may be less prone to feelings of shame, as well as be less likely to conform to masculinity norms.

Religion and Shame

Religious beliefs and doctrines can be the source of one's shame; however, religion and spirituality can also be transformative (McNish, 2013; Park, 2016). For men, a potential source of shame can be the notions of manhood based in one's religion that have been internalized. Men with chronic shame may have a God image that is consistent with and reinforcing of their self-image of being unlovable and unworthy because of their mistakes or failures, often conceived of as sinning (Park, 2016). Conversely, "divine grace" can be a very powerful antidote to shame (Fowler, 1996), as "grace works to remove the experience of rejection that lies at the heart of shame" (McNish, 2013, p. 192).

It is important to distinguish between shame and guilt within the context of religion. Some authors have argued that, within Christianity in particular, the focus has been on guilt for one's sins and forgiveness and not the experience of grace that frees one from shame (Hearn, 2015). However, men who are shame-prone may not see themselves as worthy of God's forgiveness, which can exacerbate feelings of shame (Albers, 1995; Exline, Wilt, Stauner, Harriott, & Saritoprak, 2017). In a qualitative study of Protestant Christians in Finland, most of whom were men, who had a history of substance abuse and were in recovery, it was noted that the participants' experience of their religion emphasized guilt and forgiveness, and in some way addressed shame, but they had difficulty distinguishing between guilt and shame (Lund, 2017). As such, Christian messages of forgiveness did not help with feelings of shame, because it was addressing the wrong problem. When a person feels shame, it is the whole self that is affected, and therefore God's forgiveness of deeds or behaviors is not sufficient.

"Connectedness, identity, and acceptance are at the core of what is needed to transform shame" (Park, 2016, p. 365). Indeed, feeling disconnected from God (spiritual struggles) and dissatisfaction with one's congregation were related to feelings of shame in a sample of graduate and undergraduate students in the United States (Murray & Ciarrocchi, 2007). As such, it can be argued that although shame may not be directly addressed in one's religion, and that the emphasis is on guilt and forgiveness, there is the potential for the transformation of shame through involvement in faith communities. In this regard, involvement in a congregation where God's complete acceptance of us is the doctrine may counteract feelings of shame. In the study of Protestant Christians in Finland who were in recovery, the researcher proposed that some type of spiritual experience in terms of grace, in the Christian sense, was helpful in their recovery, as well as a congregation that was non-shaming (Lund, 2017).

Culture and Shame

Eastern and Western cultures have been characterized as shame and guilt cultures respectively. Research has shown differences in shame and guilt and their relationship to other variables in collectivistic (Eastern) versus individualistic (Western) cultures (see Novin, Rieffe, & Meerum Terwogt, 2011). Thus, shame may be very important to a man whose cultural background is collectivist. He may be more sensitive to and care more about what others think of his actions, in particular his family and friends. However, it should be noted that shame may have more deleterious effects for men from individualist cultures than men from collectivist cultures. This may at first seem counterintuitive, but the rationale is one in which shame and guilt function the same way in different cultures; in collectivist cultures shame motivates social behavior that benefits interpersonal relationships, whereas guilt does so in individualist cultures (Novin et al., 2011). In a study of Dutch (individualist) and Moroccan (collectivist) adolescents, the Moroccan adolescents reported more feelings of shame than the Dutch adolescents; and shame, not guilt, was positively associated with psychosocial functioning (Novin et al., 2011).

In an interesting study that examined cultural differences in shame and guilt between Chinese and US preschool children (Zhang, 2011), the children were exposed to a "mishap task" in which a doll broke while they played with it. The session was videotaped and trained coders rated the children's shame-related behaviors in terms of withdrawal from the experimenter and nervous behaviors. Additionally, the parents had completed questionnaires on their child's shame-related behaviors. The results showed that Chinese parents reported more shame-related behaviors for their children than the US parents did. After the mishap, shame-related behaviors had increased for all children, except that the Chinese children did not show an increase in nervous behaviors. This research suggests possible differences in men's experience of shame based on cultural background, such that men from an individualist culture may be more affected by feelings of shame than men from collectivist cultures.

Conceptualization, Assessment, and Counseling Interventions

Conceptualization

Feelings of shame may underlie the presenting problem of a man who is seeking psychological help. Having to seek help may bring about feelings of shame as well. Shame may be a trait, in terms of being shame-prone, or it may be experienced as a state or be situational. It can be experienced as feeling not worthy, where shame has been internalized and is more chronic and persistent, or experienced as feeling ashamed for failing to live up to expectations of oneself. Men may experience shame associated with not fulfilling the masculine ideal; for failing to meet expectations of manhood as defined by his culture or religion. Thus, shame may have a religious basis. Shame may also be what makes him conform or adhere to masculinity norms.

When shame is chronic as opposed to situational, feelings of worthlessness as opposed to any particular behavior are what require intervention. As such, feeling loved, a sense of connectedness, and accepted by others is what can counter chronic shame. Among other therapeutic strategies, religion and spirituality are potential resources in treating dispositional and situational shame.

Assessment

It should be noted that not all men in treatment will have feelings of shame. However, the following questions can be used to guide you in assessing the experience of shame in male clients.

- Is the presenting problem shame based, or at a minimum is shame related to the presenting problem?
- Is the shame chronic, or is the shame more situational?

- To what extent is the shame based on religious beliefs?
- To what extent is the shame related to conforming to or violating masculine norms?
- To what extent is the shame related to the intersection of religion and masculinity issues?
- Does the image of the desired self have masculinity and/or religious/spiritual aspects to it?

In addition, for those men who consider themselves religious or spiritual, it would be important to evaluate the client's relationship with God.

There are also assessment instruments that can be used to assist in evaluating the client's experience of shame. The Experiential Shame Scale (Turner, 2014) and State Shame and Guilt Scale (Marschall, Sanftner, & Tangney, 1994) are brief self-report measures that assess state shame or current feelings of shame. The Internalized Shame Scale (Cook, 1996) assesses internalized shame with regard to feelings of inferiority, worthlessness, inadequacy, and alienation, and the Test of Self-Conscious Affect-3 (Tangney, Dearing, Wagner, & Gramzow, 2000) is a measure of how likely someone is to feel shame.

Counseling Interventions

It would be important for you as the therapist to be able to differentiate shame from guilt so as to be able to do so for your client. Men may not be able to state "I feel shame" or "I feel ashamed" for something they have done or continue to do. They may be more familiar with the feeling of guilt. Consider that your client likely does not feel guilty about seeking help for his problem, rather he may feel ashamed. Therefore, we suggest that you first find out how your client feels about seeking help for his problem. He may indicate that having to do so is shameful, or a sign of weakness, because he should be able to control his feelings and behavior without any help from a therapist. Although feelings of shame should not be the focus in an initial session with the client, it is an opportunity to bring such feelings to consciousness and evaluate to what extent shame may be an issue for your client. At the same time, you will be able to evaluate whether the shame is related to his ideas about what it means to be a man. What your client will need to hear from you is that his seeking help for his problem takes strength and courage. If he sees it as weakness, you may explore with him why he thinks so and make the connection between his self-concept and those masculinity messages that have influenced how he thinks about himself. In this early stage of treatment, his ideas should not be challenged; neither should his feelings be invalidated. He needs an empathic response and to hear from you how seeking help can be considered or reframed as a strength.

Feelings of shame can be associated with any psychological issue that a male client presents with, as well as behaviors that are associated with that problem. For example, shame is often associated with depression, substance abuse, and sexual behavior. Shepard and Rabinowitz (2013) suggested that when working with a depressed man you should address the components of shame, because by doing so is to address the depression. Components of shame would be the attacks on the self, feelings of failure, pain of rejection, etc., which may be related to his not living up to the ideal masculine self. Shepard and Rabinowitz provide a model for addressing shame that involves creating an egalitarian relationship between client and therapist (relational validation), demonstrating empathy for shameful feelings as well as resistance to disclosing such feelings (accessing and acknowledging shame), help with naming and regulating feelings of shame (regulating shame), and changing shame to a more adaptive emotion such as anger, guilt, and pride (transforming shame). Joining a men's psychotherapy, counseling, or support group is recommended as well.

Substance abuse can lead to feelings of shame and shameful behaviors. Conversely, feelings of shame can lead to the abuse of substances. Such feelings may be related to not living up to male gender role expectations that have a cultural or religious basis. Given research indicating that participating in religious/spiritual activities is associated with being less likely to abuse substances (Bonelli & Koenig, 2013), such activities should be encouraged. Some clients will be involved in a 12-Step group like Alcoholics Anonymous, or it may be something to recommend. In such groups, spiritual beliefs play an important role in recovery from addiction; therefore, you should be prepared to discuss these beliefs with your client if he so chooses (Center for Substance Abuse Treatment [CSAT], 2013). The client's religious or spiritual beliefs can be used to counter certain cultural beliefs about masculinity and the use of alcohol and illicit drug use. If there has been disengagement from his religion and religious institution, he may need help reentering a faith community (e.g., a church, synagogue, or mosque), as these communities can be a source of support. For some men seeking treatment who view themselves as spiritual but not necessarily religious, focusing on spirituality as opposed to religion may be a way that they can "accept the need for a higher power or a power greater than themselves (which could be other people, nature, a spiritual being, or a deity)" (CSAT, 2013, p. 42) as they struggle with maintaining abstinence or recovery from addiction.

Religiosity and spirituality interact with people's attitudes about sex and the choices they make regarding sexual activity (Murray, Ciarrocchi, & Murray-Swank, 2007). Likewise, men's masculinity ideology is linked to their sexual attitudes and behaviors. When a man engages in sexual activities or behaviors that run contrary to his religious beliefs, some of which may be specific to how men should behave sexually, he may experience feelings of shame. Such behaviors include masturbation, using pornography, sexual infidelity, same-sex sexual activity, and promiscuous or hypersexual behavior. It would be important to assess and address feelings of sexual shame that your client may have. Shame may be a precursor or a consequence of sexual behavior. Similar to what was described with regard to substance abuse, men may engage in hypersexual behavior to avoid or alleviate feelings of shame, and they may also experience sexual shame as a consequence (Gilliland, South, Carpenter, & Hardy, 2011; Giordano, Prosek, Cecil, & Brown, 2015). Additionally, within that feeling of being disconnected from or fearful of God there can be increased feelings of unworthiness and shame. Men may likewise experience sexual shame from engaging in sexual behaviors that are considered unacceptable (Murray et al., 2007). Adams and Robinson (2001) suggested interventions that can help reduce shame in hypersexual clients. They indicated that it would first be important to differentiate between shame and guilt, and to understand the origin of the shame and its function. As such, religious and spiritual beliefs should be considered, as well as beliefs about masculinity. Subsequently, shame reduction strategies should be implemented, which include interventions such as educating the client about shame, participation in a support group, facing feelings of shame and developing ways to regulate affect, and changing negative core beliefs.

Men who have a lot of shame and self-criticism may benefit from "compassionate mind training" (see Gilbert & Procter, 2006). Briefly, the training involves the use of specific strategies to help the client extend compassion to one's self-critical thoughts and develop compassionate images and warmth directed at the self. In that warmth, care, and compassion for self originally begins from experiencing it from others toward the self, the therapeutic relationship can be such a source. Additionally, a support group for men and a faith community can be sources. A religious or spiritual image can also be a source, such as God, Jesus, or Buddha. However, the "image has to have the qualities of *wisdom, strength, warmth and nonjudgement/acceptance that is given to the person* (i.e., to experience the image coming with warmth for and directing it at, the self)" (Gilbert & Procter, 2006, p. 363). Where the God image is one that is reinforcing of his self-image of being unlovable and unworthy, the intervention would involve supporting the client in replacing his shame-based narratives with God to a new narrative of divine grace (Park, 2016).

Case Example

I (Isacco) worked with Mark at an outpatient counseling center in Pittsburgh, PA. Mark was going through a very difficult time in his marriage to Lauren. Mark identified as Catholic and had initially sought help through the sacrament of confession and pastoral counseling with a priest, Fr. Tom. After meeting with Fr. Tom for a few sessions of pastoral counseling, Fr. Tom directed Mark to seek psychological counseling as Mark's marital concerns and emotional distress intensified. Fr. Tom wisely acknowledged his limitations to working further with Mark and referred him to me. It was important to Mark and the priest that he work with a "Catholic counselor." I have come to learn that many Catholics have gone to counseling and discontinued because they have perceived the counselor as insensitive and unresponsive to their faith beliefs and practices. Therefore, I hypothesized that the stability of the therapeutic relationship and trust between Mark and I would be dependent on my ability to offer a safe, accepting environment that was also aligned with his Catholic faith.

As a practicing Catholic, I felt up to the task. However, I was keenly aware that there is a great diversity among Catholics in terms of beliefs and practices. Although Mark sought a "Catholic counselor," I tried not to make any assumptions about his beliefs and practices prior to our first session. Mark arrived on time and was clearly nervous for our first session. This was his first time seeking help outside of his Church. He was of average height and build, but I learned very quickly, he was strong. He gave me a handshake that I will never forget because of the immense strength of the grip. I like to think that I give firm handshakes, but Mark nearly broke my hand. He came dressed in a t-shirt and a pair of old jeans; his grooming is best described as "gruffy." Mark looked blue-collar to me, a typical Pittsburgh guy, who probably just came from working on his car in his garage. He was in his early 40s. I later learned that my initial impression was correct, as Mark worked in a blue-collar profession and spent a good bit of time in his garage tinkering on various manual labor projects.

Before getting into what brought Mark into counseling, he immediately asked me how I knew Fr. Tom. I explained that I have known Fr. Tom for over 15 years as a friend. I could sense that Mark and I began to form our therapeutic relationship through discussing our mutual relationship with Fr. Tom and I was proving my Catholic credibility to him. Mark's nervousness began to dissipate. He asked me a few more questions such as what parish I belonged to. I decided to be transparent and self-disclosing because of my initial conceptualization that my Catholic faith would be important to establishing a trusting therapeutic relationship with Mark. Discussing my parish also allowed me to begin asking Mark about his parish, which opened up the therapeutic dialogue to his sense of religiosity and spirituality. Mark discussed being a long-time and involved member of his faith community. His faith community was clearly a source of meaning and support to him. He also described his close adherence to the Catholic faith in his life. I affirmed and validated Mark's religious involvement and religious identity. His nervousness decreased further, and I sensed him becoming more at ease.

There was a brief moment of silence. At that point, I asked Mark what brought him into counseling. Mark had been married to Lauren for close to 15 years, but she had expressed a desire for a divorce. Mark was shocked and was in cognitive and emotional distress. He was having difficulty concentrating at work and was experiencing bouts of crying. He also had no idea how to communicate with Lauren as he described several recent attempts that all ended poorly. Mark's stated counseling goal was to reconcile with Lauren and remain married – "I want to win her back Doc." He did not believe in divorce because it was against his Catholic beliefs. Although Mark did not use the word "shame" or "ashamed," my conceptualization of Mark's presenting concerns clarified. It seemed to me that his distress was associated with the conflict between his religious identity as a practicing Catholic (i.e., Catholics do not get divorced) and the reality of his marriage (i.e., his wife wanted a divorce), which resulted in a deep sense of shame for Mark. He felt like he was not living up to the desired image of a Catholic husband and father (Tangney & Dearing, 2002).

I wanted to know more about his image of fatherhood; I asked him about his children and what kind of relationship he has with them. Mark and Lauren did not have any biological children together, but Lauren had a teenage daughter from a previous relationship and Mark had become her adopted father at a young age. By his account, Mark treated her like he would a biological child. In fact, Mark discussed all of the ways in which he provided for her over the years – Catholic school, braces, new clothes, vacations, to name a few. As he discussed providing for his daughter, he began to emphasize all of the "extra jobs" that he had taken over the years to have extra money. He then generalized to his wife and how the additional jobs allowed for them to have a summer cabin in the woods for vacations. At this point, Mark did not sob but his face took on a sharply contorted and strained expression – a blend of confusion, disgust, and sorrow. I can only liken it to if he had just eaten an extremely sour and spicy food that he wanted to spit out. My conceptualization broadened at this point as Mark's description of how he related to his wife and daughter included prominent themes of a man as a provider and breadwinner. Finally, after some prompting to put words to his facial expression, he wondered aloud in exasperation how a successful provider and breadwinner could become divorced. His masculinity ideology contributed to his conflict and experience of shame. In other words, Mark had been doing what he thought a man should do in a marriage, only he was experiencing failure instead of bliss.

After a few sessions, I understood Mark as a good man who did not have the necessary tools in his toolbox to make his marriage work. His operating models of manhood and fatherhood limited his participation in the family to financial contributions. Although breadwinning is important to providing for the basic needs, it was clear that his wife wanted more from Mark, had tried to tell him that, but he did not understand her requests for intimacy. She wrote him a letter expressing as much. He read me the letter in a session and it was heartbreaking both to hear a woman ask for a deep emotional connection to her husband and a husband unable to understand the request and flounder. I asked Mark if he responded to the letter, which he had not. We used a couple sessions to draft a response letter. The letter-writing exercise facilitated emotional expression and processing from Mark. He was able to express other emotions beyond shame such as grief, loss, heartbroken, confusion, and a deep desire to make the marriage work. The letter-writing exercise also opened the therapeutic window to explore Mark's masculinity ideology. We discussed what it was like for him to express a broader range of emotions and, in particular, to his wife and another adult man.

He acknowledged that it was foreign to him and unexpectedly, he found it helpful and refreshing to "let go" of the emotions that he had been bottling up. I used his Catholic faith and asked him to think of ways that Jesus may provide an alternative model of manhood beyond providing and breadwinning. We read some scripture passages about Jesus caring for the sick, helping an outcast woman, and sobbing in the garden prior to His death. Mark's insight increased and he began to understand that he needed to broaden his core beliefs of what is a successful father and husband.

At this point in counseling, I also began working with Catholic dioceses as a psychological expert on annulment cases. An annulment is a term used in Canon Law (i.e., Church Law) to indicate that a marriage failed because of an intrinsic problem that existed prior to the marriage and that problem was a significant reason for a divorce. I used that knowledge to ask Mark about the beginning of his relationship with Lauren such as how they met, how he became an adopted father, and if there were any "warning signs" of marital conflict early in their relationship. Mark revealed that Lauren had a trauma history, which was the primary reason why she did not stay with her daughter's biological father. In Mark, Lauren found safety, stability, and a man that cared for her. Yet, because of her own unhealed traumatic scars, she also lacked emotional intimacy and effective communication skills. By the time Mark started counseling, they were sleeping in separate beds in different rooms. He could not recall the last time they engaged in sexual intimacy. I was careful not to blame Lauren while I discussed with Mark how it takes two people to make a marriage work and, similarly, it takes two people for a marriage to fail.

Mark realized that he had taken sole blame for the marriage failings, which only exacerbated his shame. He appreciated the additional Catholic perspective on marriage and divorce. Taken together, his shame lessened, and he saw his wife in a more compassionate light. I asked Mark if he could also see himself more compassionately. He seemed confused. I explained that since he was able to see his wife with more compassion, that maybe he could see himself more compassionately – perhaps as God saw him. Mark described feeling loved and forgiven by God no matter what. It was a theme we returned to as we wrapped up counseling. Mark convinced Lauren to go to couples counseling to work on both of their issues as a couple, which led to him ending his individual counseling with me. As far as I know, Mark and Lauren are still married.

References

Adams, K.M., & Robinson, D.W. (2001). Shame reduction, affect regulation, and sexual boundary development: Essential building blocks of sexual addiction treatment. *Sexual Addiction & Compulsivity, 8*(1), 23–44.

Albers, R.H. (1995). *Shame: A faith perspective.* New York, NY: Haworth Press.

Benetti-McQuoid, J., & Bursik, K. (2005). Individual differences in experiences of and responses to guilt and shame: Examining the lenses of gender and gender role. *Sex Roles, 53*(1/2), 133–142.

Bonelli, R.M., & Koenig, H.G. (2013). Mental disorders, religion and spirituality 1990 to 2010: A systematic evidence-based review. *Journal of Religion & Health, 52*(2), 657–673.

Center for Substance Abuse Treatment (CSAT). (2013). *Treatment issues for men. Addressing the specific behavioral health needs of men.* Rockville, MD: Substance Abuse and Mental Health Services Administration. (Treatment Improvement Protocol (TIP) Series, No. 56.) Retrieved from www.ncbi.nlm.nih.gov/books/NBK144290/?report=printable.

Cook, D.R. (1996). Empirical studies of shame and guilt: The Internalized Shame Scale. In D.L. Nathanson (Ed.), *Knowing feeling: Affect, script, and psychotherapy* (pp. 132–165). New York, NY: Norton.

Dearing, R.L., Stuewig, J., & Tangney, J.P. (2005). On the importance of distinguishing shame from guilt: Relations to problematic alcohol and drug use. *Addictive Behaviors, 30*(7), 1392–1404.

Del Rosario, P.M., & White, R.M. (2006). The Internalized Shame Scale: Temporal stability, internal consistency, and principal components analysis. *Personality and Individual Differences, 41*(1), 95–103.

Efthim, P.W., Kenny, M.E., & Mahalik, J.R. (2001). Gender role stress in relation to shame, guilt, and externalization. *Journal of Counseling & Development, 79*(4), 430–438.

Exline, J.J., Wilt, J.A., Stauner, N., Harriott, V.A., & Saritoprak, S.N. (2017). Self forgiveness and religious/spiritual struggles. In L. Woodyatt, E.L. Worthington, Jr., M. Wenzel, & B.J. Griffin (Eds.), *Handbook of the psychology of self-forgiveness* (pp. 131–145). New York, NY: Springer.

Ferguson, T.J., & Crowley, S.L. (1997). Gender differences in the organization of guilt and shame. *Sex Roles,* 37(1/2), 19–44.

Fowler, J.W. (1996). *Faithful change: The personal and public challenges of postmodern life.* Nashville, TN: Abingdon Press.

Gilbert, P., & Procter, S. (2006). Compassionate mind training for people with high shame and self-criticism: Overview and pilot study of a group therapy approach. *Clinical Psychology and Psychotherapy, 13*(6), 353–379.

Gilliland, R., South, M., Carpenter, B.N., & Hardy, S.A. (2011). The roles of shame and guilt in hypersexual behavior. *Sexual Addiction & Compulsivity, 18*(1), 12–29.

Giordano, A.L., Prosek, E.A., Cecil, A.L., & Brown, J. (2015). Predictors of hypersexual behavior among college men and women: Exploring self-conscious emotions. *Journal of Addictions & Offender Counseling, 36*(2), 113–125.

Haidt, J. (2003). Elevation and the positive psychology of morality. In C.L. Keyes & J. Haidt (Eds.), *Flourishing: Positive psychology and the life well-lived* (pp. 275–289). Washington, DC: American Psychological Association.

Hearn, R. (2015). The Church's other mission: Ministry to the shamed – Recognising and responding to brokenness. *Crucible, 6*(2), 1–12. Retrieved from www.crucibleonline.net/wp-content/uploads/2016/08/Hearn-Ministry-to-the-Shamed-Crucible-6-2-May-2015.pdf.

Jakupcak, M., Tull, M.T., & Roemer, L. (2005). Masculinity, shame, and fear of emotions as predictors of men's expressions of anger and hostility. *Psychology of Men & Masculinity, 6*(4), 275–284.

Kolves, K., Ide, N., & De Leo, D. (2011). Marital breakdown, shame, and suicidality in men: A direct link? *Suicide and Life-Threatening Behavior, 41*(2), 149–159.

Lewis, H.B. (1971). *Shame and guilt in neurosis.* New York, NY: International Universities Press.

Lewis, M. (1992). *Shame: The exposed self.* New York, NY: The Free Press.

Lewis, M. (2010). Self-conscious emotions. Embarrassment, pride, shame, and guilt. In M. Lewis, J.M. Haviland-Jones, & L.F. Barrett (Eds.), *Handbook of emotions* (3rd ed.) (pp. 742–756). New York, NY: The Guilford Press.

Lund, P. (2017). Christian faith and recovery from substance abuse, guilt, and shame. *Journal of Religion & Spirituality in Social Work: Social Thought, 36*(3), 346–366.

Lutwak, N., & Ferrari, J.R. (1996). Moral affect and cognitive processes: Differentiating shame from guilt among men and women. *Personality and Individual Differences, 21*(6), 891–896.

Lutwak, N., Ferrari, J.R., & Cheek, J.M. (1998). Shame, guilt, and identity in men and women: The role of identity orientation and processing style in moral affects. *Personality and Individual Differences, 25*(6), 1027–1036.

Lynch, J.S., Hill, E.D., Nagoshi, J.L., & Nagoshi, C.T. (2012). Mediators of the shame-guilt-psychological adjustment relationship. *Scandinavian Journal of Psychology, 53*(5), 437–443.

Marschall, D., Sanftner, J., & Tangney, J.P. (1994). *The State Shame and Guilt Scale.* Fairfax, VA: George Mason University.

McNish, J.L. (2013). *Transforming shame: A pastoral response.* New York, NY: Routledge.

Murray, K., & Ciarrocchi, J.W. (2007). The dark side of religion, spirituality and the moral emotions: Shame, guilt, and negative religiosity as markers for life dissatisfaction. *Journal of Pastoral Counseling, 42*, 22–41.

Murray, K., & Ciarrocchi, J.W, & Murray-Swank, N.A. (2007). Spirituality, religiosity, shame and guilt and predictors of sexual attitudes and experiences. *Journal of Psychology and Theology, 35*(3), 222–234.

Neff, K. (2003). Self-compassion: An alternative conceptualization of a healthy attitude toward oneself. *Self and Identity, 2*(2), 85–101.

Ng, M.N. (1981). Internal shame as a moral sanction. *Journal of Chinese Philosophy, 8*(1), 75-86.

Novin, S., Rieffe, C., & Meerum Terwogt, M. (2011). Guilt, shame, and anger in monocultural and bicultural adolescents. Retrieved from https://openaccess.leidenuniv.nl/bitstream/handle/1887/17713/03.pdf?sequence=7.

Park, C.J. (2016). Chronic shame: A perspective integrating religion and spirituality. *Journal of Religion & Spirituality in Social Work: Social Thought, 35*(4), 354-376.

Reigeluth, C.S., & Addis, M.E. (2016). Adolescent boys' experiences with policing of masculinity: Forms, functions, and consequences. *Psychology of Men & Masculinity, 17*(1), 74–83.

Reilly, E.D., Rochlen, A.B., & Awad, G.H. (2014). Men's self-compassion and self-esteem: The moderating roles of shame and masculine norm adherence. *Psychology of Men & Masculinity, 15*(1), 22–28.

Rice, S.M., Aucote, H.M., Moller-Leimkuhler, A.M., Parker, A.G., Kaplan, R.A., Seidler, Z.E., . . . & Amminger, G.P. (2016). Conformity to masculine norms and the mediating role of internalised shame on men's depression: Findings from an Australian community sample. *International Journal of Men's Health, 15*(2), 157–164.

Schoenleber, M., Sippel, L.M., Jakupcak, M., & Tull, M.T. (2015). Role of trait shame in the association between posttraumatic stress and aggression among men with a history of interpersonal trauma. *Psychological Trauma: Theory, Research, Practice, and Policy, 7*(1), 43–49.

"Self-Conscious Emotions" (n.d.). Retrieved from www.google.com/search?q=elementaleducation.com%2Fwp-content%2Fuploads%2F...%2F7%2F4f06c70dbc8d94.85111226.docx&ie=utf-8&oe=utf-8&client=firefox-b.

Shepard, D.S., & Rabinowitz, F.E. (2013). The power of shame in men who are depressed: Implications for counselors. *Journal of Counseling & Development, 91*(4), 451–457.

Stuewig, J., Tangney, J.P., Heigel, C., Harty, L., & McCloskey, L. (2010). Shaming, blaming, and maiming: Functional links among the moral emotions, externalization of blame, and aggression. *Journal of Research in Personality, 44*(1), 91–102.

Tangney, J.P. (1991). Moral affect: The good, the bad, and the ugly. *Journal of Personality and Social Psychology, 61*(4), 598–607.

Tangney, J.P., Burggraf, S.A., & Wagner, P.E. (1995). Shame-proneness, guilt-proneness, and psychological symptoms. In J.P. Tangney & K.W. Fischer (Eds.), *Self-conscious emotions: The psychology of shame, guilt, embarrassment, and pride* (pp. 343–367). New York: Guilford Press.

Tangney, J.P., & Dearing, R.L. (2002). *Shame and guilt*. New York, NY: Guilford.

Tangney, J.P., Dearing, R.L., Wagner, P.E., & Gramzow, R. (2000). *The Test of Self-Conscious Affect-3* (TOSCA-3). Fairfax, VA: George Mason University.

Tangney, J.P., Stuewig, J., & Mashek, D.J. (2007). Moral emotions and moral behavior. *Annual Review of Psychology, 58*, 345–372.

Turner, J.E. (2014). Researching state shame with the Experiential Shame Scale. *The Journal of Psychology, 148*(5), 577–601.

Wright, F. (1987). Men, shame and antisocial behavior: A psychodynamic perspective. *Group, 11*(4), 238–246.

Wright, K., Gudjonsson, G.H., & Young, S. (2008). An investigation of the relationship between anger and offence-related shame and guilt. *Psychology, Crime & Law, 14*(5), 415–423.

Zhang, D. (2011). Cultural differences in shame and guilt between American and Chinese preschoolers (Master's thesis). Retrieved from https://dspace.library.colostate.edu/bitstream/handle/10217/46731/Zhang_colostate_0053N_10605.pdf?sequence=1.

6 Men and Forgiveness

Forgiveness is an important teaching in the major world religions such as Judaism, Christianity, Islam, Buddhism, and Hinduism (Toussaint, Williams, Musick, & Everson-Rose, 2008). For example, Christianity teaches to forgive "seventy times seven" or without any limits (Matthew: 18:22, New American Bible Revised Edition [NABRE]). Those involved in the world religions will also seek forgiveness from God (or the deity figure) for their sins, transgressions, and mistakes. Thus, forgiving others and being forgiven are generalized religious and spiritual practices that are described as "wiping the slate clean" (Allais, 2008). Given the religious and theological context of forgiveness, it has traditionally been associated with the psychological study of religion and spirituality. In the psychology field, few religious/spiritual constructs have garnered as much attention as forgiveness. Dr. Everett L. Worthington, a psychologist and professor at Virginia Commonwealth University, is the father of forgiveness research in psychology. A brief glimpse into his research productivity on the topic reveals hundreds of peer-reviewed articles, book chapters, mentored student dissertations, and about 8 authored books over the past 30 years. Needless to say, this chapter relies on his expertise. We would be remiss not to acknowledge his substantial contributions to this area.

Forgiving and seeking forgiveness are aspirational and fraught with interpersonal, psychological, and spiritual challenges. As such, forgiveness (giving and receiving) is often considered a difficult journey rather than an isolated, simple, and singular action. Men may be less willing to forgive others and themselves, while being vulnerable to expressing anger and hostility due to gender role socialization. There are tremendous benefits to forgiving, which increases the importance of removing barriers to forgiveness. By not forgiving, men miss out on positive intrapsychic and interpersonal outcomes such as decreased stress and improved relationships. Counselors are ideally positioned to help men through the process of forgiving others, self-forgiveness, and perceiving forgiveness from their God. Despite a robust literature on forgiveness, implementation of forgiveness-based interventions in clinical settings with men is minimal. This chapter will provide counselors with a clear guide on integrating forgiveness in clinical practice.

Regardless of men's ignorance, resistance, or hesitancy in relation to forgiveness, forgiveness is relevant in clinical practice with men presenting with a variety of presenting concerns. For example, they may feel wronged by another person, perceive interpersonal conflict, are in the midst of a divorce or marital stress, and are feeling hurt, betrayed, and wounded by another person. In such situations, they are in a victim role in relation to the person perpetrating the offense; thus, counseling assists him in forgiving the perpetrator. In other situations, men may be the perpetrator. They have hurt someone in their life and/or committed an egregious mistake. Counseling focuses on helping him forgive himself and to seek forgiveness from the divine. This chapter will help counselors to conceptualize, assess, and intervene with men when forgiveness is relevant to the presenting concerns and achieving positive therapeutic outcomes.

Defining Forgiveness

Forgiveness entails multifaceted and complex human experiences. Given such complexity, the psychology scholarship contains many terms. This section will identify and define the terms to clarify how forgiveness will be used in this chapter. The prevailing definition of forgiveness is "a prosocial change toward a perceived transgressor, and includes the reduction of negative (and in some cases the increase of positive) thoughts, emotions, and motivations toward the offender that might eventuate in changed behaviors" (Davis, Worthington, Hook, & Hill, 2013, p. 233). The definition packs a punch so to speak and highlights the key components to forgiveness that warrant further discussion. First, forgiveness is often situated within an interpersonal dynamic, in which one person is the transgressor and the other person is the victim. Forgiveness in this interpersonal dynamic is focused on how the victim will forgive the transgressor. The victim experiences stress due to the offense and other emotions toward the transgressor such as sadness, hurt, disappointment, indignation, anger, and hostility. The result of such emotions is a tendency of the victim to avoid the transgressor, hold a grudge, or to seek revenge (McCullough, 2000). Avoidance, resentment, revenge-seeking emotions, thoughts, and behaviors are termed "unforgiveness" (Worthington, Witvliet, Pietrini, & Miller, 2007). Unforgiveness is correlated with increased stress. Thus, forgiveness is considered a positive coping process in response to stress that requires motivation by the victim to enact behaviors that decrease unforgiveness, which, in turn, reduce stress and negative emotions. Clients that reach a point of forgiveness have a "moving on" experience as previous negative emotions are alleviated, there is less distress, and a sense of reconciliation. As a point of clarification, forgiveness is not minimizing, overlooking, or excusing an offense.

The vast amount of research devoted to forgiveness has reported generally positive physical, mental, and interpersonal benefits (Fehr, Gelfand, & Nag, 2010). The positive health benefits are attributed to the transformation from unforgiveness to forgiveness. Turning unforgiveness to forgiveness can be a difficult process, especially, in isolation. Interpersonal conflicts and problems are seemingly inevitable. Thus, being a victim of an interpersonal offense, or perpetrating an offense/committing a mistake, are common occurrences that can be experienced across a variety of specific presenting concerns by clients. Taken together – the difficulty of coming to a point of forgiveness by oneself, the benefits of forgiveness, and the frequency of such offenses – have all reinforced the integration of forgiveness in clinical practice.

The forgiveness scholarship entails other types and dimensions of forgiveness that are also worth defining, as they illuminate the fullness of forgiveness and generate more clinical implications. Decision-to-forgive or decisional forgiveness is applicable when counseling the victim as it entails a commitment by the victim to apply effort and energy to reduce unforgiveness toward the transgressor (Davis et al., 2013). A primary component of the forgiveness definition posited here is the decrease in negative emotions toward the transgressor. Decisional forgiveness focuses counseling on working with victims to feel less negatively toward the transgressor and move away from unforgiving. Scholars in the forgiveness literature have debated the emotional changes needed to achieve forgiveness. There is a consensus that forgiveness includes the decrease of negative emotions toward the transgressor, as mentioned. There is a growing consensus, but still some debate, about the victim experiencing an increase in positive emotions as part of forgiveness. Thus, there will be variability in how counselors facilitate positive emotional changes with men depending on individual and contextual factors. Emotional forgiveness is the extent to which some victims experience positive emotions while forgiving, such as empathy, compassion, and love (Worthington et al., 2007). Emotional forgiveness entails the facilitation of replacing negative emotions with positive emotions, which can be a focus of forgiveness-based interventions with victims of an offense. Some forgiveness scholars and counselors would consider a decrease in negative emotions to be a sufficient indicator of forgiveness, while other clinical situations may progress to include an increase in positive emotions as part of the forgiveness process.

Decisional and emotional forgiveness are points of change in counseling. Both can be addressed in counseling because forgiveness has intrapersonal and interpersonal components (Miller & Worthington, 2010). While forgiveness is often situated within an interpersonal context, some clients can experience forgiveness toward the transgressor without interacting with the transgressor. For these clients, their journey to forgiveness takes place within their mind, heart, and soul. Other clients may use counseling to approach the transgressor and engage in interpersonal forgiveness. In other words, a client may exhibit decisional and emotional forgiveness as an internal process of change or through external communication with the transgressor by rebuilding trust and reconciliation. Both intrapersonal and interpersonal components of forgiveness include key ingredients of decreasing negative emotions, exploration of transforming negative emotions into positive emotions, facilitating empathy, and de-emphasizing the negative attributions toward the transgressor (Miller & Worthington, 2010).

In addition to decisional and emotional forgiveness, there is dispositional and state forgiveness. Dispositional forgiveness is often termed "forgivingness" and refers to an ingrained characteristic within an individual to forgive others (Worthington et al., 2007). In other words, some people have a forgiving personality. Counselors will not likely need to implement forgiveness-based interventions with individuals with a forgiving personality. Those with a forgiving personality are simply more likely to forgive the transgressor on their own, without the need for a mental health intervention. State forgiveness is consistent with how we have been discussing forgiveness to this point in the chapter. State forgiveness is a response to a specific situation, event, trigger, or offense that causes distress and harm to an individual (Worthington et al., 2007). Thus, counselors are more likely to encounter clients who need assistance developing and exhibiting state forgiveness.

Forgiveness entails four common dimensions. To this point in the chapter, we have been describing forgiveness within the interpersonal dimension, i.e., how an individual forgives a transgressor. Much of the forgiveness research and scholarship has focused primarily on the interpersonal dimension. The other three dimensions of forgiveness are self-forgiveness, seeking and feeling forgiven by the divine, and seeking (and receiving) forgiveness as a transgressor (Toussaint et al., 2008). Self-forgiveness is emerging as more prominent as more emphasis has been placed on the intrapsychic component of forgiveness rather than an exclusive focus on the interpersonal component. A quote attributed to Dalai Lama VIV states, "We can never obtain peace in the outer world until we make peace with ourselves," which highlights the importance of self-forgiveness. Leading scholars in this area (Hall & Fincham, 2005) defined self-forgiveness in psychology as involving motivation to decrease self-retaliatory thoughts, feelings, and behaviors, and to increase self-benevolent thoughts, feelings, and behaviors. In other words, when an individual commits a transgression, they feel guilty and shameful and "beat themselves up" over the transgression. In such instances, clients need to reaffirm violated values and to return to a positive self-regard to experience self-forgiveness (Griffin et al., 2015).

The forgiveness from God dimension entails feelings of approval, condemnation, favor, or forgiveness from the transgressor's God (Walker & Gorsuch, 2002). Men's perceptions of being forgiven by God will be tied to their religious affiliation, theistic beliefs, and God image. Perceived forgiveness from God often facilitates self-forgiveness (McConnell & Dixon, 2012), indicating a tight connection between the two dimensions of forgiveness. The tight connection often reflects an individual's religious belief in a personal God; for example, the individual has difficulty forgiving themselves if they do not feel forgiven by their God. The fourth dimension, seeking forgiveness as a transgressor, has been less examined in the scientific literature within an external, interpersonal context. Rather, the seeking forgiveness as a transgressor has been studied in the intrapsychic and divine contexts, in line with the self-forgiveness and divine forgiveness dimensions.

Forgiveness with Men

Research has identified some gender differences between men and women in this area, suggesting that there is a gendered component to forgiveness. The identified differences do not apply to all men, and we caution against stereotyping. The subsequent sections will help counselors to better understand the unique aspects of forgiveness with individual men. Counselors will learn how some men may struggle with forgiveness and express divergent emotions after an interpersonal offense. Some men will find self-forgiveness difficult to achieve and are wracked by guilt and shame. An effective clinical approach needs to account for the gendered component of forgiveness.

Generally speaking, women have been found to be more forgiving than men (Miller & Worthington, 2010). Specific differences among the various dimensions of forgiveness reinforce that general finding. For example, women have been found to be more forgiving of others, forgiving of themselves, to perceive being forgiven by God, and to seek forgiveness with more regularity when compared to men (Toussaint et al., 2008). In addition, men are more likely to express anger and shame as part of unforgiveness as well as to seek revenge rather than engage in the process of forgiveness (Hammond, Banks, & Mattis, 2006). Shame is an especially powerful emotion experienced by men, which hinders therapeutic progress (see Chapter 5). Self-forgiveness may be particularly difficult for men because of their proneness toward shame after committing an interpersonal offense (e.g., romantic infidelity, workplace conflict, combat-killing) (Griffin et al., 2015). The statistics illustrate the gender differences but also imply that men are likely to lose out on the benefits of forgiveness and experience compounding psychological distress through anger, shame, and revenge-seeking.

Take a moment to consider popular culture's representations of offended men. There is a whole genre of movies with revenge as the central theme (e.g., *Braveheart*, *Man on Fire*, *Death Wish*, *The Punisher*) that star leading men (e.g., Mel Gibson, Denzel Washington, Charles Bronson, and Jon Bernthal respectively). Indeed, the movies reflect the statistics and perpetuate a stereotype; when a man experiences a transgression, it is a forgone conclusion that he will seek revenge through a rampaged-filled path of destruction. There seem to be few (if any) movies with a lead male actor that sets out on a journey to forgive their transgressor. In movies and in real life, revenge continues to foster negative outcomes while forgiveness cultivates resolution and positive outcomes. One of the most dramatic examples of a man demonstrating forgiveness in the last half century is Pope John Paul II. He survived an assassination attempt in 1981, and in 1983, he visited the prison cell of the would-be assassin to forgive him. In a quote attributed to the pontiff, he eloquently summarized the difficulty of forgiveness as well as a spiritual basis needed for him to forgive:

> Forgiveness is above all a personal choice, a decision of the heart to go against the natural instinct to pay back evil with evil. The measure of such a decision is the love of God who draws us to himself in spite of our sin. It has its perfect exemplar in the forgiveness of Christ, who on the Cross prayed: "Father, forgive them; for they know not what they do" (Luke 23:34).

Therefore, men should not be excused from forgiveness or considered incapable of engaging in the process of forgiveness. Men's religion and spirituality may be facilitating factors to help them make the choices to forgive others and themselves. Counseling will likely require a skillful integration of forgiveness with men to accomplish such a goal.

There are multiple theories and hypotheses to explain the stated gender differences with forgiveness and to enhance a counselor's ability to better understand forgiveness with male clients. Scholars have yet to identify the exact reason why women are more forgiving than men. Some explanations have focused on gender differences in moral development, with men having been found to focus more on law, order, and justice compared to women, which fosters the vengeance and revenge-seeking among men (Miller, Worthington, & McDaniel, 2008). Other scholarship has highlighted women's collectivistic tendencies that are more congruent to reconciling interpersonal offenses versus men's individualistic tendencies that de-emphasize forgiveness to achieve group harmony (Toussaint et al., 2008). Such hypotheses have the potential to be helpful to conceptualizing men in counseling. However, the above explanations have been posited as tentative hypotheses and lack currency with established models of the psychology of masculinities. Rather, a within-group approach to understanding men's forgiveness has been called for to better address the needs of men (Hammond et al., 2006).

Conceptualization, Assessment, and Counseling Interventions

Conceptualization

The conceptualization section will provide theoretical explanations for the gendered elements of forgiveness. We focus on integrating gender role socialization theories with forgiveness to guide counselors.

Masculinity Ideology

Traditional masculinity in the United States and other countries focuses on reinforcing expectations for men to be stoic, strong, invulnerable, and independent (Levant, 1996). Understanding men's adherence or non-adherence to traditional expectations of masculinity is an important component to a clinical conceptualization in regard to forgiveness. Walker and Doverspike (2001) authored an initial study among Christian men and their forgiveness experiences in relation to their masculinity ideology. They found that stricter adherence to a traditional masculinity ideology hindered men's self-described experiences of forgiveness. Such a finding fits with similar findings discussed in this book; i.e., adherence to traditional masculinity norms and roles are likely to decrease men's involvement in religious and spiritual practices and activities. Forgiveness has deep spiritual, philosophical, and theological roots and contexts. Thus, the acts of forgiveness are often associated with religious/spiritual practices. As a result, men adhering to a strict traditional masculinity will not engage in forgiveness because they are not involved in religious and spiritual activities.

Traditional masculinity is multifaceted and a conceptualization is helped by examining specific aspects of masculinity. For example, a man that has internalized the masculine norm of stoicism will find it difficult to engage in forgiveness because the process requires an emotional skillset. Recall that the basic definition of forgiveness is a decrease in negative emotions and generating positive emotions regarding the offender and/or self (Hammond et al., 2006). At its core, forgiveness is an emotional journey. Men adhering to higher expectations of traditional masculinity often experience "normative male alexithymia," which is a difficulty identifying, naming, and expressing emotions that boys and men experience due to gender role socialization (Levant, 2001). Such men will find engaging in forgiveness interventions to be difficult because they lack the emotional skillset to do so.

Men may not forgive others because they view it as a sign of weakness rather than strength. As a result, those men are likely to exhibit anger and revenge-seeking as a sign of their strength and masculinity. Conversely, men that do not exhibit a strict or rigid adherence to traditional expectations of masculinity are more likely to be open to forgiveness from the onset of counseling. Similarly, men that adhere to non-traditional masculine ideologies may be more emotionally skilled and, thus, apt at demonstrating forgiveness in response to interpersonal offenses.

Precarious Manhood Theory

First, as reported earlier in the book, men are generally less religious than women. According to precarious manhood theory, men may avoid religion/spirituality because they consciously or unconsciously equate religious/spiritual activities with femininity. As a result, men avoid feminine activities that are considered "unmanly" by others in order to preserve their sense of manhood in social contexts (Vandello & Bosson, 2013). In a similar way, men associate forgiveness with a feminine religiosity, which in turn, leads to avoidance of forgiveness and a reluctance to engage in the process of forgiveness to maintain their sense of manhood, especially in relation to other men. For example, in a 2006 study (Wade & Goldman, 2006) about a group intervention for forgiveness, the male participants did not experience a reduction in desires for revenge over time and they expressed less empathy for the offender when there were more men in the group intervention. The authors questioned the utility of a group intervention for men in the future because it was apparent that the social norms among the male participants interfered with forgiveness. Such research findings speak to the importance of incorporating societal expectations of masculinity into a clinical conceptualization. Men are likely to be influenced by societal expectations of how to express their masculinity within a social context in response to interpersonal offenses. Counselors may first observe anger and shame as well as a desire to seek revenge or avoid forgiveness because of their motivation to maintain their sense of manhood with others.

Masculine Gender Role Stress Theory

Being the victim of an interpersonal offense evokes hurtful feelings and stress. Similarly, making a mistake or committing a transgression elicits guilt and shame, which contributes to stress. Both instances create stress for men, which is why unforgiveness is correlated with stress and forgiveness is considered a coping response to stress. Men may find it difficult to enact forgiveness to cope with the stress because of additional stress stemming from their masculine gender role. Men may feel intense demands to uphold male gender roles and learn to adopt increasingly rigid gender roles as a way to avoid social punishment and gain social rewards for being masculine. Masculine gender role stress (MGRS) is one possible outcome of male gender role rigidity (McCreary et al., 1996). MGRS is defined as "the cognitive appraisal of specific situations as stressful for men" (Eisler & Skidmore, 1987a, p. 125). Men may experience stress from the interpersonal offense (as a victim or perpetrator). In deciding on how to respond to the interpersonal offense, some men may experience increasing stress in the situation because they consider forgiveness as a possible response to the offense but appraise forgiveness as a challenge to their masculine role. As a result, men become fearful of showing forgiveness because such thoughts, feelings, and behaviors are not congruent with societal expectations of masculinity. The stress and fear lead men to think and behave in ways that they consider congruent with societal expectations of masculinity such as anger and revenge-seeking. Men with higher levels of MGRS have demonstrated higher levels of anger, fear, and engagement in high-risk behavior (Isacco & Wade, 2017). Therefore, a key part of a clinical conceptualization is determining the level of gender role stress and its impact on their sense of forgiveness.

Assessment

As described earlier, forgiveness is complex and multifaceted, which can be experienced and expressed in diverse ways. Thus, assessing "forgiveness" and the various types and dimensions with different men requires a multi-pronged approach from counselors. Part of assessing forgiveness with men is also assessing their masculinity. This section will describe assessment strategies for both forgiveness and masculinity in relation to forgiveness.

Assessing Forgiveness

Generally speaking, forgiveness is likely to be relevant for male clients who experience an interpersonal hurt or who commit an interpersonal offense. Those two situations are common among therapy clients and can be accompanied by an array of unresolved feelings such as shame, anger, guilt, sadness, anxiety, and depression. The assessment process starts by gaining information about the specifics of the situation and related feelings. Is he a victim or offender? If he is a victim, what kind of interpersonal offense did he experience (e.g., conflict with a family member, work colleague, spouse, romantic partner)? If he is a perpetrator, what offense did he commit? What is the perceived impact on the victim?

After understanding the situation better, the counselor can assess his feelings about the situation, keeping in mind that he may be more prone to anger, revenge-seeking, and/or stoicism due to gender socialization factors. Yet, beneath those emotions, he may be experiencing deeper shame and guilt as well as a wound in need of healing. An assessment of feelings may help the counselor to estimate where he is on their forgiveness journey. Counselors can utilize informal, exploratory questions to assess his unforgiveness and forgiveness. Specifically, we suggest asking about their feelings about forgiving the person, what their religion teaches them about forgiveness, and how they might want to pursue forgiveness. When self-forgiveness is salient, the counselor can guide the questions so that he engages in self-reflection by examining how he would forgive himself.

This chapter defined several types and dimensions of forgiveness, which informal questioning may not be able to fully assess. There are associated formal assessments for many of those types and dimensions, which can be used in clinical practice. See Table 6.1 for a list and short descriptions that are most appropriate for adult male clients in individual counseling while demonstrating appropriate psychometric properties.

The forgiveness literature and research as well as this chapter largely purports that forgiveness is healing, healthy, and helpful to the therapeutic process. However, it is not always a given that forgiveness is the therapeutic goal or will have a positive impact on his psychological health. Some scholarship has pointed to situations and instances in which forgiveness and self-forgiveness hinders health and wellbeing. Therefore, the assessment phase can identify when forgiveness might be cautioned. According to Wohl and McLaughlin (2014), forgiveness does not benefit partners in chronic, high-conflict relationships, as forgiving facilitates the reoffending of negative behavior over time. A similar dynamic has been noted with self-forgiveness, i.e., the more people forgive themselves for an ongoing negative behavior (e.g., smoking), the less likely they are to cease the negative behavior. Therefore, a key assessment question to ask a male client is, is forgiveness maintaining a negative status quo? If so, promoting forgiveness in therapy would not be appropriate.

Assessing Masculinity Ideology in Relation to Forgiveness

An assessment of masculinity ideology will enhance clinical conceptualizations related to forgiveness. As mentioned, "masculinity" and "traditional masculinity" are complex and diverse. It is not the most helpful to understand traditional masculinity, as a whole, in relation to forgiveness. Rather, we have information about specific aspects of masculinity that are most likely to impact forgiveness, such as emotionality, masculine gender role stress, aggression, and independence. Therefore, it is more helpful to assess those specific parts of masculinity with men in the context of forgiveness. Counselors can utilize informal, exploratory questions to assess the specific aspects of their masculinity. Some example questions include the following:

- How do you express emotions?
- Is expressing emotions difficult?
- What emotions are you most likely to express in your daily life?
- Are you an independent person?
- How do you try to be connected to other people?
- How do you respond to stressful situations?
- Are you likely to respond to stress with aggression?

Masculinity ideology is expressed in diverse and at times, unconscious, ways. Informal questions may not be able to fully assess his conscious understanding of his masculinity ideology in relation to forgiveness. Men may benefit from using formal assessments rather than open-ended questions. Counselors may be able to gather more accurate data from the formal assessments as men have prompts to respond to with the instruments. See Table 6.2 for a list and short descriptions that are most appropriate for adult male clients in individual counseling while demonstrating appropriate psychometric properties.

Overall, a thorough assessment of forgiveness and masculinity ideology in relation to forgiveness with informal questions and formal assessment tools will help the counselor to confirm or rule out hypotheses generated in their clinical conceptualization and inform the next phases of the treatment process.

Counseling Interventions

Forgiveness is the rare area in the psychology of religion and spirituality with a robust empirical base that has evolved to rigorous randomized control trials studies. Over ten years of clinical research has shown that forgiveness interventions promote forgiveness while also increasing hope, psychological wellbeing, and decreasing depression, anxiety, and anger (Wade, Hoyt, Kidwell, & Worthington, 2014). As mentioned earlier, group counseling focused on forgiveness with men may not be effective given the social norms of masculinity. For male clients, we focus on findings from studies for individual counseling and workbook-based interventions that can complement individual counseling.

Men are likely to seek counseling for other reasons beside forgiveness. More often than not, men are not even likely to consider forgiveness as an option to responding to a hurt and offenses (Wade & Goldman, 2006). However, that does not mean that counseling cannot address forgiveness. The benefits of forgiveness are clear; men may need collaborative psychoeducation within individual counseling to introduce forgiveness into the clinical process. Counselors can tactfully introduce the topic as an initial intervention, deconstruct why he may not have considered it, and explore if he would be open to beginning the process of forgiveness.

Once forgiveness has been introduced, and assuming he agrees to work on forgiveness, counselors may progress in counseling using two established treatment models. The first model, often termed "The Enright Model" (Enright & Fitzgibbons, 2000), includes four phases: (1) uncovering negative feelings about the offense, (2) deciding to pursue forgiveness about the specific offense, (3) working towards understanding the offending person, and (4) discovery of positive feelings. The Enright Model has been shown to be effective with an array of people, with various concerns (Wade et al., 2014). The second model is called the REACH model (Worthington, 2001) and entails five steps: (1) recalling the hurt and the associated emotions, (2) empathizing with the offender, taking a different perspective, (3) exploring forgiveness as an altruistic response to the offense, (4) making a commitment to forgive, and (5) holding on to forgiveness during times of anger, bitterness, or uncertainty.

Similar phases and steps have been proposed to address self-forgiveness. To address self-forgiveness, a counselor can utilize these steps (Griffin et al., 2015): (1) identify the offense that he perpetrated, (2) receive divine forgiveness and repair social relationships, (3) decrease negative thoughts and ruminations about the perpetrated transgression, (4) recall the hurt, be empathetic toward self, and give forgiveness as an altruistic gift to self, (5) rebuild self-acceptance, and (6) commit to living more virtuously and learning from the mistake(s). Whether for forgiving others or self-forgiveness, the phases and steps are meant as a guide to counseling rather than prescriptive, linear rules that must be followed.

As mentioned earlier in the conceptualization section, a key part to counseling is understanding his masculinity ideology and gender role socialization history and its impact on his sense of forgiveness. Counselors may integrate a workbook to help him forgive others or for self-forgiveness as a complementary tool to the therapeutic process. Workbooks for both purposes have been researched in a few studies and have been shown to be effective (e.g., Griffin et al., 2015; Harper et al., 2014). As a bonus, the workbooks are freely available at: www.evworthington-forgiveness.com/diy-workbooks. A workbook option may appeal to men with restrictive emotionality for a couple reasons. First, discussing and expressing emotions with another person may be difficult due to gender role socialization influences (e.g., normative male alexithymia). Individual writing can be an effective intermediate step toward emotional expression in an interpersonal context to promote forgiveness. Second, expressive writing interventions have been shown to help men with restrictive emotionality to feel less psychological distress and more connected to a romantic partner – both of which are important to the forgiveness journey (Wong & Rochlen, 2009). Thus, the workbook may serve an important function for men with restrictive emotionality. In addition, if normative male alexithymia manifests in individual counseling, counselors may promote forgiveness by first focusing on the cognitive and behavioral aspects of the process and then working on the affective aspects later in counseling. Men with restrictive emotionality and normative male alexithymia would likely benefit from a structured and psychoeducational approach to addressing the affective aspects of forgiveness.

For men that view forgiveness as overly feminine and/or a sign of weakness, counselors can focus on reframing forgiveness as a sign of strength and an indicator of positive masculinity. Integration of their religious beliefs and teachings may be helpful in this regard as the major religions all promote forgiveness. Moreover, spirituality is focused on transcendence and connection with self, others, and the divine; forgiveness fosters those outcomes while unforgiveness creates friction, tension, disconnect, and conflict. Therefore, men striving to live in congruence with their religious teaching on forgiveness and to experience a heightened spiritual life may be motivated to work towards forgiveness in counseling. To capitalize on that motivation, counselors can provide relevant sacred reading based on their religious affiliation and spiritual leanings (Cook, Dixon, & Fukuyama, 2011). For example, assigning a Bible passage such as The Parable of the Unforgiving Servant (Luke 17) for Christian men can serve as a catalyst for processing forgiveness in counseling. Discussing religious and spiritual role models who exhibit forgiveness such as John Paul II provides alternative models of masculinity that can make forgiveness more acceptable.

Integrating religion and spirituality in counseling also helps to address receiving divine forgiveness. Receiving divine forgiveness is related to self-forgiveness and forgiveness with others. Self-forgiveness is rooted in one's personal relationship with God for many male clients with theistic beliefs (McConnell & Dixon, 2012). Counselors can draw upon relevant religious teachings of a benevolent God and personal divine relationship with men who are affiliated to religions with such beliefs, which decreases shame and self-condemnation associated with transgressions and promotes self-forgiveness. By drawing upon relevant sacred readings and God images to integrate into counseling interventions to promote forgiveness, counselors may also be building a stronger therapeutic alliance with men by offering interventions that are culturally congruent with their religious and spiritual beliefs.

Summary and Conclusions

Forgiveness is a challenging religious and spiritual journey. Forgiveness is well researched in the psychological field, which has led to a strong empirical base for counseling interventions. The general findings of over 20 years of research indicate that forgiveness and self-forgiveness are positive and healthy outcomes. Gender differences identified in research studies indicates that there is a gendered component to forgiveness as women have been found to be more forgiving than men. Counselors are guided to take a within-groups approach to conceptualization, assessment, and clinical techniques as forgiveness and masculinity ideology are both complex and expressed differently by diverse men. Such an approach enhances the probability of men to experience the positive outcomes associated with forgiveness.

Case Example*

When Louis presented for the initial intake session at the outpatient mental health clinic, he was direct, blunt, and highly critical. He commented on how uncomfortable my office chairs were, joked about the lack of windows in my office, and disclosed his pessimistic beliefs about the utility of psychotherapy. He was well educated and exhibited a high-culture persona. He displayed an interesting knowledge of linguistics and classical literature and was fluent in four modern languages, proficient in two ancient languages, and accented his conversations with literary references. Some of his learned qualities made sense when he described his parents. Louis' father and mother were highly educated from Ivy League schools. He described his father as an aloof academic – the type of man who would philosophize about work around the house, but never lift a finger to help. His mother was a psychologist – gentle, nurturing, and warm by his account. She practiced psychotherapy until recently retiring to tend to her garden.

I asked Louis why he decided to attend counseling despite not believing he could be helped. He explained that he was 48 years old, depressed, fatigued, irritable, and pessimistic about his life. He has been living with such symptoms for a long time and he feared that his symptoms were becoming "ingrained" into his personality. Louis did not have children, was not married, and did not have a professional career. My initial conceptualization focused on his masculinity as Louis had not met the typical developmental markers of manhood. I hypothesized that part of his depression may be related to experiencing Masculine Gender Role Stress (MGRS) as he was self-critical for not living up to societal ideals of masculinity.

Throughout the course of counseling, which included approximately 27 sessions over a year, Louis uncovered a deep sense of personal inadequacy and shame. Indeed, part of his shame related to his masculinity as he "was not the man that I wanted to be"; neither was he the son that his parents had envisioned. They were accomplished professionals in their respective fields and, as their only son, he senses a deep disappointment from them regarding his lack of accomplishment. In addition, he had well-discerned and articulated moral ideals and was quick to tear himself down anytime he failed to uphold his ideals. He described himself as a "secular Christian," which Louis explained as meaning he did not belong to a particular church or Christian denomination but accepted Jesus as his Savior and aimed to live according to a "biblical moral code." He had a deep appreciation and yearning for harmony, human connection, and service to others. Louis highlighted moments in his life where he went beyond all reasonable expectations to serve those in need. He detailed numerous events where he stood up to injustices often at his own expense such as being fired from jobs. Friendships and family were of the utmost importance, even though his relationships with many people were strained.

His strict moral code and self-criticalness impacted his interpersonal relationships. When he encountered people who did not meet his expectations, he was reminded of his own imperfections, and defended himself by aggressively expressing his dissatisfaction with other people's behaviors. Louis' conflict between his high ideals and the inability for himself or others to meet those ideals manifested as internalized and externalized anger. He did not have compassion for himself or others. The paradox became evident. Despite wanting to follow the teachings of Jesus, which focused on mercy, forgiveness, and compassion, Louis was unable to forgive himself or others. He was not able to exhibit self-compassion because his anger overwhelmed more rational thought processes. My conceptualization broadened and I viewed Louis as clearly struggling with self-forgiveness. His struggle with self-forgiveness seemed to have an existential component. He was unable to forgive himself for not being the man that he, his parents, religious beliefs, and society expected him to become.

In addition, I learned that Louis had difficulty forgiving other people. The primary object of his interpersonal dissatisfaction and anger was his father, the distant and aloof academic. We decided to enter the arena of father-son relations slowly. Initially, our time was spent exploring the numerous faults of his father – personality traits, behaviors, attitudes, and past parenting behavior. He expressed affective states that accompanied his thoughts and experiences with his father. Needless to say, anger and resentment were omnipresent. Louis was high in psychological mindedness and developed cognitive insight about how his anger stemmed from underlying feelings of hurt. His masculinity made it easier for him to express an aggressiveness toward his father rather than emotional pain. When I normalized this tendency among men, he appeared to have greater internal freedom to discuss the ways he had been hurt by his father. Identifying and expressing feelings about an offense are initial steps of both the Enright and REACH models.

Following those models, I urged Louis to identify specific instances of feeling hurt by his father and what he wanted from his father now. He explained with strong conviction that he wanted a father who was affectionate, attentive, and willing to spend quality time with his son. The absence of these traits seemed to be more distressing than anything his father had ever done to him. We arrived at this point after about 15 sessions and the emotional pain from the father-son relationship began to drive the counseling process with more urgency. I remember my focus shifting from his words to my own thoughts. I did not believe Louis' feelings and thoughts about his father were irrational. It's reasonable to want an affectionate, attentive, and present father. However, Louis' expectations for his father overpowered his ability to see his father as a human being with limitations. Perhaps if he was able to acknowledge his father's limitations, he could garner some compassion. And with compassion, he might be able to move toward forgiveness. I hypothesized that Louis may be more capable of forgiving his father if he understood him more deeply and experienced some empathy toward his father (Enright & Fitzgibbons, 2000; Worthington, 2001). I asked Louis whether he thought his father was capable of being the attentive, affectionate, and present man he wanted him to be. Louis wanted me to elaborate. I explained that maybe his father was limited. He might have been a brilliant academic but perhaps he lacked the relational skills to foster the sort of relationship Louis desired. After my disclosure, Louis appeared to be drawing connections in his mind without articulating them. He took the words a step further. Louis explained that he never thought about his father as a person with limitations. His father was an intelligent and accomplished man. Limited was not a term that he associated with his father.

Working from this alternative perspective, Louis started to express compassion toward his father. We imagined what it would be like to have difficulty developing meaningful relationships with others and a son. We imagined having a strained marriage, a dissatisfied wife, and not having the conflict resolution skills to make positive changes. He was beginning to see his father as a person with skill deficits rather than a father who did not love his son. Louis noted that it was harder in some ways to acknowledge his father's limitations than to be angry with him. What made it more difficult? The recognition of his father's limitations was painful. After Louis stepped outside of his expectations and into his father's shoes, he was able to develop compassion for the aloof academic. We sat together in silence with his emotions. After moments passed, I asked Louis whether he might be able to forgive his father for his limitations. Louis voiced that he could. The forgiveness that Louis offered in our session was not in the presence of his father. It did not need to be. As subsequent sessions revealed, it changed the way he viewed his relationships, the expectations he holds for others, and the value of compassionate perspective taking. The forgiveness Louis extended to his father opened the doors for personal healing. Our counseling refocused on his self-forgiveness. If Louis was able to understand the limitations of his father and forgive, I asked him if it was possible for him to understand his own limitations as a man and forgive himself? Louis recognized that there were similarities between the experiences. We discussed some passages from the Bible about forgiveness, and I made the point that forgiveness is a core teaching of Jesus. Louis concluded, "If Jesus can forgive me, then I have to forgive myself." The last few sessions focused on helping Louis accept the man that he is, including his mistakes and strengths. My clinical observations at the end of counseling Louis was that he was less judgmental of himself and others and that his affective expressions of anger and aggression had subsided. He seemed more content and smiled more. My observations mirrored his self-report as Louis expressed feeling less depressed and more invigorated to enter his fifties with purpose rather than baggage.

*Please note: portions of the case were provided and written by Domenick Tirabassi, MS.

Table 6.1 Forgiveness Assessment Tools

Assessment Tool	*Description*
The Transgression-Related Interpersonal Motivation Inventory – Revised (McCullough et al., 2010)	18-item, self-report instrument. Assesses avoidance, revenge, and benevolence motivation. Has been translated into several languages including Dutch, Japanese, Chinese, and Arabic.
Forgiveness Scale (Crescioni, Baumeister, Ainsworth, Ent, & Lambert, 2016)	38-item, self-report instrument. Assesses forgiveness of others, receiving others' forgiveness, and receiving forgiveness from God.
The Decision to Forgive Scale (Davis et al., 2015)	5-item, self-report instrument that measures one's decision to forgive a specific offense.

(continued)

Table 6.1 (continued)

Assessment Tool	*Description*
The Forgiveness Likelihood Scale (Rye et al., 2001)	10-item, self-report instrument that examines one's tendency to forgive across situations.
The Heartland Forgiveness Scale (Yamhure Thompson et al., 2002)	18-item, self-report instrument that measures dispositional forgiveness. Assesses unforgiveness (and forgiveness of self, others, and situations.
The State Self-Forgiveness Scale (Wohl, DeShea & Wahkinney, 2008)	17-item, self-report instrument that assesses self-forgiveness for specific transgressions.
The Differentiated Process Scale of Self-Forgiveness (Woodyatt & Wenzel, 2013)	19-item, self-report instrument that assesses the processes driving self-forgiveness such as self-punitiveness, pseudo self-forgiveness, and genuine self-forgiveness.

Table 6.2 Masculinity Ideology Assessment Tools

Assessment Tool	*Description*
Conformity to Masculine Norms Inventory (Mahalik et al., 2003)	94-item, self-report instrument that assesses the extent to which a male conforms or does not conform to the actions, thoughts, and feelings that reflect masculinity norms in the dominant culture in US society. Three sub-factors are most relevant to forgiveness: emotional control, violence, dominance.
Masculine Gender Role Stress Scale (Eisler & Skidmore, 1987b)	40-item, self-report instrument that assesses the degree to which men cognitively appraise how stressful specific situations are to their masculinity. The emotional inexpressiveness subscale is most relevant to forgiveness and measures situations that require the expression of tender emotions such as love, fear, and hurt.
Male Role Norms Inventory (Levant et al., 1992)	57-item, self-report instrument of traditional masculinity ideology. Four subscales of male norms are most relevant to forgiveness: avoidance of femininity, self-reliance, aggression, and restrictive emotionality.

References

Allais, L. (2008). Wiping the slate clean: The heart of forgiveness. *Philosophy & Public Affairs, 36*(1), 33–68.

Cook, S.W., Dixon, L.S., & Fukuyama, M.A. (2011). Integrating sacred writings in therapy. In J.D. Aten, M.R. McMinn, & E.L. Worthington Jr. (Eds.), *Spiritually oriented interventions for counseling and psychotherapy*. (pp. 227–301). Washington, DC: American Psychological Association.

Crescioni, A.W., Baumeister, R.F., Ainsworth, S.E., Ent, M., & Lambert, N.M. (2016). Subjective correlates and consequences of belief in free will. *Philosophical Psychology, 29*(1), 41–63.

Davis, D.E., Worthington Jr, E.L., Hook, J.N., & Hill, P.C. (2013). Research on religion/spirituality and forgiveness: A meta-analytic review. *Psychology of Religion and Spirituality, 5*(4), 233–241.

Davis, D.E., Hook, J.N., Van Tongeren, D.R., DeBlaere, C., Rice, K.G., & Worthington, E.L., Jr. (2015). Making a decision to forgive. *Journal of Counseling Psychology, 62*(2), 280–288.

Eisler, R.M., & Skidmore, J.R. (1987a). Masculine gender role stress: Scale development and component factors in the appraisal of stressful situations. *Behavior modification, 11*(2), 123–136.

Eisler, R.M., & Skidmore, J.R. (1987b). Masculine Gender Role Stress Scale (Assessment instrument). doi:10.1037/t27379-000.

Enright, R.D., & Fitzgibbons, R.P. (2000). *Helping clients forgive: An empirical guide for resolving anger and restoring hope*. Washington, DC: American Psychological Association.

Fehr, R., Gelfand, M.J., & Nag, M. (2010). The road to forgiveness: A meta-analytic synthesis of its situational and dispositional correlates. *Psychological Bulletin, 136*(5), 894–914.

Griffin, B.J., Worthington, E.J., Lavelock, C.R., Greer, C.L., Lin, Y., Davis, D.E., & Hook, J.N. (2015). Efficacy of a self-forgiveness workbook: A randomized controlled trial with interpersonal offenders. *Journal of Counseling Psychology, 62*(2), 124–136.

Hall, J.H., & Fincham, F.D. (2005). Self-forgiveness: The stepchild of forgiveness research. *Journal of Social and Clinical Psychology, 24*(5), 621–637.

Hammond, W.P., Banks, K.H., & Mattis, J.S. (2006). Masculinity ideology and forgiveness of racial discrimination among African American men: Direct and interactive relationships. *Sex Roles, 55*(9–10), 679–692.

Harper, Q., Worthington, E.L., Griffin, B.J., Lavelock, C.R., Hook, J.N., Vrana, S.R., & Greer, C.L. (2014). Efficacy of a workbook to promote forgiveness: A randomized controlled trial with university students. *Journal of Clinical Psychology, 70*(12), 1158–1169.

Isacco, A.J., & Wade, J.C. (2017). A review of selected theoretical perspectives and research in the psychology of men and masculinities. In R.F. Levant & Y. Wong (Eds.), *The psychology of men and masculinities* (pp. 139–168). Washington, DC: American Psychological Association.

Levant, R.F. (1996). The new psychology of men. *Professional psychology: Research and practice, 27*(3), 259–265.

Levant, R.F. (2001). Desperately seeking language: Understanding, assessing, and treating normative male alexithymia. In G.R. Brooks & G.E. Good (Eds.), *The new handbook of psychotherapy and counseling with men: A comprehensive guide to settings, problems, and treatment approaches, Vol. 1 & 2* (pp. 424–443). San Francisco, CA: Jossey-Bass.

Levant, R.F., Hirsch, L., Celentano, E., Cozza, T., Hill, S., MacEachern, M., . . . & Schnedeker, J. (1992). The male role: An investigation of norms and stereotypes. *Journal of Mental Health Counseling, 14,* 325–337.

Mahalik, J.R., Locke, B.D., Ludlow, L.H., Diemer, M.A., Scott, R.P.J., Gottfried, M., & Freitas, G. (2003). Development of the conformity to masculine norms inventory. *Psychology of Men & Masculinity, 4*(1), 3–25.

McConnell, J.M., & Dixon, D.N. (2012). Perceived forgiveness from God and self-forgiveness. *Journal of Psychology and Christianity, 31*(1), 31–40.

McCreary, D.R., Wong, F.Y., Wiener, W., Carpenter, K.M., Engle, A., & Nelson, P. (1996). The relationship between masculine gender role stress and psychological adjustment: A question of construct validity? *Sex Roles, 34*(7–8), 507–516.

McCullough, M.E. (2000). Forgiveness as human strength: Theory, measurement, and links to well-being. *Journal of Social and Clinical Psychology, 19*(1), 43–55.

McCullough, M.E., Luna, L.R., Berry, J.W., Tabak, B.A., & Bono, G. (2010). Transgression-Related Interpersonal Motivations Inventory – Revised (Assessment instrument). doi:10.1037/t30045-000.

Miller, A.J., & Worthington Jr, E.L. (2010). Sex differences in forgiveness and mental health in recently married couples. *The Journal of Positive Psychology, 5*(1), 12–23.

Miller, A.J., Worthington Jr, E.L., & McDaniel, M.A. (2008). Gender and forgiveness: A meta-analytic review and research agenda. *Journal of Social and Clinical Psychology, 27*(8), 843–876.

Rye, M.S., Loiacono, D.M., Folck, C.D., Olszewski, B.T., Heim, T.A., & Madia, B.P. (2001). Forgiveness Likelihood Scale (Assessment instrument). doi:10.1037/t48847.000.

Toussaint, L.L., Williams, D.R., Musick, M.A., & Everson-Rose, S.A. (2008). The association of forgiveness and 12-month prevalence of major depressive episode: Gender differences in a probability sample of US adults. *Mental Health, Religion and Culture, 11*(5), 485–500.

Vandello, J.A., & Bosson, J.K. (2013). Hard won and easily lost: A review and synthesis of theory and research on precarious manhood. *Psychology of Men & Masculinity, 14*(2), 101–113.

Wade, N.G., & Goldman, D.B. (2006). Sex, group composition, and the efficacy of group interventions to promote forgiveness. *Group Dynamics: Theory, Research, and Practice, 10*(4), 297–308.

Wade, N.G., Hoyt, W.T., Kidwell, J.E., & Worthington Jr, E.L. (2014). Efficacy of psychotherapeutic interventions to promote forgiveness: A meta-analysis. *Journal of Consulting and Clinical Psychology, 82*(1), 154–170.

Walker, D.F., & Doverspike, D. (2001). The relationship between forgiveness experiences and the masculine gender role among Christian men. *Journal of Psychology and Christianity, 20*(1), 29–39.

Walker, D.F., & Gorsuch, R.L. (2002). Forgiveness within the Big Five personality model. *Personality and Individual Differences, 32*(7), 1127–1138.

Wohl, M.J., DeShea, L., & Wahkinney, R.L. (2008). State Self-Forgiveness Scale (Assessment instrument). doi:10.1037/t30116-000.

Wohl, M.J., & McLaughlin, K.J. (2014). Self-forgiveness: The good, the bad, and the ugly. *Social and Personality Psychology Compass, 8*(8), 422–435.

Wong, Y.J., & Rochlen, A.B. (2009). Potential benefits of expressive writing for male college students with varying degrees of restrictive emotionality. *Psychology of Men & Masculinity, 10*(2), 149–159.
Woodyatt, L., & Wenzel, M. (2013). Differentiated Process Scale of Self-Forgiveness (Assessment instrument). doi:10.1037/t41494-000.
Worthington, E.L., Jr. (2001). *Five steps to forgiveness: The art and science of forgiving.* New York, NY: Crown Publishers.
Worthington, E.L., Witvliet, C.V.O., Pietrini, P., & Miller, A.J. (2007). Forgiveness, health, and well-being: A review of evidence for emotional versus decisional forgiveness, dispositional forgivingness, and reduced unforgiveness. *Journal of Behavioral Medicine, 30*(4), 291–302.
Yamhure Thompson, L., Snyder, C.R., Hoffman, L., Michael, S.T., Rasmussen, H.N., Billings, L.S., . . . & Roberts, D.E. (2002). Heartland Forgiveness Scale (Assessment instrument). doi:10.1037/t00957-000.

7 Pornography Use and Spiritual Issues with Men

A priest once told me (Isacco) that if the Bible said not to do something, the people at the time were doing it! For example, going back to the Old Testament thousands of years ago, the people were warned not to fornicate or to commit adultery. Needless to say, the topic of sexuality has been around for a long time within religious communities. Today, the major world religions continue to have theological beliefs and moral teachings about sexuality, sexual behavior, and sexual virtue. Although there are as many teachings about sexuality as there are world religions, there are some similarities, such as the prohibition against adultery. Further, the three Abrahamic religions (Judaism, Christianity, and Islam) teach against pornography. We identified problematic pornography consumption as a clinical concern among men that also overlaps with religion and spirituality.

Measured by several types of metrics, Internet pornography is "trending up." Internet pornography is described as a $10–14 billion industry that accumulates more yearly revenue than several professional sports leagues combined (Szymanski & Stewart-Richardson, 2014). It is estimated that there are approximately 4.2 million pornography websites, which is 12% of total websites. In 2016, one of the most popular pornography websites reported that 4.6 billion hours of pornographic videos were watched worldwide. The website was visited approximately 23 billion times, meaning that around 44,000 people visited the site every minute.

The Internet has increased the frequency and societal acceptance of pornography use. No longer does a man have to sneak out under the cover of darkness and buy an adult magazine at the local convenience store. The rise of Internet pornography in the United States and other Western countries is facilitated by the "3 As": anonymous browsing, affordability (often free), and accessibility. Almost any type of pornographic video or image is a click away and viewed from the privacy of an individual's smartphone. Some sample statistics highlight the impact of the 3 As on contemporary viewing patterns. Using data from the General Social Survey, 62% of men and 36% of women aged 18–26 years old viewed a pornographic video in the past year between 2008 and 2012 compared to 45% of men and 28% of women of the same age range between 1973 and 1980 (Price, Patterson,

Regnerus, & Walley, 2016). In 1992, 405 million adult videos were sold or rented; the number more than doubled in 2006 to 957 million, due to the ease of finding a video on the Internet (Ropelato, 2006). It is worth noting that some countries, such as Indonesia, have strict anti-pornography laws and government-sponsored censorship of pornographic content from the Internet. Thus, the three As are not universally applicable. This chapter focuses primarily on research and clinical scholarship within the United States and similar countries.

In a complex body of literature, studies have consistently shown that there are significant gender differences in the use of Internet pornography. Specifically, young adult men (approximately 18–28 years old) have been found to have more favorable attitudes about pornography, consume more pornography, and experience more sexual addiction symptoms related to pornography compared to women (e.g., Riemersma & Sytsma, 2013). We have heard counselors refer to pornography consumption as the "common cold" of sexual concerns among men. Consider some sample statistics (e.g., Albright 2008 in Levin, Lillis, & Hayes, 2012; Döring, 2009; Riemersma & Sytsma, 2013):

- In a study of young adults in the United States ages 18–26 years old, nine out of ten men reported using pornography compared to one out of three women.
- 67% of men in the United States viewed pornography as acceptable compared to 49% of women.
- In a study of 15,245 adults in the United States, 75% of men viewed pornography compared to 41% of women.
- In a study among Norwegian men and women, men used more pornographic magazines, videos, and Internet sites than women.
- Similarly, in a sample of Canadian adults, 72% of men compared to 24% of women had used Internet pornography in the past 12 months.

According to Perry (2017), the profile of a typical user of Internet pornography is a young man with less religiosity, more sexual permissive views, of higher socioeconomic status, and more liberal political views. For men (e.g., Philaretou, Mahfouz, & Allen, 2005), pornography use is often correlated with negative outcomes across life domains – psychological, financial, occupational, emotional, and interpersonal. Given the increase of Internet pornography in society, the clear gender difference in use, and the associated negative outcomes, counselors will likely encounter pornography-related problems in men.

Why do men use more pornography than women? What effect does religion and spirituality have on men's pornography use? What effect does the man's pornography use have on his psychological, interpersonal, religious, and spiritual functioning? And what can counselors do to help men live more sexually healthier lives? The purpose of this chapter is to answer those questions by providing clinical tools to conceptualize, assess, and intervene with men experiencing problems with pornography consumption.

Clarifying Terms and Definitions

Similar to other behaviors, pornography use can be conceptualized along a health continuum. Frequency, type of use, underlying problems, and associated outcomes are just some of the variables that contribute to understanding where the health behavior falls along the continuum, from healthy and adaptive to unhealthy and problematic. For example, some people do not drink any alcohol while others drink moderately, and some people drink to excess to the point of alcoholism. Even one alcohol beverage can be problematic for some people, whereas another person may consume three alcohol beverages without incident. The same can be said of individual patterns of pornography use as well as associated outcomes. Some men do not view pornography, some view a little, and some view pornography compulsively.

This chapter focuses on men that use pornography in an unhealthy and maladaptive way.

Table 7.1 provides an overview of terms that have been used to describe the problematic or addictive side of the continuum with pornography use. For this chapter, we will use the term Problematic Pornography Consumption (PPC), which has been defined as powerful urges/impulses that are difficult to stop or control and lead to some degree of functional impairment in at least one of the following domains: legal, occupational, social/interpersonal, physical, emotional, spiritual, and psychological (Twohig, Crosby, & Cox, 2009). For example, unhealthy pornography use among men has been associated with body image dissatisfaction, permissiveness toward casual sex, engagement in condomless sex, sexual aggression, sexual objectification of women, lower levels of self-worth, and higher levels of depression (e.g., Miller, Hald, & Kidd, 2018; Nelson, Padilla-Walker, & Carroll, 2010; Szymanski & Mikorski, 2016).

However, studies have reported on both the positive and negative outcomes associated with pornography use (e.g., Grubbs, Exline, Pargament, Volk, & Lindberg, 2017). The mixed findings among scientific studies and determining the degree of dysfunction associated with pornography use have created a spirited debate in the behavioral health fields (e.g., psychology, psychiatry). The debate is largely focused on how to categorize pornography use that is clinically problematic, distressful, and impairing to an individual. The DSM-5 acknowledged behavioral addiction in the renamed chapter "Substance Use and Addictive Disorders," which includes a "Non-Substance-Related Disorders" subchapter (Love, Laier, Brand, Hatch, & Hajela, 2015). However, a pornography use subtype diagnosis was not included in the DSM-5 despite a large body of psychological and neuroscientific research indicating that an addiction model applies to Internet-related behaviors such as pornography use (Love et al., 2015). For example, individuals can develop an Internet Pornography Addiction (i.e., sexual addiction) that is neurologically similar to an alcohol or substance addiction. Although a sexual addiction subtype diagnosis was not included in the DSM-5, counselors have recognized that pornography use can increase to the level of causing significant distress and impairment in the lives of their clients. In such situations, counselors have referred to such pornography use as a sexual addiction and diagnosed clients with Sexual Disorder, Not Otherwise Specified (Isacco, Tirabassi, Porada, & Meade, 2018). To be clear, there is not an Internet Pornography Addiction Disorder in the DSM-5. The World Health Organization recently recognized compulsive sexual behavior as a mental health disorder and classified it in the International Classification of Diseases (ICD-11) as a subtype of an impulse control disorder.

Other psychologists, counselors, and psychiatrists have been reluctant to put pornography use into an addiction model on par with alcohol and substances or label with a DSM-5 diagnosis. Rather, other terms have been used such as "clinical syndrome" (Karila et al., 2014) or a "perceived addiction" (Grubbs et al., 2017). Perceived addiction overlaps with actual addictive behaviors but focuses more on how individuals label themselves. The term perceived addiction reflects the general debate in the field as there is a recognition of a problem with the definition, but a caveat that an individual's perception is different from their actual pornography use. As a point of contrast, there is not a *perceived* Alcohol Use Disorder.

All things being considered, no matter the label, category, diagnosis, or definition, if a client has a treatment goal to stop a behavior that is causing distress and impairment, counseling is well positioned to assist the client to meet that goal. In that context, decreasing pornography use is a reasonable treatment goal to work on in counseling. This chapter focuses on decreasing PPC with men and how masculinity, religion, and spirituality are part of the conceptualization, assessment, and counseling interventions.

Men, Masculinity, and Problematic Pornography Consumption

The statistics describing gender differences in pornography use between men and women clearly indicate that men consume more pornography than women. This section offers explanations for the gender difference and the particular harmful effects on men and their relationships (interpersonal and divine).

By most accounts (Mikorski & Szymanski, 2017), heterosexual men view pornography that sexually objectifies women, includes women as "props" for men's pleasure, and increasingly view content that is verbally and/or physically aggressive toward women. Given such tendencies toward objectification, scholars have viewed men's pornographic consumption through Mahalik and colleagues' (2003) Masculinity Norms Theory. In particular, men adhering to the masculinity norms of playboy, power over women, and violence view pornography in such a way that objectifies women (Mahalik et al., 2003; Mikorski & Szymanski, 2017). "Playboy" refers to men's expectations and desires to be sexually promiscuous. "Power Over Women" is the expectation that men are dominant over women. "Violence" refers to the view that men are expected to display aggression and physical force. Taken together, men adhering to expectations of masculinity such as "Playboy," "Power Over Women," and "Violence" are likely to view pornography. In a reinforcing cycle, the viewing of pornography compounds the adherence to such hypermasculine norms and roles (Mikorski & Szymanski, 2017).

In line with the Masculine Norms Theory of Mahalik is "Centerfold Syndrome" put forth by Brooks (1995). According to Brooks, society is proliferated with sexually objectifying portrayals of women that contribute to socializing men to develop nonrelational sexual attitudes, interactions, and self-schemas. The centerfold syndrome posits five primary hypotheses about heterosexual men's sexual objectification (Wright & Tokunaga, 2015): (1) voyeurism: men learn to believe that voyeurism is natural and inevitable; (2) sexual reductionism: men develop sexually reductionist thoughts and evaluations of women; (3) masculinity validation: men believe that their masculinity ideology is validated through the sexual conquest of women; (4) trophyism: men assess women as "trophies" to gain social status; and (5) nonrelational: men ascribe to a recreational, nonrelational sexual philosophy. The five hypotheses may interact with each other. For example, a nonrelational sexuality reflects a masculinity ideology that promotes sexual conquest rather than sexual intimacy and a reduction of women to sexual objects instead of as a person with dignity.

Men steeped in the centerfold syndrome are likely to view pornography because of the associated tendency to objectify women. Moreover, viewing pornography further reinforces the centerfold syndrome as men are "rewarding" the learned cognitive scripts by their engagement in viewing objectifying media (Wright & Tokunaga, 2015). In other words, men exposed to pornographic centerfolds will adhere more to the centerfold syndrome. Pornography use does not require an intimate, interpersonal relationship and promotes detachment and avoidance. Pornography use in conjunction with reductionist and objectifying masculine norms add up to negative factors in a romantic relationship, not to mention sexual immaturity in men. Counselors may encounter a couple of types of men because of the centerfold syndrome. First, some men may lack experience in romantic relationships because they have essentially been attached to virtual representations of a sexual partner on the Internet. Second, other men may present to counseling with a history of conflictual romantic relationships because they have been enacting harmful schemas and attitudes that are incompatible with an intimate, egalitarian relationship.

Gender Role Conflict Theory (GRC; O'Neil, 2008) has also been used to explain men's pornography consumption. GRC is defined as a psychological state in which gender socialization has negative consequences on self and others (O'Neil, 2008). Men experience gender role conflict when they rigidly adhere to restrictive and sexist gender roles that devalue and violate self and others. GRC involves subcomponents such as success, power, competition, restrictive emotionality, restrictive sexual behavior, and conflicts between work and family relations. According to O'Neil (2008), in a major review of the theory and psychosocial outcomes, GRC was linked to sexual entitlement and sexual aggression in samples of men. In the context of men's pornography use, men experiencing GRC are likely to lack emotional expression, have difficulty with intimacy in interpersonal relationships, and, thus, become prone to relationship dissatisfaction. As a result, men may use pornography to avoid intimacy in romantic relationships and to compensate for their interpersonal deficits (Szymanski & Stewart-Richardson, 2014).

The theoretical explanations have primarily focused on heterosexual men. Gay and bisexual men as well as men who have sex with men (MSM) (Chapter 8) also use pornography and may be susceptible to similar masculinity influences that were described above. For example, gay men may be drawn to pornography use because of sexual objectification and nonrelational attitudes about sex. Yet, considering any unique features among gay men is important. For instance, it is important to know that researchers of MSM purposely avoid the word "pornography" to avoid negative connotations and instead use the term "sexually explicit online media" or SEOM or SEM for short (Nelson, Pantalone, Gamarel, & Simoni, 2016). Although not conclusive, some research indicates that gay men use more pornography than heterosexual men (Stein, Silvera, Hagerty, & Marmor, 2012) and hold more positive attitudes about pornography. Recent studies have reported that 96–98% of MSM view Internet pornography (Schrimshaw, Antebi-Gruszka, & Downing, 2016). Similarly, in a study of 1,333 US MSM, 97% reported positive attitudes about sexually explicit media as having a positive effect on their sexual knowledge, enjoyment of and interest in sex, and understanding of their sexual orientation (Hald, Smolenski, & Rosser, 2013). One theoretical framework for such findings is that gay men may lack positive role models, availability of partners, and sexual education and, as a result, turn to the Internet for sex information and sexual activity. To that point, Mustanski, Lyons, and Garcia (2011) reported that gay men are more likely to "come out" on the Internet, use the Internet to find their first sexual partner, and continue to use the Internet to access pornography. Sexual minority men are likely to develop problematic or addictive patterns of pornography use, similar to heterosexual men. Although there is no research on sexual minority men, PPC, and relationship difficulties, it is just as likely that PPC can have a negative effect on intimacy in romantic relationships for sexual minority men.

Psycho-Social Health Outcomes for Men and Their Partners

The combination of such gender norms, roles, and conflict with PPC has negative effects on men and their relationships. In terms of relationships, PPC has been associated with decreased interpersonal skills as well as problems with communication and conflict resolution in relationships (Riemersma & Sytsma, 2013). Given the neurological basis of sexual behavior, studies have found biological effects such as young men with PPC having difficulty achieving an erection or sexual arousal with a romantic partner despite being capable of doing so with Internet pornography (Love et al., 2015). Many counselors may assume that if a man comes to counseling for a sexual concern, the problem is likely related to erectile dysfunction. Men may perceive a lack of self-confidence or sexual attraction to their partner are the contributing problems to their erectile dysfunction. They may not link their problematic pornography use as a factor contributing to their erectile dysfunction. Establishing the biological link between PPC and erectile dysfunction may provide motivation for men to decrease their pornography use.

Gay men may experience different or similar consequences as heterosexual men. In terms of unique consequences for gay men, there is a lot of attention paid to the effect of pornography use on risky sexual behaviors that may increase the risk of HIV, AIDs, or other sexually transmitted infections (STI). For example, some studies have found an association between viewing unprotected anal sex on the Internet with engaging in unprotected anal intercourse behavior (Stein, Silvera, Hagerty, & Marmor, 2012), while other studies did not find such an association (Schrimshaw et al., 2016). Gay men exhibiting compulsive use of pornography in line with our definition of PPC has been linked to internalized homonegativity, low sexual self-esteem, earlier onset of sexual activity, more sexual partners, and increased sexual risk-taking (Nelson, Pantalone, Gamarel, & Simoni, 2016). Taken together, gay men are susceptible to similar negative effects as heterosexual men, with the added concern that SEOM may contribute to risky sexual behavior that increases the risk of HIV/AIDS.

The effects of pornography use are not limited to men, but also to their partners. Conformity to the playboy and violence masculine norms is associated with increased pornography use as well as making unwanted body evaluations of women and unwanted sexual advances toward women, which increases the risk for sexual violence (Mikorski & Szymanski, 2017). On the more extreme end of the continuum, pornography use has been linked to men perpetrating sexual assault and domestic violence against women. Studies about women's experiences of their male partner's pornography use have found that women felt betrayed, confused, unhappy about their body, undesirable, and decreased sexual satisfaction and relationship satisfaction, as well as feelings of anger, depression, low self-esteem, distress, and victimization (Szymanski, Feltman, & Dunn, 2015). In other words, women have described their male partner's pornography use in similar ways as an affair. In a study of 359 young adult college women, even women that held positive attitudes of pornography experienced decreased relationship trust and more psychological distress in relation to their male partner's pornography use (Szymanski, Feltman, & Dunn, 2015).

In a review of the literature about the centerfold syndrome, Wright (2012) identified adverse effects for women and men. Sexual objectification has been linked to body shame, body dissatisfaction, appearance and safety anxiety, self-objectification, depression, sexual passivity, eating disorders, and low self-esteem among various groups of women. For men, objectifying women has been associated with sexual aggression. In his vast clinical experience, Dr. Brooks (1995) observed that men exhibiting the centerfold syndrome have difficulty forming and maintaining relationships with women, exhibiting unrealistic expectations for their partner's physical appearance, difficulty with fidelity, and less sexual satisfaction in the actual romantic relationship. Overall, such studies and clinical evidence point to the need to conceptualize a man's PPC not only within an individual perspective but also a relational context. Thus, couple counseling may be an important component to treatment.

Religion, Spirituality, and Pornography Consumption

As mentioned earlier, the major world religions generally teach against viewing pornography. It is common for religious groups and individuals to speak out against pornography while many religious self-help books and websites focus on decreasing pornography use (e.g., *Every Man's Battle*). Religion/spirituality may be a protective factor against pornography use because men abstain from viewing pornography on religious-moral grounds (Short, Kasper, & Wetterneck, 2015). As mentioned earlier, Perry (2017) identified that less religious men are more likely to view pornography than religious men. For the purposes of this chapter, we do not focus on religious men who are successfully abstaining from pornography because it is unlikely that their pornography use would be a salient clinical issue. The type of man that is relevant for this chapter is one who is religious and spiritual, has tried unsuccessfully to decrease his PPC, has been experiencing distress, and has a functional impairment in at least one life domain. Below are some religious/spiritual issues that counselors should be prepared to integrate into counseling with men who fit this profile.

Perception of Pornography Use and Distress

Religious men are situated within the norms and attitudes of their faith. Thus, they are likely aware of their religious community's anti-pornography stance, teachings, and programming. His disapproval of his pornography use is steeped in his faith's teaching and accompanying moral code. As a result, he may perceive this pornography use as further down on the unhealthy side of the spectrum than a less religious or non-religious man. Earlier in the chapter, we discussed new literature that used the term perceived addiction to pornography (Grubbs et al., 2017). Due to their faith's anti-pornography teachings and their inability to conform to such teachings, religious men may more readily perceive that they are addicted to pornography, which increases their distress level. Edger (2012) stated that self-identified sexual addicts, i.e., those who perceive an addiction, present with higher levels of problematic symptoms compared to individuals that do not self-identify as addicts. For religious men, such a difference may be explained by them recognizing the depth of their problems and being in the action stage of change, while an individual that does not self-identity may be minimizing the impact of their pornography use and are still in a precontemplation or contemplation stage of change. Conversely, some religious men may perceive an addiction to pornography and are highly distressed when, in fact, they are not actually addicted to pornography. Such men benefit from psychoeducation about what constitutes an addiction as well as counseling to help them reduce their use of pornography to a degree that is more in line with their religious and spiritual beliefs.

Moral Incongruence

It is common for religious men to think and feel like pornography is "wrong," "sinful," and "immoral," but those thoughts and feelings may not prevent pornographic viewing behaviors. Capturing the essence of that seeming paradox is the saying, "I believe it is wrong, but I still do it" (Nelson, Padilla-Walker, & Carroll, 2010). Although religiosity and spirituality may be protective for some men against the use of pornography, religious men still use pornography despite their sincere desire to cease such behavior. As a result, religious men in that paradoxical state experience a constellation of guilt, shame, internal conflict, divine struggle, and moral incongruence when they view pornography. Chapter 5 thoroughly addresses men and shame while Chapter 3 addresses divine struggle. We will quickly note in this chapter that pornography use contributes to religious men feeling shame, questioning their faith, feeling disconnected from the Sacred, avoiding their religious community, and disengaging from their religious practices (Isacco et al., 2018). In other words, the risk of pornography use among religious men is that it makes them less religious and spiritual for a period of time (Perry, 2016). Findings from the same study by Perry (2016) indicate that it is possible for religious men to eventually return back to their God and religious community due to moral justification or to solicit divine help with their PPC out of desperation.

We discuss moral incongruence in this chapter because it is an important topic in the professional literature about pornography and religion (and we covered shame and divine struggle in other chapters). Moral incongruence is defined as "engaging in an activity that violates the sacred values of oneself and one's community" (Perry & Whitehead, 2018, p. 2). Religious men are prone to experiencing moral incongruence when they view pornography, which contributes to increased intrapsychic distress because they are acting in a manner that conflicts with their deeply held beliefs and values. Simply put, incongruence between sexual values and sexual behavior is inherently distressing (Grubbs & Perry, 2019). Moral incongruence is proving to be a significant indicator of the level of distress and even psychopathology that male pornography users experience. For example, in a large longitudinal study, Perry (2018) found that men who reported more moral incongruence about their pornography use were more prone to depressive symptoms over a six-year period. Conversely, the same study implied that depressed men who did not consider pornography to be immoral were more likely to view more pornography as a maladaptive coping tool. Scholars have not examined moral congruence with gay men. Yet, gay men are likely to have more permissive attitudes about pornography use and, as a result, a working hypothesis is that they may experience less moral incongruence with viewing pornography. However, such a hypothesis may not be applicable to all gay men, especially gay men who adhere to religious and spiritual beliefs that oppose pornography.

Thus, counselors need to be aware of their client's sense of morality in general and, specifically, their moral beliefs about pornography in relation to their pornography use.

Conceptualization, Assessment, and Counseling Interventions

Conceptualization

The integration of the psychology of masculinity and the psychology of religion provide important insights into how and why men with PPC present to counseling. First, some men come to counseling with the explicit presenting concern of pornography use and state that their treatment goal is to decrease and/or eliminate their pornography use. This type of man likely has some (or all) of these indicators:

- maladaptive learning of gender norms about sexuality, which has developed into a conscious or unconscious sexual objectification of others.
- high religiosity and experiencing moral incongruence, which is contributing to increased distress.
- multiple failed attempts at stopping the PPC, which has revealed a lack of volitional control and behavior with compulsive and addictive qualities.
- negative consequences in their life such as marital discord, inability to complete work tasks because of time spent viewing pornography, negative emotions (frustration, desperation, anxiety, depression), or difficulty in interpersonal relationships.

Men that fit with this profile type may be in the action stage of change, but due to the nature of the PPC, have had difficulty making the desired changes.

A second type of man comes to counseling and describes other presenting concerns (e.g., depression, anxiety, work, relationships) instead of pornography use and, thus, states associated treatment goals (e.g., improve relationships). However, for these men, pornography use is conceptualized as a latent, contributing problem to their presenting concerns. In this clinical context, counselors should conceptualize men's initial assertion that their pornography use is not a problem as a form of minimization and denial stemming from a range of possible reasons such as cognitive dissonance, shame, embarrassment, or lack of knowledge about addictive behaviors (Grubbs & Perry, 2019). During the assessment and counseling process, men that fit this second profile type may develop a conscious understanding of how their pornography use is negatively impacting their lives. Similar indicators of PPC may then become clearer such as maladaptive learning of sexually objectifying gender norms, moral incongruence, and lack of volitional control to cease the PPC.

Other chapters have discussed the importance of attachment style to men's health (see Chapter 3). Attachment style is also important in the context of men and PPC. Scholars have linked anxious and avoidant attachment styles to gender role conflict, which in turn, was all linked to male pornography use, poor relationship quality, and less sexual satisfaction (Szymanski & Stewart-Richardson, 2014). Counselors can conceptualize men's maladaptive pornography use as stemming from an anxious-avoidant attachment style with primary caregivers. One specific manner in which an anxious-avoidant attachment style facilitates pornography use among adult men is through experiential avoidance. According to Levin et al. (2012), experiential avoidance is defined as engaging in any behavior with the goal to reduce or avoid difficult emotions. For men, pornography viewing has been associated with depression, anxiety, stress, and poor social functioning. Thus, to avoid the negative emotions in the psychological and social domains, men view more pornography in a negative reinforcing loop. Men with difficulty expressing emotions and/or with poor emotional intelligence in relationships turn to pornography as an escape, fantasy, and to control their private experiences with negative emotions rather than to express or reveal those emotions to another person in the public domain. Therefore, in such situations, pornography use is an unhealthy coping response by men or a means of self-soothing to cope with comorbid mood disorders (anxiety and depression; Riemersma & Sytsma, 2013). Such a pattern is more common among men with restrictive emotionality as an aspect to their gender role conflict, who have internalized the masculine norm of emotional stoicism, and/or experienced anxious-avoidant attachment styles during their childhood with primary caregivers.

Counselors may also conceptualize PPC from an addictions model (Bőthe et al., 2018). According to an addictions model, PPC includes six core elements: (1) salience or the importance of pornography to the person's life; (2) mood modification, which is the subjective emotional experience from pornography use; (3) conflict, which includes the person's interpersonal and/or intrapsychic conflict; (4) tolerance or the process of increasing more pornography use to achieve the same level of desired mood modification; (5) relapse, which is the tendency to continue to use pornography despite repeated efforts to stop; and (6) withdrawal, which is unpleasant feelings that emerge when pornography use is stopped. Similar to other addictions, men may turn to pornography to cope with a difficult life experience(s), and in the process, the pornography use may escalate to a problematic level that exacerbates their distress and contributes to other functional impairments in their life. We agree with Bőthe and colleagues (2018) that problematic and addiction are overlapping constructs along the same continuum.

Assessment

This chapter adheres to a similar assessment approach put forth by Isacco and colleagues (2018) by asking about content, frequency, volitional control, functional impairment, and specific issues with masculinity and religiosity. A comprehensive assessment includes a combination of open-ended and closed questions within a clinical interview and throughout the counseling process. The use of assessment tools is also helpful. At least initially, men may struggle with an open conversation about their pornography use. Sexual problems such as pornography have been described as existing in the shadows or darkness, emphasizing the often hidden and isolative nature of the problem (Carnes, 2001). Stigma, shame, and guilt are just a few barriers to self-disclosures about PPC, particularly among religious/spiritual clients. Aspects of gender role socialization such as stoicism, gender role conflict, and the centerfold syndrome may further impede easy self-disclosure. It can be helpful to administer brief, self-report scales to gather additional information that sheds light on the scope, level of distress, varying degrees of risk, specific behaviors, and motivations of PPC that might not readily be disclosed during the clinical interview. Some men respond well to a closed-ended, direct assessment in a test format that provides prompts of specific behaviors and attitudes. We recommend four scales, which are listed in Table 7.2.

Assessing content reveals specific fantasies as well as the viewing of softcore and hardcore material, types of fetishes, and possible psychological conflicts such as violence and aggression. Asking if the man is viewing child pornography content is a significant ethical and legal issue. Adult pornography is a legal form of personal expression in the United States and other countries. Child pornography – defined as producing, disseminating, viewing, and/or possessing pornographic material (e.g., images and videos) that includes children/minors under the age of 18 in a sexual act and may include sexual exploitation, abuse, and trafficking – is illegal (Mapes, 2015). To help avoid an ethical dilemma that may rupture the therapeutic alliance, counselors should include a statement on their informed consent document about their possible role as a mandated reporter in response to disclosures about child pornography (Isacco et al., 2018).

To date, studies have estimated that viewing pornographic content anywhere between 6 and 11 (and over) hours per week is an indicator of compulsive and addictive pornography consumption (Baltazar, Helm Jr., McBride, Hopkins, & Stevens 2010; Levin et al., 2012). Although frequency is not the exclusive indicator of compulsive and addictive behavior, it is important to assess in the context of the additional information.

- How often do you view pornography?
- How many hours/minutes per day? How many hours per week?
- How recent have you viewed pornography?
- Is the amount of time viewing pornography interfering with other aspects of your life?

As mentioned earlier in the chapter, volitional control is an important component to categorizing pornography use as problematic, compulsive, or addictive. Therefore, the assessment process benefits from inquiring about impulse control, urges, and the degree of difficulty controlling the PPC. Some men will begin counseling with the explicit goal to decrease their pornography use. They are initiating counseling because of their inability to stop the pornography use on their own. Other men may learn that they need to decrease their pornography use through the counseling process, but are unable to do so on their own.

- To what extent are you able to control or not control your pornography consumption?
- Do you want to stop viewing pornography?
- What have you tried to help you stop viewing pornography?
- What has been helpful and what has not been helpful?

Along with volitional control, functional impairment is a key indicator of the degree of dysfunction associated with PPC. What problems in your life are related to PPC? Specific probes in the various domains such as vocational/occupational, legal, interpersonal/social, marital/familial, psychological, emotional, spiritual, and/or physical. When assessing volitional control and functional impairment, the Problematic Pornography Consumption Scale (PPCS) may be useful because it is based on an addictions model and provides additional information about relevant factors such as mood modification, tolerance, relapse, and withdrawal (Bőthe et al., 2018).

Religious men are known to have tried a range of religious and spiritual behaviors to decrease their pornography use such as prayer, confession, spiritual direction, talking to a pastor, offering sacrifices, fasting, and other such spiritual efforts. For religious men demonstrating indicators of PPC, engagement in such religious and spiritual behaviors has likely led to a range of outcomes such as disappointment, anger, and learned helplessness to temporary relief to spiritual healing to seeking the Sacred out of desperation. Religious men in counseling because of PPC have likely been unsuccessful at decreasing their pornography use with the religious and spiritual resources.

Thus, the need for counseling. Even then, some aspects of their religion and spirituality may be helpful in their pursuit of decreasing pornography use.

- What religious and spiritual resources or tools have you tried?
- How helpful have those religious and spiritual resources been in decreasing your pornography use?
- How can your religion and spirituality help you decrease your pornography use?

Counselors can assess moral incongruence by asking about his sexual values and moral beliefs about pornography and comparing those to his pornography use. Some questions include the following:

- What religious and moral beliefs do you hold about pornography?
- Are you living in accordance with those beliefs and values?
- Are you experiencing distress related to your inability to live according to your morals?

As described earlier, assessing masculinity ideology is an important part to understanding pornography use. The relevant areas of masculinity included conformity to masculine norms (playboy, violence, dominance over women), gender role conflict, experiential avoidance, and the centerfold syndrome. We discussed how to assess Mahalik et al.'s (2003) masculine norms and O'Neil's (2008) gender role conflict in Chapter 2. Therefore, we focus on the assessment strategy for experiential avoidance and the centerfold syndrome. Two scales are listed in Table 7.2. In addition, the Pornography Consumption Inventory measures emotional avoidance as a motivation for using pornography. Below are open-ended questions to use that address experiential avoidance:

- When faced with stress, do you approach or avoid?
- How comfortable are you expressing negative emotions in front of others?

Some parts of the centerfold syndrome may be assessed in other parts of the assessment process. For example, voyeurism may be accounted for when asking about frequency and content. Additional open-ended questions assess other components of the syndrome and may facilitate a re-evaluation of their attitudes and behaviors about their sexuality in relation to women. Counselors should stay attuned to how men talk about women and identify some indicators of centerfold syndrome. In Table 7.3 we also provide some common scripts that men say, which may be indicative of centerfold syndrome (Wright, 2012), with corresponding sample questions for counselors to use.

In summary, assessing PPC in conjunction with related masculinity and religious issues is multidimensional and goes beyond simply asking about the frequency of pornography use. By conducting a thorough assessment, the counselor gains a clearer understanding of how problematic the pornography use is, the role of masculinity in his use of pornography, the mental health effects, and the degree of moral incongruence.

Counseling Interventions

Despite the surge in research about Internet pornography, the relative recency of the phenomena and the ongoing debate in the mental health professions about the topic have prevented a "gold standard" therapy to emerge in the helping fields. This section integrates a spiritually sensitive approach (Isacco et al., 2018) with techniques that fall under the Cognitive Behavioral Therapy umbrella.

The spiritually sensitive approach to addressing PPC put forth by Isacco and colleagues (2018) is comprised of four phases: (1) assessment (described above), (2) identification of spiritual concerns (occurs in assessment phase), (3) addressing the PPC and associated spiritual concerns, and (4) use of spiritual tools to decrease PPC. Initially, this approach is most relevant for the first type of man described in the conceptualization section, i.e., the man who is overtly religious and wants to decrease his PPC. For such clients, it is important to note that this approach functions under the primary assumption that counselors should exercise multicultural competence in regard to his religious and spiritual beliefs. We know that some counselors have a personal bias that minimizes PPC, while other counselors may over-pathologize pornography use. Neither bias is helpful to this type of client. Therefore, a critical intervention to offer in the early stages of counseling is validation of the concern in the context of his religious and spiritual beliefs. Counseling that attempts to reframe or abandon the client's faith beliefs and sexual morality will be ineffective, culturally incompetent, and is not advised (Grubbs et al., 2017; Isacco et al., 2018).

Phases 1 and 2 are addressed in the assessment process. Therefore, we focus this section on phases 3 and 4 and how to address any spiritual struggle related to PPC. The counselor can spend some time exploring the spiritual struggle with the client to facilitate resolution. Resolution of a spiritual struggle is a process and occurs on a continuum, ranging from unresolved to complete resolution. The counselor can use three strategies for resolving a spiritual struggle: spiritual meaning-making, transforming images of God, and resolving spiritual inconsistencies (Pargament, 2011). Transforming God images was discussed thoroughly in Chapter 3 and resolving spiritual inconsistencies is addressed below in the context of moral incongruence. Therefore, we focus this section on spiritual meaning-making, which is helping men to make sense out of the spiritual struggle associated with PPC. To foster spiritual meaning-making, the counselor assists him in taking a wider and deeper perspective on his PPC. The counselor prompts him to consider any adaptive meanings to his struggle with PPC from a spiritual perspective. For example, he may discuss ways in which he has learned to surrender control of his life over to God or to find some value in suffering.

To take the spiritual meaning-making a step further, the counselor integrates relevant spiritual tools in counseling (Plante, 2009). Chapter 4 comprehensively addresses prayer. In the context of PPC, prayer may be a specific spiritual tool worth integrating with a religious man. As discussed earlier, experiential avoidance is a common pathway to PPC, as men learn to use pornography as a maladaptive coping process to deal with negative emotions such as anxiety. Thus, he would benefit by learning a new positive coping skill (i.e., prayer) to counteract the experiential avoidance habit. Prayer facilitates approaching behaviors in the man as he talks to his God, and in the spiritual dialogue, he may find more meaning in the PPC struggle (Anderson & Nunnelley, 2016). Prayer also has a soothing quality similar to mindfulness, which, in turn, helps to reduce his anxiety. Counseling may need to assist him in establishing a new prayer routine or remaining accountable with the existing prayer practices.

Cognitive Behavioral Therapy (CBT) Techniques

Acceptance and Commitment Therapy (ACT) is considered part of a new wave of counseling that falls under the CBT umbrella. The basic definition of ACT is that it is a process-based intervention that "targets inner experiences (thoughts, feelings, bodily sensations) and utilizes behavior change strategies, targets problems as they are presently occurring, and has an empirical focus" (Twohig & Crosby, 2010, p. 2). The goal is to facilitate change in the relevant processes, which will impact the desired outcomes. ACT has been utilized to decrease PPC (Twohig & Crosby, 2010) and may be particularly helpful to addressing moral incongruence with religious men because of its focus on aligning values with actions.

ACT may be an appropriate starting point for non-religious men (Chapter 9) who oppose pornography use for secular ethical-moral reasons. For example, some non-religious men have aimed to decrease their pornography use after learning about the growing neuropsychological research findings documenting the harmful effects of pornography on individuals, relationships, and families. Thus, non-religious men that come to counseling may oppose pornography and seek to live a more congruent lifestyle between their sexual behaviors and values, ethical code, and moral compass.

Twohig and Crosby (2010) developed and tested an eight-session ACT for PPC, which led to deceased pornography use. We briefly review the eight sessions. Session 1 entails reviewing the informed consent and establishing the mutually agreed upon treatment goal to reduce pornography viewing. The counselor provides some initial psychoeducation about how pornography viewing regulates inner experiences in the short term but that sustained viewing over time negatively affects his quality of life (e.g., romantic relationships, erectile dysfunction, emotional expression). In addition, the counselor introduces the paradoxical nature of battling to control urges to view pornography, only for the man to end up viewing pornography anyway. Session 2 picks up on that latter theme and expands on the reality that sexual arousal is a normal part of being human rather than something that needs to be suppressed. The counselor explores the idea of accepting sexual arousal and the urge to view pornography rather than controlling and battling those urges.

Session 3 re-emphasizes acceptance of sexual arousal and urges and reinforces the agreed upon goal of not viewing pornography. Next, the counselor introduces values into the session and prompts him to develop behavioral commitments in line with his values. For example, rather than commit to not viewing pornography, the counselor encourages him to commit to other related-behaviors such as praying, being intimate with a romantic partner, or talking with a friend. The counselor checks in with him about his commitment to those values-based behaviors throughout the counseling process.

In sessions 4 through 6, the counselor facilitates contact with his inner experiences without verbal disclosures (diffusion) and to understand himself as the context of those inner experiences (self as context) rather than defined by the urges and thoughts to view pornography. As mentioned earlier in the chapter, some men may have difficulty expressing their thoughts and feelings about their PPC, thus diffusion may be particularly helpful given the limitations of language. Self-as-context is facilitated through mindfulness exercises for non-religious clients and/or through contemplative prayer practices for the appropriate religious client. Finally, in sessions 7 and 8, the counselor helps him to reinforce his values and related behavioral commitment through further defining his values and analyzing the importance of congruence between values and behaviors. Although Twohig and Crosby did not mention it specifically, it is easy to see the possible integration of moral (in)congruence in such discussions. The final session includes developing a plan to prevent relapse by solidifying the behavioral commitments that align with his values.

In addition to ACT, counselors can use cognitive therapy techniques to challenge maladaptive masculinity scripts that are contributing to PPC (Brooks, 1995; Elder, Brooks, & Morrow, 2012; Mahalik et al., 2003; Wright, 2012). The masculinity scripts of playboy, dominance of women, and violence are likely the most relevant in the context of men's PPC. Therefore, when a man comes to counseling for PPC, the counselor can monitor for client language that is indicative of those masculinity norms. Challenging the norms and scripts as a first response by a counselor is likely to evoke defensiveness with him as masculinity is learned and protected over time. Thus, when a maladaptive masculinity script is first identified, the counselor explores the positive functions of the script(s). For example, learning to enact violence helped him to avoid bullying as an adult or had an occupational value (e.g., military, sports). Adhering to a playboy script helped him achieve a high social status among his male peer group. After allowing space to nonjudgmentally explore the potential positive value of the masculinity scripts, the counselor shifts the focus to the costs of the scripts. The counselor can frame the shift as a normative process of looking at both benefits and costs of an issue. Next, the counselor prompts the client to connect the costs of the masculinity scripts to the PPC and related concerns (e.g., marital discord, communication problems).

The third step involves helping him to develop more flexible and adaptive masculinity scripts, which promote more positive sexual behaviors rather than PPC. For example, counselors may draw from the line of research about women's descriptions of their male partner's pornography (Szymanski, Feltman, & Dunn, 2015) by asking him to see his pornography use through his partner's perspective (i.e., perspective-taking). Perspective-taking, which is the ability to see a situation from another person's viewpoint, facilitates insight into how their pornography use is having a negative impact on his partner. As such, the new perspective-taking may evoke an empathetic response from him toward his partner that deviates from the playboy and dominance scripts.

The assessment section describes several indicators of the centerfold syndrome that counselors may identify during counseling. When indicators of the centerfold syndrome are identified, the counselor assists him to connect the PPC with lessons learned from his masculinity socialization (Elder et al., 2012). Masculinity socialization begins in childhood and continues through adulthood; often, men will carry wounds from his childhood and adolescence that are adversely impacting him as an adult. For example, he may have been rejected by female peers during his adolescence because of his unflattering appearance, which contributed to low self-esteem and anxiety in female relationships. As a result, he increasingly turned to pornography viewing as an adult rather than to risk having continued defeating experiences with women. Counselors provide the safety, trust, and empathy so he can evaluate those painful experiences in light of his current struggles. In such situations, counseling becomes a process of deep emotional healing for him that helps to enact transformative changes in their intimate relationships with others and by default, their use of pornography.

Summary and Conclusions

Internet pornography use has generated increased attention, research, and debate within the mental health professions. Given the emergence of the 3 As and gender socialization factors in the United States and similar countries, counselors are likely to see an increase in men struggling with Internet pornography use – a term that we called Problematic Pornography Consumption in this chapter. Religious men, in particular, struggling with PPC may experience increased distress, spiritual struggles, and moral incongruence. A spiritually sensitive approach to counseling that integrates cognitive behavioral interventions (e.g., ACT, cost-benefit analysis of masculinity scripts) is beneficial to help men decrease their PPC and to live in greater accordance with their values.

Case Example

My (Isacco) private practice is primarily focused on the psychological evaluation of applicants to serve in ministerial roles (e.g., priests, clergy, deacons, sub-deacons) within church organizations. The evaluations are somewhat unique because the church organization is my client and often requests certain information to be included in the psychological report that I submit. The sexuality of the applicant has become an increasingly salient topic to assess in the psychological evaluations since news of the sexual abuse scandal within the Catholic Church broke in 2002. Therefore, I have asked hundreds of men about their sexual identity, sexual history and experiences, and sexual behaviors. The questions range from normative experiences such as dating to sexual deviancy, fetishes, and addictions. Within this context, I routinely assess an applicant's pornography use through open-ended questions and self-report tools. This case example will focus on the assessment process of identifying PPC rather than counseling interventions. I will also provide some conceptualization to help explain the etiology of the PPC.

I met George in my private practice for a psychological evaluation as part of his admission application to a seminary, which is a school for training to be a priest. Similar to other applicants, George appeared nervous. He was very quiet and stoic. Yet, he had a squirrelly quality to him, very shifty and his eyes darted around the room quite frequently. For example, he regularly moved his body back and forth in his seat. He would answer a question and his eyes would look to the left, then to the right, and back to the left again. He seemed unsettled and uncomfortable.

George was about 22 years old, was clean-cut, and was of average height and build. Many people would look at him and consider him "a nice young man." And indeed, much of the public information about George fit a profile that was congruent with a young man pursing the priesthood. His family-of-origin was devoutly Catholic and very religious. George grew up in a large family, with many siblings, and his parents homeschooled him and his siblings. He was an altar boy at the local parish and was told repeatedly by parishioners that he "would make a great priest." They were, of course, giving him a compliment because they saw a religious young man who seemed like a natural fit to be a religious leader. Similarly, his parents were very encouraging of George to pursue the priesthood. They were very proud to have a son applying to the seminary and it was a major point of conversation in their community. To sum up how George was perceived by others – simply put, he was the "golden boy."

The clinical interview proceeded through various sections such as psychosocial history, mental health, physical health, and family-of-origin dynamics until I transitioned to psychosexual history. I give a verbal indicator of this transition and provide each applicant with a heads-up that we will now be talking about sexual issues. I noticed George tense up a little bit (e.g., clenched jaw, shoulders squeezed inwards) and his eyes darted around the room. He quietly said "ok" but nothing else. In regard to pornography, I started by asking him if he does or does not use pornography. George answered "yes," which is an opt-in answer for a more extensive assessment (Isacco et al., 2018). After a series of open-ended questions, I learned that George viewed pornography everyday for approximately two hours per day. He viewed the pornography primarily at night, after 10 pm, when his roommates were asleep. George expressed frustration with his pornography viewing and stated a desire to stop. However, his attempts to stop had been unsuccessful. When asked what he has tried to stop the behavior, George described several religious and spiritual activities. For example, praying to God, frequenting the sacrament of confession, and discussing his struggles with a priest. My concerns increased when he discussed associated compulsive behavior such as going to confession two or three times per week. Most Catholics go to confession once or twice a year and even the most active Catholics that I know use the sacrament of confession about three times per month. For George, these religious/spiritual behaviors were not helping to decrease his pornography use. He was experiencing a great deal of guilt and shame as the pornography use was incongruent with his moral code, family-of-origin values, and religious beliefs. According to George, this pattern of using pornography, trying to stop, going to confession had been going on since his adolescence (about six years). He had never sought mental health counseling or any other psychological tool to help him with his pornography use.

To complement his self-report to open-ended questions and to gather more assessment data, I administered three paper-pencil self-report measures about pornography use. First, I used the Internet Sex Screening Test (ISST). The ISST is a 34-item, self-report assessment of problematic sexual feelings, behaviors, and compulsions on the Internet. Scores can range from 0–25. Scores ranging from 1–8 indicate "low risk," 9–18 indicate "at-risk" sexual behavior, and a score of 19 or above indicate high risk for sexual behavior and the likelihood of corresponding impairment in some areas of life. George scored a 20, indicating that he is in the high-risk category. In addition, he scored 7/9 on an embedded set of items intended to screen for sexual addiction, including a self-perception that he considered himself a sexual addict.

Second, George completed the Pornography Consumption Inventory (PCI). The PCI is a 15-item, self-report assessment of motivations for pornography consumption. The PCI assesses four motivations: (1) emotional avoidance, (2) sexual curiosity, (3) excitement seeking, and (4) sexual pleasure. Scores can range from 15–75, with higher scores indicating greater tendencies to use pornography, per the four motivations. George's total score was 54. When assessed per the four motivations, he was using pornography primarily to avoid and/or unhealthily cope with negative emotions (emotional avoidance). In other words, he was not using pornography out of curiosity, to seek excitement, or for sexual pleasure but as a distraction and/or to cope with negative emotions.

Third, I administered the Hypersexual Behavior Inventory (HBI-19). The HBI-19 is a 19-item, self-report assessment of sexual fantasies, urges, behaviors, thoughts, and feelings that may be problematic and cause distress. Scores can range from 19–95, with a score of 53 or above indicative of problematic hypersexual behavior. George's total score was 66, which was above the cut-off and indicative of hypersexual behavior. In particular, George's score indicated a perceived inability to control hypersexual behaviors that he wants to stop.

Finally, I assessed any functional impairments. George was finishing up his undergraduate degree at a large public university. He was passing his classes and was scheduled to graduate in a few months. He was also able to maintain a part-time job on campus. By his account, his family relationships were good, and he got along well with his roommates. George's functional impairment appeared to be in the vocational domain as he had trouble seeing himself as worthy and "holy" to be a priest. In addition, he was using pornography to cope with and to avoid negative emotions. He was experiencing a heightened level of psychological consternation about his inability to stop a behavior that he desperately wanted to stop. Thus, spiritually, he felt like he was "letting God down" and was disconnected from God. Based on the assessment information, I considered George to be exhibiting the indicators of PPC and his pornography use had an addictive quality.

Conceptually, I understood the etiology of George's PPC as stemming from a couple of sources. First, his family of origin contributed to his PPC by placing many expectations on George about his future and decision-making. George lacked a sense of control, autonomy, and individuation from his parents in order to take responsibility for his decisions as a young man. The pornography use developed as a way for George to have a sense of control over his environment. He could view any image, at any time, without any one's permission. In addition, pornography use was an unconscious rebellion from his family of origin's religiosity. Second, although George desired to make decisions as a young man, he had experienced maladaptive gender role socialization. Specifically, he did not develop a broader array of healthy coping skills and believed that men should be stoic and not show emotions. By the time that I met with George for the psychological evaluation, he was unable to express any positive emotions either. He believed that any emotional expression was unmanly and, thus, he fit the profile of a young man with gender role conflict. His pornography use became problematic because he increasingly turned to pornography as a form of emotional avoidance. Thus, as the pornography use increased and became tied to maladaptive coping, an addiction formed. George wanted to stop the pornography use but could not because he had not resolved his family-of-origin or manhood issues that perpetuated the PPC.

Based on this psychological evaluation, I expressed significant concerns about his admission application to the seminary. In addition, I recommended that he begin to utilize several psychological tools to help him with his pornography addiction such as mental health counseling, bibliotherapy (e.g., *Integrity Restored: Helping Catholic Families Win the Battle Against Pornography* by Dr. Peter Kleponis), and technology (accountability apps and software, e.g., *Covenant Eyes*) for his laptop and smartphone. The issues and behaviors were long term and deeply ingrained. I gave George a guarded prognosis because he was young enough to make some significant progress. He is not a priest and has continued to discern his vocation.

Table 7.1 Terms and Definitions

Term	*Definition*
Problematic Pornography Consumption	Can be triggered, is persistent and intrusive, and influenced by powerful urges/impulses that are difficult to stop or control. PPC likely impacts at least one of the following domains: legal/occupational, social, physical, other pain, financial, and psychological/spiritual. (Twohig et al., 2009)
Problematic Use of Internet Pornography	Frequent to the point of excess or compulsion, triggered by an urge and difficult to control, aimed at attaining a positive emotional state or escaping a negative emotional state, and continues despite adverse consequences and personal distress and/or impairment. (Kor et al., 2014)
Pornography Addiction	Pornography consumption that is addictive in the neurological sense: impacting the motivation, reward, and memory systems of the brain. (Hilton, 2013)
Internet Sex Addiction	Recurrent, intrusive sexual fantasies or urges, and the compulsion to repeatedly engage in sexual behaviors to cope, despite a detrimental impact on the individual's life. (Griffiths, 2012)

(continued)

Table 7.1 (continued)

Term	*Definition*
Hypersexual Disorder	Any sexual behavior that one feels cannot be controlled and negatively impacts their life. (Kafka, 2014)
Nonparaphilic Hypersexual Behavior	Nonparaphilic sexual fantasies that are intense, recurring, and lead to negative consequences and significant distress, that impair an individual in one or more areas of functioning. (Hook, Reid, Penberthy, Davis, & Jennings, 2014)
Perceived Pornography Addiction	The feeling that pornography usage is compulsive or out of control, and an inability to stop, despite the experience of severe or significant consequences. (Grubbs et al., 2017)
Compulsive Use of Internet-Based Sexually Explicit Material	Characterized by difficulty keeping oneself from accessing sexually explicit material (SEM) online, despite the intention to stop, thinking about and looking forward to the material when not engaged with it, neglecting to complete important life tasks or obligations because of SEM, or preferring SEM to spending time with significant others. (Downing, Antebi, & Schrimshaw, 2014)
Compulsive Sexual Behavior	Persistent and repetitive sexual impulses or urges that become a central focus of an individual's life, which they feel they cannot resist or control, and leads to feelings of distress and the neglecting of self-care and personal responsibility. (Krueger, 2016)
Sexual Dysfunction Unspecified	302.70 (F52.9) Issues of sexual functioning that cause significant distress, but do not fit any other DSM-5 diagnoses relating to sexual function. (American Psychiatric Association, 2013)
Impulsive-Compulsive Internet Sexual Behavior	Frequent and intrusive thoughts about sex and sexual behaviors, which an individual feels are out of control. This behavior is cyclic, triggered by an impulsive drive, and continued compulsively. (Mick & Hollander, 2006)

Table 7.2 Assessments Related to Problematic Pornography Consumption

Scale	*Description*
The Internet Sex Screening Test (ISST)	The ISST is a 34-item, self-report assessment of problematic sexual feelings, behaviors, and compulsions on the Internet. Scores can range from 0–25. Scores ranging from 1–8 indicate "low risk;" 9–18 indicate "at-risk" sexual behavior; 19 + indicate high risk for sexual behavior and the likelihood of corresponding impairment in some areas of life. (Delmonico & Miller, 2003)
The Pornography Consumption Inventory (PCI)	The PCI is a 15-item, self-report assessment of motivations for pornography consumption. The PCI assesses four motivations: (1) emotional avoidance, (2) sexual curiosity, (3) excitement seeking, and (4) sexual pleasure. Scores can range from 15–75, with higher scores indicating greater tendencies to use pornography, per the four motivations. (Reid et al., 2011)
The Hypersexual Behavior Inventory (HBI-19)	The HBI-19 is a 19-item, self-report assessment of sexual fantasies, urges, behaviors, thoughts, and feelings that may be problematic and cause distress. Scores can range from 19–95, with a score of 53 or above indicative of problematic hypersexual behavior. (Reid et al., 2011)
Problematic Pornography Consumption Scale (PPCS)	The PPCS is an 18-item, self-report assessment of problematic pornography consumption based on addiction theory, which clustered the items into six subscales: (1) salience, (2) mood modification, (3) conflict, (4) tolerance, (5) relapse, and (6) withdrawal. Scores can range from 18–126, with higher scores indicating more problematic pornography use. (Bőthe et al., 2018)
Centerfold Syndrome	Centerfold Syndrome has been assessed on a self-report tool using a 31-item index based on Brook's conceptualization and hypotheses. The 31 items are clustered into 5 subscales: (1) voyeurism, (2) sexual reductionism, (3) masculinity validation, (4) trophyism, and (5) nonrelational Sex. Higher scores reflect stronger adherence to the Centerfold Syndrome. (Wright & Tokunaga, 2015)
The Acceptance and Action Questionnaire – II (AAQ-II)	The AAQ-II is a 7-item measure of experiential avoidance. Higher scores reflect a stronger tendency to experientially avoid. (Bond et al., 2011)

Table 7.3 Assessing Centerfold Syndrome

Centerfold Syndrome Components	*Indicator Scripts*	*Sample Question during Counseling*
Voyeurism	"Women make good eye candy." "I like going to the gym to look at women." "Men are visual people. It's natural to look at women."	Do you find yourself looking at women a lot?
Sexual Reductionism	"I'm a leg [fill in women's body part] guy."	Do women fill other roles in your life beyond sex?
Masculinity Validation	"A man finds one [a woman] and then forgets them." "Something is wrong with a guy who turns down a chance to have sex."	Have you viewed women as a sexual conquest?
Trophyism	"I haven't found a hot enough woman to date." "My friends are jealous of my girlfriend."	What attributes other than physical appearance do you value in a woman?
Nonrelational Sex	"The best sex is with no strings attached." "I'm not looking for anything serious." "I enjoy sexual experiences without someone else."	How do you relate to women other than through sexual experiences?

References

American Psychiatric Association. (2013). *Diagnostic and statistical manual of mental disorders: DSM-5*. Washington, DC: American Psychiatric Association.

Anderson, J.W., & Nunnelley, P.A. (2016). Private prayer associations with depression, anxiety and other health conditions: An analytical review of clinical studies. *Postgraduate Medicine, 128*(7), 635–641.

Baltazar, A., Helm Jr, H.W., McBride, D., Hopkins, G., & Stevens Jr, J.V. (2010). Internet pornography use in the context of external and internal religiosity. *Journal of Psychology and Theology, 38*(1), 32–40.

Bond, F.W., Hayes, S.C., Baer, R.A., Carpenter, K.M., Guenole, N., Orcutt, H.K., Waltz, T., & Zettle, R.D. (2011). Preliminary psychometric properties of the Acceptance and Action Questionniare – II: A revised measure of psychological flexibility and experiential avoidance. *Behavior Therapy, 42*, 676–688.

Bőthe, B., Tóth-Király, I., Zsila, Á., Griffiths, M.D., Demetrovics, Z., & Orosz, G. (2018). The development of the Problematic Pornography Consumption Scale (PPCS). *Journal of Sex Research, 55*(3), 395–406.

Brooks, G.R. (1995). *The centerfold syndrome: How men can overcome objectification and achieve intimacy with women*. San Francisco, CA: Jossey-Bass.

Carnes, P. (2001). *Out of the shadows: Understanding sexual addiction*. Center City, MN: Hazelden Publishing.

Delmonico, D.L., & Miller, J.A. (2003). The internet sex screening test: A comparison of sexual compulsives versus non-sexual compulsives. *Sexual and Relationship Therapy, 18*(3), 261–276.

Döring, N.M. (2009). The Internet's impact on sexuality: A critical review of 15 years of research. *Computers in Human Behavior, 25*(5), 1089–1101.

Downing, M.J., Antebi, N., & Schrimshaw, E.W. (2014). Compulsive use of Internet-based sexually explicit media: Adaptation and validation of the Compulsive Internet Use Scale (CIUS). *Addictive Behaviors, 39*(6), 1126–1130.

Edger, K. (2012). Evangelicalism, sexual morality, and sexual addiction: Opposing views and continued conflicts. *Journal of Religion and Health, 51*(1), 162–178.

Elder, W.B., Brooks, G.R., & Morrow, S.L. (2012). Sexual self-schemas of heterosexual men. *Psychology of Men & Masculinity, 13*(2), 166–179.

Griffiths, M.D. (2012). Internet sex addiction: A review of empirical research. *Addiction Research & Theory, 20*(2), 111–124,

Grubbs, J.B., Exline, J.J., Pargament, K.I., Volk, F., & Lindberg, M.J. (2017). Internet pornography use, perceived addiction, and religious/spiritual struggles. *Archives of sexual behavior, 46*(6), 1733–1745.

Grubbs, J.B., & Perry, S.L. (2019). Moral incongruence and pornography use: A critical review and integration. *The Journal of Sex Research, 56*(1), 29–37.

Hald, G.M., Smolenski, D., & Simon Rosser, B.R. (2013). Perceived effects of sexually explicit media among men who have sex with men and psychometric properties of the Pornography Consumption Effects Scale (PCES). *The Journal of Sexual Medicine, 10*(3), 757–767.

Hilton, D.L. (2013). Pornography addiction: A supranormal stimulus considered in the context of neuroplasticity. *Socioaffective neuroscience & psychology, 3*, 20767.

Hook, J., Reid, R., Penberthy, K., Davis, D., & Jennings, D.J. (2014). Methodological review of treatments for nonparaphilic hypersexual behavior. *Journal of Sex & Marital Therapy, 40*(10), 294–308.

International Classification of Diseases (ICD–11) (2018). World Health Organization, Retrieved from https://icd.who.int/browse11/l-m/en#/http://id.who.int/icd/entity/1630268048.

Isacco, A., Tirabassi, D., Porada, K., & Meade, K.A. (2018). Using a spiritually sensitive approach to treat problematic pornography consumption. In T.G. Plante (Ed.), *Healing with spiritual practices: Proven techniques for disorders from addictions and anxiety to cancer and chronic pain* (pp. 222–238). Santa Barbara, CA: ABC-CLIO.

Kafka, M.P. (2014). What happened to hypersexual disorder? *Archives of Sexual Behavior, 43*(7), 1259–1261.

Karila, L., Wéry, A., Weinstein, A., Cottencin, O., Petit, A., Reynaud, M., & Billieux, J. (2014). Sexual addiction or hypersexual disorder: Different terms for the same problem? A review of the literature. *Current Pharmaceutical Design, 20*(25), 4012–4020.

Kor, A., Zilcha-Mano, S., Fogel, Y.A., Mikulincer, M., Reid, R.C., & Potenza, M.N. (2014). Psychometric development of the Problematic Pornography Use Scale. *Addictive Behaviors, 39*, 861–868.

Krueger, R.B. (2016). Diagnosis of hypersexual or compulsive sexual behavior can be made using ICD-10 and DSM-5 despite rejection of this diagnosis by the American Psychiatric Association. *Addiction, 111*(12), 2110–2111.

Levin, M.E., Lillis, J., & Hayes, S.C. (2012). When is online pornography viewing problematic among college males? Examining the moderating role of experiential avoidance. *Sexual Addiction & Compulsivity, 19*(3), 168–180.

Love, T., Laier, C., Brand, M., Hatch, L., & Hajela, R. (2015). Neuroscience of internet pornography addiction: A review and update. *Behavioral Sciences, 5*(3), 388–433.

Mahalik, J.R., Locke, B.D., Ludlow, L.H., Diemer, M.A., Scott, R.P., Gottfried, M., & Freitas, G. (2003). Development of the Conformity to Masculine Norms Inventory. *Psychology of Men & Masculinity, 4*(1), 3–25.

Mapes, B.E. (2015, September). Child pornography and the law. *The Pennsylvania Psychologist Quarterly*.

Mick, T., & Hollander, E. (2006). Impulsive-compulsive sexual behavior. *CNS spectrums, 11*, 944–955.

Mikorski, R., & Szymanski, D.M. (2017). Masculine norms, peer group, pornography, Facebook, and men's sexual objectification of women. *Psychology of Men & Masculinity, 18*(4), 257–267.

Miller, D.J., Hald, G.M., & Kidd, G. (2018). Self-perceived effects of pornography consumption among heterosexual men. *Psychology of Men & Masculinity, 19*(3), 469–476.

Mustanski, B., Lyons, T., & Garcia, S.C. (2011). Internet use and sexual health of young men who have sex with men: A mixed-methods study. *Archives of Sexual Behavior, 40*(2), 289–300.

Nelson, K.M., Pantalone, D.W., Gamarel, K.E., & Simoni, J.M. (2016). A new measure of the perceived influence of sexually explicit online media on the sexual behaviors of men who have sex with men. *Journal of Sex Research, 53*(4–5), 588–600.

Nelson, L.J., Padilla-Walker, L.M., & Carroll, J.S. (2010). "I believe it is wrong but I still do it": A comparison of religious young men who do versus do not use pornography. *Psychology of Religion and Spirituality, 2*(3), 136–147.

O'Neil, J.M. (2008). Summarizing 25 years of research on men's gender role conflict using the Gender Role Conflict Scale: New research paradigms and clinical implications. *The Counseling Psychologist, 36*(3), 358–445.

Pargament, K.I. (2011). *Spiritually integrated psychotherapy: Understanding and addressing the sacred*. New York, NY: Guilford Press.

Perry, S.L. (2016). From bad to worse? Pornography consumption, spousal religiosity, gender, and marital quality. *Sociological Forum, 31*(2), 441–464.

Perry, S.L. (2017). Does viewing pornography diminish religiosity over time? Evidence from two-wave panel data. *The Journal of Sex Research, 54*(2), 214–226.

Perry, S.L. (2018). Pornography use and depressive symptoms: Examining the role of moral incongruence. *Society and Mental Health, 8*(3), 195–213.

Perry, S.L., & Whitehead, A.L. (2018, online January). Only bad for believers? Religion, pornography use, and sexual satisfaction among American men. *The Journal of Sex Research*, 1–12. doi:10.1080/00224499.2017.1423017.

Philaretou, A.G., Mahfouz, A.Y., & Allen, K.R. (2005). Use of Internet pornography and men's well-being. *International Journal of Men's Health, 4*(2), 149–169.

Plante, T.G. (2009). *Spiritual practices in psychotherapy: Thirteen tools for enhancing psychological health*. Washington, DC: American Psychological Association.

Price, J., Patterson, R., Regnerus, M., & Walley, J. (2016). How much more XXX is Generation X consuming? Evidence of changing attitudes and behaviors related to pornography since 1973. *The Journal of Sex Research, 53*(1), 12–20.

Reid, R.C., Li, D.S., Gilliland, R., Stein, J.A., & Fong, T. (2011). Reliability, validity, and psychometric development of the Pornography Consumption Inventory in a sample of hypersexual men. *Journal of Sex & Marital Therapy, 37*, 359–385.

Riemersma, J., & Sytsma, M. (2013). A new generation of sexual addiction. *Sexual Addiction & Compulsivity, 20*(4), 306–322.

Ropelato, J. (2006). *2006 & 2005 US Pornography Industry Revenue Statistics. TopTenREVIEWS.* Retrieved from: http://internet-filter-review.toptenreviews.com/ internet-pornography-statistics.html.

Schrimshaw, E.W., Antebi-Gruszka, N., & Downing, M.J. (2016). Viewing of Internet-based sexually explicit media as a risk factor for condomless anal sex among men who have sex with men in four U.S. cities. *PLoS ONE, 11*(4), e0154439. doi:10.1371/journal.pone.0154439.

Short, M.B., Kasper, T.E., & Wetterneck, C.T. (2015). The relationship between religiosity and internet pornography use. *Journal of Religion and Health, 54*(2), 571–583.

Stein, D., Silvera, R., Hagerty, R., & Marmor, M. (2012). Viewing pornography depicting unprotected anal intercourse: Are there implications for HIV prevention among men who have sex with men? *Archives of Sexual Behavior, 41*(2), 411–419.

Szymanski, D.M., Feltman, C.E., & Dunn, T.L. (2015). Male partners' perceived pornography use and women's relational and psychological health: The roles of trust, attitudes, and investment. *Sex Roles, 73*(5–6), 187–199.

Szymanski, D.M., & Mikorski, R. (2016). External and internalized heterosexism, meaning in life, and psychological distress. *Psychology of Sexual Orientation and Gender Diversity, 3*(3), 265–274.

Szymanski, D.M., & Stewart-Richardson, D.N. (2014). Psychological, relational, and sexual correlates of pornography use on young adult heterosexual men in romantic relationships. *The Journal of Men's Studies, 22*(1), 64–82.

Twohig, M.P., & Crosby, J.M. (2010). Acceptance and commitment therapy as a treatment for problematic internet pornography viewing. *Behavior Therapy, 41*(3), 285–295.

Twohig, M.P., Crosby, J.M., & Cox, J.M. (2009). Viewing Internet pornography: For whom is it problematic, how, and why? *Sexual Addiction & Compulsivity, 16*(4), 253–266.

Wright, P.J. (2012). Show me the data! Empirical support for the "Centerfold Syndrome." *Psychology of Men & Masculinity, 13*(2), 180–198.

Wright, P.J., & Tokunaga, R.S. (2015). Activating the centerfold syndrome: Recency of exposure, sexual explicitness, past exposure to objectifying media. *Communication Research, 42*(6), 864–897.

8 Gay Men and Religion

Although the title of this chapter refers to "gay" men, there will be men who are seeking counseling who do not identify as gay. A term often used to describe a diverse group of men is "men who have sex with men," or MSM. Another term is "same-sex attracted men," or SSA men. Such men may identify as gay, homosexual, or bisexual, whereas some will not. They may identify as heterosexual or straight. Some men who do not identify as gay may identify as homosexual. These men do not identify with the label of "gay" because they do not identify with gay men or gay culture. There are also men who may be confused about their sexual orientation, and may or may not have had a sexual experience with another man. In this chapter, we address MSM and SSA men who are seeking help and how religion or spirituality are issues that should be considered and integrated into the counseling or psychotherapy.

Much of the literature and research on this topic is not specific to MSM and SSA men, rather it pertains to the lives of LGB or LGBTQ individuals (lesbian, gay, bisexual, transgender, and queer), or the gay community. For the purposes of this chapter, we will refer only to men, although what will be presented is or may be applicable to lesbian and transgender individuals as well. Where the findings are specific only to men, this will be noted.

Religious Involvement, Spirituality, and Gay Men

Given most US religious denominations condemn same-sex behavior as sinful (Barnes & Meyer, 2012), one would assume that gay and bisexual men would be less likely to be involved in religious organizations or institutions. However, research indicates otherwise. Sherkat (2002) investigated religious commitment in six sexuality groupings: female and male heterosexuals, female and male bisexuals, and lesbians and gay men. Gay men and heterosexual females had almost the same rates of church attendance, and gay men were more active in religious organizations than male heterosexuals. With regard to spirituality, Barnes and Meyer (2012) showed that LGBs were more likely to consider themselves spiritual than in the general population, and gay/bisexual males were more likely than lesbian/bisexual females to consider themselves very spiritual (57% vs. 46%).

It is possible that if being religious is viewed as not masculine and associated with femininity, then being a gay male would allow for less conflict with regard to being religious, if such gay men do not endorse traditional notions of masculinity. However, most mainstream religions are rejecting of homosexuality, which is equated with femininity or non-adherence to traditional gender roles. This is somewhat of a paradox. What may allow some men to be religious and/or spiritual is their nontraditional masculinity. On the other hand, those men who hold traditional attitudes about masculinity will be less likely to be religious or spiritual, although some religious men may be more drawn to more masculine forms of religion and spirituality, such as the masculine spirituality of the men's movement and the evangelical Promise Keepers. However, such spiritual and religious movements are heteronormative (Gelfer, 2009).

Noting that research on gay Christian men has typically neglected the topic of masculinities, Sumerau (2012) examined how gay Christian men in an LGBT Christian Church constructed their identities as men by what he determined were "compensatory manhood acts." Some of the ways in which the men constructed their identities as men included defining themselves as fatherly guides and financial providers; stressing emotional control as central to manhood, and the inherent rationality of men made them more suited for leadership in the church; and emphasizing monogamy in intimate relationships and responsible sexual conduct that is consistent with Christianity. Sumerau concluded that these manhood acts compensated for their subordination as gay men in relation to the masculine ideal.

In addition to any other issues that male clients present despite their sexual orientation and religious identity, or that may contribute to the presenting problem, it would be important to evaluate whether sexual identity and religious or spiritual identity are areas of conflict and if such conflict is related to the presenting problem. However, for the most part, the research indicates that religiosity is associated with poor mental health for gay men, not spirituality (Harari, Glenwick, & Cecero, 2014). For some religious men, there may be conflict about their sexual identity that is related to their religious identity. Conversely, conflict about their religious identity may be related to their sexual identity. Such conflict may result from religious teachings that were psychologically damaging, affecting the emotional wellbeing of gay men. Essentially, the counselor will need to address what has been referred to in the literature as internalized homophobia and internalized homonegativity, which in this instance is a result of the religious homonegativity experienced by the client. Ultimately, and ideally, the therapeutic outcome is resolution of the client's identity conflict.

Religious Homonegativity

The term "homonegativity" broadly defined refers to negative reactions to homosexuality (Hudson & Ricketts, 1980), which include attitudes, beliefs, and behaviors of individuals and institutions that are negative toward sexual minorities or are anti-gay. For some MSM, their religious upbringing will have included a condemnation of homosexuality or hearing anti-gay messages. However, the anti-gay messages and heteronormative values espoused will differ among religious affiliations. For example, "six passages from the Bible (Genesis, 19:1–28; Leviticus, 18:22, 20:13; Romans, 1:26,27; I Corinthians, 6:9; I Timothy, 1:10) have generally been used to support the contention that homosexuality is a sin" (Rodriguez, 2009, p. 9). Conservative Protestants (e.g., Southern Baptists, Pentecostals, and Evangelicals) are more likely to view the contents of the Bible as literally true, morally object to homosexuality, view homosexuals as contaminating society, and have lower levels of tolerance than mainline Protestants, Catholics, and those with no religious affiliation (Burdette, Ellison, & Hill, 2005). Jäckle and Wenzelburger (2015) conducted a multilevel analysis of 79 countries and found religious people were more homonegative than non-religious people, although there were clear differences among people in the level of homonegativity based on religious affiliation. From most to least homonegative were Islam, Catholicism/ Protestant Free Churches/Orthodox Christianity, Traditional (European) Protestantism, Hinduism, Buddhism/Taoism/Confucianism, and Atheism (Judaism was not included in their study). Additionally, those whose religious motivation was extrinsic as opposed to intrinsic were more likely to have negative attitudes toward gay and lesbian people.

The Torah, with respect to Orthodox Judaism, prohibits any sexual activity between two men. According to the halakhah (Jewish religious law), "sexual intercourse between men is an egregious transgression, whereas sex between two women is also forbidden, but its moral, social, and religious consequences are not as severe as in the case of two men" (Shilo, Yosef, & Savaya, 2016, p. 1553). The story of Lot in the Qu'ran has been used for the stance on the immorality of same-sex sexuality in the religion of Islam (Jamal, 2001). Traditional Islamic law, which is derived from the Qu'ran and applied to the lives of Muslims, considers homosexuality a grave sin. Muslim Americans tend to be less accepting of homosexuality than Americans as a whole, with those who have a low level of religious commitment being more accepting than those high in religious commitment (Pew Research Center, 2011). Sikh, Hindu, and Buddhist religions do not have any teachings or text that are homonegative or against homosexuality.

In a study on homonegativity, one in three gay men reported having experienced homonegativity in a religious environment (Christman, 2012). Experiencing religious anti-gay messages in religious settings can lead to feelings of depression, sensitivity to rejection, lack of resilience, and lack of social support (Lassiter, Grov, Ventuneac, Starks, & Parsons, 2015). The effects of religious homonegativity may be intensified for African-American MSM due to the importance of religion among African-Americans, as a result of the historical role of the Church in the African-American community (Quinn, Dickson-Gomez, & Kelly, 2016). However, religious African-American MSM may resist leaving their church community given the importance that it has in their lives. Similarly, some White evangelical and Mormon gay men would rather stay connected with their church community than leave it despite the anti-gay religious rhetoric.

Religious homonegativity experienced in a religious setting is often experienced in one's family environment as well, which can only exacerbate one's level of distress or discontent. In a qualitative study of gay men brought up in Polish Catholic families highly involved in religion, the researchers observed that the men were unable to differentiate between attitudes about sexuality held by their parents or grandparents from those of the Church. Further, it was not evident which was more stressful for them, the religious homonegativity experienced in the religious setting or from one's family (Pietkiewicz & Kołodziejczyk-Skrzypek, 2016). This religion-sexuality related distress can persist even after having rejected one's religious beliefs and allegiances (Sowe, Brown, & Taylor, 2014).

Internalized Homonegativity

Internalized homonegativity is when negative attitudes toward homosexuality are accepted or incorporated into the self as guiding principles about oneself and others (Mayfield, 2001). These beliefs and attitudes are learned or unconsciously assimilated, and research indicates internalized homonegativity may be greater for males (Sowe et al., 2014). When the religious environment is or has been pervasively homonegative, gay men may view their sexuality as sinful or inferior, resulting in a greater degree of internalized homonegativity (Sowe et al., 2014). For many MSM, religious homonegativity can cause them to question their sexual and religious identities, and create feelings of worthlessness, depression, and shame (Jeffries, Dodge, & Sandfort, 2008; Quinn et al., 2016).

Generally, research shows a positive relationship between internalized homophobia and religious participation and religious commitment. When MSM feel that homosexuality is rejected by their religion and family, and the more important religion is to their family, the more they will experience internalized homonegativity (Sowe et al., 2014). Internalized homonegativity has been associated with not disclosing to others about one's sexuality, a lack of connectedness with the LGB community, having a poor sense of self, and psychological distress (Sowe et al., 2014). Only one study has examined religiosity, homonegativity, and masculinity in sexual minority men. The study involved bisexual Latino men and found that religiosity was positively associated with homonegativity and having a masculine identity (Severson, Munoz-Laboy, & Kaufman, 2014).

However, for some gay men, affiliation with a gay affirming religion can have psychological benefits, counteracting the effects of homonegativity. For example, involvement in gay affirming organized faith groups predicted lower internalized homophobia and higher spirituality, which was associated with better mental health outcomes (Lease, Horne, & Noffsinger-Frazier, 2005).

Identity Conflict: Gay Identity and Religious/Spiritual Identity

The process of identity formation can be a difficult process for some MSM who are religious. Because of a conflict between one's sexuality and religious beliefs, it can make it difficult to identify as gay or bisexual or come out to others. Likewise, it can make it difficult to identify with a religion that is condemning of one's sexuality. What makes this difficult is the feelings of shame and anxiety that are associated with this identity conflict (Rodriguez, 2009). The causes or sources of the conflict can be characterized as "*extrinsic*, coming from outside of the individual and more dependent on acceptance by others, and *intrinsic*, coming from within the individual and generally held as internalized moral ideals" (Rodriguez, 2009, p. 10). Examples of extrinsic sources include adherence to religious doctrines that are anti-gay, acceptance of the negative perspectives of other gay men, and contradicting friends' and family members' religious beliefs, while intrinsic examples include fear of retribution from God and believing that being gay and religious is incompatible (Rodriguez, 2009).

The response to identity conflict can result in the rejection of a gay identity or religious identity, separation of the gay self from the religious self, or integration of one's gay and religious identities (Beagan & Hattie, 2015). There are a variety of reasons as to why MSM will respond to the religious-sexual identity conflict in either of these ways. We argue that integration of identities to resolve the conflict is the ideal outcome. However, we recognize that this resolution may not be possible or desirable for all clients.

Several authors have noted how some individuals manage integrating their religious and sexual identities (Dahl & Galliher, 2009; McGlasson & Rubel, 2015; Rodriguez, 2009; Schuck & Liddle, 2001):

- Reading literature related to the issue of religious and sexual identity conflict.
- Talking with others who can relate to the experience and have dealt with it.
- Re-establishing one's relationship with God.
- Getting involved with organizations that have a positive stance on homosexuality and religion.
- Realization and acceptance of one's sexual identity.
- Identifying as spiritual rather than religious.
- Reinterpreting religious teachings.
- Remaining religious but stop attending a religious institution.
- Renunciation of religious authority (from religious institutions, family members, and community), or rejection of a former religious affiliation, and the development of a new healthy spirituality.

Dahl and Galliher (2009) investigated the process of religious and sexual identity integration in a sample of lesbian, gay, bisexual, queer, and questioning young adults aged 18 to 24 years old. They assessed degree of identity integration and frequency of being simultaneously religious and open about their sexuality. For degree of integration 42% responded "not at all" and 42% responded "somewhat," and for frequency 57% responded "never" and 39% responded "sometimes." Thus, the authors concluded most did not integrate their sexual and religious identities. However, for some individuals integration was not relevant because they no longer identified as religious or with a religion. For those in which there was integration of religious and sexual identities, there were several factors identified that aided in this process. Some of these included knowledge of biblical and religious readings (49%), support of friends involved in the church (31%), and involvement in an affirming religious organization (27%).

It should be noted that for some gay men, involvement in a gay affirming religious organization, congregation, or place of worship has particular benefits for integration of identities; because in addition to religious homonegativity, they may experience prejudicial attitudes within the gay community about their religiousness. O'Brien (2004) described the "double stigma" experienced by gay Christians because of their being denounced by Christians for their homosexuality and rejected by other gays for their religiousness. However, in his interviews with gay Christians, several interviewees explained that the term double stigma did not best characterize their experience, rather "it was about 'living a contradiction that defines who I am'" (p. 181). Thus, their experience of identity integration was in reconciling this contradiction in identities. Having a community of like others in this regard can be supportive of one's identity and mental health. Conversely, feeling marginalized within the gay community or by other gays, as well as feeling marginalized by one's religious community, can be detrimental to one's identity and mental health.

Although involvement in a gay affirming church can be a means by which some men achieve integration of their religious and sexual identities, others may not feel comfortable with attending a "gay church," especially those men who were raised with conservative religious beliefs (Kubicek et al., 2009). Additionally, some Black gay Christians may feel uncomfortable with attending gay affirming churches because most gay affirming churches are predominately White and are not compatible with their own cultural experiences (Pitt, 2010). Alternatively, those men who do not find a gay affirming church appealing may choose to remain in the Church and will reconcile their identities in other ways, such as those mentioned earlier.

The process of religious and sexual identity integration can result in increased spirituality and self-acceptance (Dahl & Galliher, 2012) for religious MSM. In struggling with feelings resulting from religious homonegativity experienced in one's religion and church, spirituality allows for maintaining a connection with the Church for some, whereas for others it will allow for disconnecting from the church while keeping one's faith – an identity often characterized as "spiritual but not religious." This distinction that is made between religion and spirituality can aid in the process of identity integration.

Religiosity versus Spirituality

Religiosity and spirituality are variously defined in the literature. They are related concepts and people who are religious may be spiritual as well. Generally, religiosity or religiousness refers to maintaining a system of standardized beliefs and practices relating to spirituality that are shared among the members of a religious group (Tan, 2005). People who are religious hold the beliefs of their religion and uphold the practices of their religion, such as attending a place of worship, prayer, doing good deeds, believing in God and the scriptures/religious text, observing religious holidays, etc. Some scholars (e.g., Allport & Ross, 1967; Batson, 1982) refer to religiosity as being "extrinsic" in the sense that it is the practice of a religion and is institutional in nature, and where religion is used as a means to an end. However, one can have an "intrinsic" religious orientation, in which one's religion is more internally oriented and an end in itself. An intrinsic religious orientation is often equated with the spirituality aspect of religiosity. However, spirituality has been defined without respect to religiousness, in the sense that one can be spiritual and not religious. The definitions of spirituality that have been offered in the literature typically concern a journey or search with respect to the sacred (God), thoughts and feelings about the sacred, and understanding of and relatedness to the transcendent (Vieten et al., 2013). Generally, spirituality "pertains to the sense of meaning, purpose, and morality that individuals espouse regarding their lives" (Tan, 2005, p. 136).

MSM more often identify as spiritual than religious, which may be a result of religious homonegativity. Halkitis et al. (2009) sought to identify the meanings that are constructed of the terms religiosity and spirituality by LGBT persons by asking 498 participants (52% male) to provide written responses to two open-ended questions: "What does 'spirituality' mean to you?" and "What does 'religiosity' mean to you?" They also rated themselves on how religious and spiritual they are, and how important religion and spirituality are to them (*not at all* to *very*). Their responses indicated they were more spiritual than religious, and likewise spirituality was more important to them than religion. There were no differences according to gender or race/ethnicity. Definitions of religion "focused on structured, communal forms of worship (e.g., organized worship), beliefs in and relationship with God (or a system of Gods), as well as on prescribed, rule-based patterns of devotional practice," whereas "definitions of spirituality focused on relationship with God/higher power and with self and others" (Halkitis et al., 2009, p. 260). The researchers concluded that spirituality may be how LGBT individuals differentiate religion as institutionalized beliefs and practices that may be used to support bias (e.g., anti-gay) from the "more subjectively meaningful beliefs and practices that affirm LGBT individuals' sense of worth and connectedness to others" (p. 260).

Research with MSM typically has found spirituality to be associated with positive outcomes and religiosity to be associated with negative outcomes.

For example, spiritual coping, or reliance on spirituality as a source of strength, was positively associated with self-esteem, whereas religious commitment was negatively associated (Meanley, Pingel, & Bauermeister, 2016). In a sample of gay Orthodox Jews, spirituality was positively related to life satisfaction and positive affect (e.g., experiencing positive emotions such as excitement, enthusiasm, pride, inspired, and interested), whereas religiosity was not related to either (Harari et al., 2014). In studies of African-American MSM, spirituality was negatively associated with depression and substance use (alcohol, crack, and cocaine), and positively associated with resilience and social support, whereas religiosity was positively associated with depression and using substances (Lassiter et al., 2015; Watkins et al., 2016).

However, religion or the Church may serve as a protective factor for some MSM as well as sexual minority adolescents. Lassiter (2014) noted how African-American Christian churches can be a source that affirms the masculine identity of African-American men due to the challenges to their masculinity from the hegemonic society. In a qualitative study conducted with 31 young African-American MSM, "several men reported that that their religion helped them feel empowered to confront life's challenges effectively, increased their ability to establish internal peace and helped them accept the difficult situations they faced" (Foster, Arnold, Rebchook, & Kegeles, 2011, p. 1110). In another study of ten HIV symptomatic men (nine who were African-American), African-American men viewed the Black Church as their religious and spiritual foundation, and their religious experiences as more spiritually satisfying than experiences defined as spiritual (Seegers, 2007). Although rewarding, spiritual experiences were activities that are not religious and are more solitary (e.g., meditating, exercise, being with nature), whereas religious experiences were activities that involved the church and doing for others (e.g., leading Bible study, teaching Sunday school, driving for Meals on Wheels). In a study of sexual minority adolescents, Rosario, Yali, Hunter, and Gwadz (2006) found religious participation served as a protective factor for male adolescents but not female adolescents. Male adolescents who were religiously affiliated had less suicidal ideation, used less alcohol and marijuana, and had fewer sexual experiences. One possible explanation offered was that the male adolescents had achieved better sexual and religious identity integration.

Conceptualization, Assessment, and Counseling Interventions

Conceptualization

MSM or SSA men who present for counseling may experience conflict about their sexual identity, religious/spiritual identity, and/or masculine identity. These three identities may intersect, as well as intersect with one's racial/ethnic identity, especially in racial/ethnic minority men. The concept of intersectionality concerns how the interconnectedness of multiple identities affect a person's life experiences and circumstances, as opposed to each aspect of identity in isolation; in particular, the experience of societal prejudice and discrimination (Garcia, 2017). For example, a gay man has to deal with sexual prejudice. A Black man has to deal with racial discrimination. A Black gay man will have to deal with both. He may face racism in the White gay community and sexual prejudice or homonegativity in the Black community. In addition to the experience of prejudice and discrimination, the person may feel he does not completely belong in one group or another, which can lead to feelings of isolation, anxiety, and depression (Equality Network, n.d.).

The intersection and competition of multiple identities results in incongruence (Read & Eagle, 2011). Beliefs associated with one's sexuality or sexual identity exist alongside one's religious beliefs or religious identity, and may compete with each other. The concept of incongruence is similar to that of Festinger's (1957) cognitive dissonance theory (Metin & Metin Camgoz, 2011). Cognitive dissonance theory is often referred to in the literature as a way to conceptualize this conflict in identity. MSM may reject institutional religion or a gay identity, or they may reject religion and cultivate their spiritual identity, as a way to resolve the dissonance.

Assessment

For counselors working with SSA male clients, it would be important to assess: (1) the client's religious beliefs/identity, sexual identity, and masculinity ideology; (2) the extent to which there is identity conflict; and (3) whether such conflict is related to the presenting problem.

Inquire about the client's feelings and attitudes toward his sexuality

What is the client's sexual identity and how salient is it? Does he consider himself gay, bisexual, heterosexual with same-sex attraction, homosexual but not gay? Is he confused or conflicted about his sexuality, such that there is no sexual identity? How does he feel about his sexual identity (or lack thereof)? If he has negative feelings and attitudes, or internalized homonegativity, to what extent are they due to his religion or religious beliefs? To what extent does the client feel he can express his sexual identity, and in what context does he feel he can or cannot express it?

Some men may ask whether they can change their sexual orientation or rid themselves of their same-sex attraction and seek change-oriented therapy. Professional organizations such as the American Psychological Association, American Counseling Association, and National Association of Social Workers have provided a statement on sexual orientation change efforts (SOCE) that in essence does not support their efficacy or use. It would therefore be important to understand the reasoning behind his desire to change his sexual feelings or desires. To the extent that religion underlies his reasons, the client's religious beliefs will need to be explored.

Inquire about the client's religious background, any current religious beliefs, and his spirituality

Does the client have a religious or spiritual identity; and if so, how salient is it? Does he distinguish between religion and spirituality? To what extent does his religious or spiritual identity make life harder or more fulfilling? Are the client's religious beliefs intractable? How does he use religion to cope? Pargament, Smith, Koenig, and Perez (1998) differentiated positive religious coping from negative religious coping (see Chapter 1). Does the client's use of religion include forgiveness, spiritual support, and seeking comfort in God (positive coping), or does he experience spiritual and religious discontent, God as punishing, and question the power of God (negative coping)? Is he involved in a religious community, and if so what is the nature of that involvement? To what extent does the client feel he can express his religious identity, and in what contexts does he feel he can or cannot express it?

Inquire about the client's masculinity ideology

The extent to which the client's masculinity ideology conflicts with his sexual identity and religious beliefs should be assessed. He may feel he does not live up to the masculinity ideology of his religion, or that his masculinity ideology conflicts with having a gay identity. Wade's (1998) theory of male identity can be useful in making this assessment. Wade hypothesized that some men "may have difficulty relating or feeling close to other men, feel uncomfortable in groups of men, be confused or conflicted about what it means to be a man, and basically feel different from other men" (Wade & Coughlin, 2012, p. 328) because they do not have a sense of connectedness or feelings of similarity to other men. Further, Wade offered that a man can feel conflicted about what it means to be a man due to differences in his male reference groups, referred to as "a torn allegiance." Given this conceptualization, some men may feel torn between the masculinity ideology of gay men as a reference group and the masculinity ideology of their religion or the men in their religion as a reference group. For example, in a sample of highly intrinsically religious men who had been involved in SOCE, a male identity characterized by a lack of psychological relatedness to other males received the highest endorsement, whereas a male identity characterized by feeling similar to all males received the lowest endorsement; results that were contrary to all prior studies (Karten & Wade, 2010).

The strategy would be to assess the extent to which the client feels a sense of connectedness to other men, given his masculinity ideology. What are his thoughts on what it means to be a man? Does he feel a sense of connection with other men at his place of worship? Does he feel a sense of connection with gay men? Do his beliefs about masculinity or manhood conflict with his religion? Do his beliefs about masculinity or manhood conflict with his perception of gay masculinity? If there are conflicting notions of manhood, does this result in feelings of alienation, loneliness, and insecurity?

Counseling Interventions

For men who are conflicted about their same-sex attraction, or do not want to have such feelings, the counseling goal would be to help them accept their feelings of attraction. In this regard, the client may or may not accept a gay identity; however, whatever sexual identity the client chooses for himself, acceptance of their same-sex attraction would nonetheless be of paramount importance. To the extent that religion or religious identity is in conflict with his feelings of same-sex attraction, counseling will involve working toward identity integration or personal congruence. Several models will be briefly discussed and readers should review the referenced articles for details on their application.

Some men will not have a conflict about their sexual identity but may be struggling with their religious identity. For example, the client accepts his same-sex attraction or sexuality but is having difficulty reconciling his religious beliefs or the religious teachings of his Church and/or family. Bozard and Sanders (2011) developed the GRACE model for use with LGB clients who want or need help with religious issues; in particular, those who have a desire to explore religious forms of spiritual engagement. The acronym GRACE stands for Goal exploration, Renewal of hope, Action, Connection, and Empowerment. To briefly summarize the model, the counselor explores the client's religious history and feelings about religion; identifies what kind of religious life the client would like to have; increases the client's awareness of possible options for positive religious engagement (e.g., gay affirmative places of worship); assists with seeking a religious connection in a new community and/or a new way of understanding and relating to God; and promotes empowerment.

Most models of counseling and psychotherapy that are described in the literature that address identity conflict suggest that the counselor do the following therapeutic strategies (see Haldeman, 1996; Harari et al., 2014; Kocet, Sanabria, & Smith, 2011; Kubicek et al., 2009; Lassiter, 2014; Pietkiewicz & Kołodziejczyk-Skrzypek, 2016):

- Ascertain the significance of religion and spirituality in the client's life.
- Explore unresolved feelings or conflicts that are about religion/spirituality.
- Analyze meanings ascribed to being gay, with reference to religion.
- Develop a better understanding of what spirituality means to the client.
- Identify ways to integrate religious/spiritual beliefs with the client's sexual identity.
- Help the client maximize the benefits of their religion and minimize the negative aspects.
- Assist in seeking and connecting with religious support groups for sexual minorities.
- Provide knowledge and emotional support.

Buchanan, Dzelme, Harris, and Hecker (2001) offered a narrative perspective that can be used with men who identify as gay and are experiencing conflict with their religious identity. This conflict or struggle between identities has become an internalized discourse, or a person's dominant story, in which religious beliefs are unquestioned and are assumed realities. The narrative perspective explores these beliefs for their underlying influences and effects. Externalizing conversations change the internalized discourse to one that is external and exposed, which then can be acted upon. The therapist attempts to deconstruct the problematic narrative, and through this process identify the client's preferred ways of being. Buchanan and colleagues provided examples of questions that the therapist can use to explore the client's extrinsic/religious beliefs, attitudes, and practices; explore his or her intrinsic/spiritual beliefs, attitudes, and practices; and deconstruction questions for both religion and spirituality. The authors noted that although the narrative perspective they offered emphasized the exploration and deconstruction of the client's spiritual/religious beliefs, this same process can be adapted for clients whose issues concern their sexual identity.

Throckmorton and Yarhouse (2006) developed "sexual identity therapy" to treat clients who are experiencing sexual identity conflicts. Such conflicts occur when there is dissonance between one's sexual feelings and one's personal values; for example, when a man's feelings of same-sex attraction conflict with his religious beliefs and values. The objective or outcome of the therapy is sexual identity synthesis characterized by personal congruence. During the assessment phase, it is vital to assess the consequences of same-sex attraction or a gay identity for the client with respect to other aspects of his identity and his familial attachments; recognizing that the consequences could possibly be undesirable, placing the other aspects of his identity at risk. However, it is also possible that synthesis of a gay or homosexual or bisexual identity would be the preferred treatment strategy. Counselors assist clients with clarifying their values to be able to determine what the client prefers as a course of action. Counseling may primarily involve providing support as the client considers and mulls over his options. As he begins to take action toward synthesis, therapeutic interventions are employed to help him accept his thoughts, feelings, and desires, gain self-awareness and self-acceptance, and pursue the behavior he personally values while refraining from unvalued behaviors.

Tan and Yarhouse (2010) applied the practice of mindfulness to sexual identity therapy as a way for clients to become aware of their feelings of same-sex attraction without judgment or self-condemnation. The strategy involves acknowledging and accepting one's feelings and behaviors without necessarily approving or condoning them, which may run contrary to their religious values. With acceptance there is no judgment of right or wrong, good or bad that may evoke feelings of distress. Thus, same-sex attraction loses its valence and is no longer viewed as a problematic experience. The authors suggested a variety of mindfulness exercises that can be used for "acceptance of same-sex attraction, managing compulsivity, navigating religious identity conflicts, dealing with emotional reactivity, and enhancing sexual intimacy" (p. 505).

Bibliotherapy

Bibliotherapy can be a useful intervention whereby books and websites that address religious and sexual identity conflict can normalize the client's experience and facilitate analyzing, questioning, and scrutinizing of religious ideology (Bayne, 2016). Schuck and Liddle (2001) identified the most helpful books that participants in their study used in resolving conflict between their sexuality and religion:

- McNeill's (2015) *The church and the homosexual.*
- Boswell's (1980) *Christianity, social tolerance, and homosexuality.*
- Helminiak's (1994) *What the Bible* really *says about homosexuality.*
- Piazza's (1997) *Holy homosexuals: The truth about being gay or lesbian and Christian.*
- Scanzoni and Mollenkotts's (1978) *Is the homosexual my neighbor?*
- Spong's (1992) *Rescuing the Bible from fundamentalism: A bishop rethinks the meaning of scripture.*
- Williams's (1992) *Spirit and the flesh: Sexual diversity in American Indian culture.*

Additionally, Bowland, Foster, and Vosler (2013) suggested two resources that address alternative ways of interpreting religious texts:

- Scanzoni and Mollenkott's (1994) *Is the homosexual my neighbor? A positive Christian response* (revised and updated version of the above).
- Nelson's (1978) *Embodiment: An approach to sexuality and Christian theology.*

Organizations

Several authors have identified organizations that are supportive of sexual minority individuals with a religious identity (Buchanan et al., 2001; Minwalla, Simon Roser, Feldman, & Varga, 2005; Schuck & Liddle, 2001). These organizations include places of worship and other organizations or groups that are considered gay affirming or welcoming. Below are some examples:

- Courage, a nationally founded religious organization for gay Catholics.
- Integrity (for Episcopalians).
- "Open and Affirming Churches" program (United Church of Christ).
- "Welcoming Congregations" program (Unitarian-Universalist).
- Unity Church.

- Metropolitan Community Church (Christian).
- Al-Fatiha is an Internet-based organization within Islam.
- The Episcopal Church.
- The Evangelical Lutheran Church of America.
- Friends General Conference (Quakers).
- The Presbyterian Church.

Counselors should assist the client in identifying ways and places that he can be involved within an affirming religious community, if he has no affiliation or the affiliation that he currently has is unsatisfying to him and his religion is a salient aspect of his identity. He may or may not be aware of such opportunities. It may be that he does not need or want to have such involvement. However, we recommend that this be explored and then encouraged if there is any ambivalence.

Case Example

Andrew came to the university counseling center on the recommendation of one of his professors with whom he had a close and supportive relationship. He was a piano performance major in his senior year, which required several hours daily of individual practice in addition to classes and other course work. However, recently he was not able to practice and was having difficulty with performing academically as well, and both he and his teacher were quite concerned about it. In the initial interview with Andrew I (Wade) inquired about when he first started having these difficulties. He stated that after the Christmas holiday when he returned for the second semester he was unable to concentrate and was finding it difficult to be motivated to perform. After asking about what had happened over the winter break, he told me a story about how his family confronted him about his sexuality and told him he could not return home unless he stopped being a homosexual. Andrew asked if I could help him get his family to accept him.

Andrew was 22 years old, White, and from an upper middle-class Catholic family. He was very attractive and somewhat feminine in his demeanor. Upon meeting him, I had the immediate impression that he was gay, and I thought most people who met him would have the same impression. He was tall, of average build, impeccably dressed, and exceedingly well groomed. He did not look like a college student, rather he looked like a male model. He was somewhat grandiose as he talked about himself and his talent, but he was also a perfectionistic and overly self-critical. He came from an intact, religious family and had an older brother who was 24 years old. The family was well known in their community and they attended church weekly. There were several priests and nuns in his extended family.

The confrontation about his sexuality was as a result of Andrew's older brother finding some emails on Andrew's computer that were from a guy whom Andrew had been dating. His brother told their mother who told their father, and the three of them brought Andrew into the living room one evening and confronted him, asking him if he was homosexual and what the emails were about. Andrew felt attacked and did not know how to respond. His father was the primary inquisitor, but Andrew felt his mother and brother did nothing to support him. They all believed him to be a sinner and that he needed to stop sinning. Andrew relayed to me how his father asked him whether he had had sex with a female, and that since he never had he was told that he needed to have sex with a woman in order to cure him of his homosexuality. His father said he would rather have a criminal as a son than a son who is homosexual. Andrew would no longer be a member of the family if he continued to be a homosexual. He was not to return home and they would not attend his graduation, unless he were to stop being a homosexual.

His story was tragic, and it was a painful story to tell and hear as he cried telling it. It was surprising to me that his family had not considered that Andrew was gay; they had responded as if it were a total shock to them. It occurred to me that maybe their eyes were closed to his being gay because of their strong religious beliefs, such that it was impossible to think they had a gay son and brother – kind of like hearing that your son or brother is a mass murderer. Although the signs were there, it is too incredible to believe. This, as well as other parts of his story, signaled to me that it was not likely that his family would accept him unless he were to live as heterosexual. I explained to Andrew that I would not be able to get his family to accept him. What I could help him with was being able to deal with being rejected by his family. His inability to concentrate and to practice was because of the traumatic experience of being rejected by his family over the winter break. Not only was it the rejection but also the ultimatum in which he must decide what to do. I told him I could help him with making a decision about what to do as well.

Our initial sessions focused on his sexual identity. His sexual identity intersected with his religious identity, but it was not clear initially which was more salient. He felt he was gay, and he did not feel that he could be heterosexual, but he also thought maybe he should try to be heterosexual. After the family confrontation, he stopped seeing the guy he had been dating. He was somewhat confused about whether being gay was a sin or not, because his family said that it was a sin and he was "evil," and he had heard people in his community express such views. Yet, he did not think that God viewed him as a sinner or evil for being gay. With regard to internalized homophobia, it was minimal. Nonetheless, the combination of his family's recent condemnation and rejection of him for being gay, compounded by a religious background environment that was anti-gay, Andrew was considering conversion therapy. Our counseling sessions were consistent with sexual identity therapy (Throckmorton & Yarhouse, 2006). We examined the pros and cons, so to speak, of his not acting on his same-sex attraction and pursuing heterosexual romantic and sexual relationships. He thought his "choice" was to not be his authentic self and be miserable but still be a part of his family, or be his authentic self but be miserable without his family. With support, lots of discussion, and clarification of his values he came to the conclusion that he may be *less* miserable if he can live as a gay man even if his family never accepts him.

When we discussed his religious beliefs and identify and the extent to which they conflicted with his sexuality, Andrew did not have negative feelings about his religion or feel that there was much conflict. What was problematic for him was that he grew up in a church community, a parish, and the rejection by his family meant he could no longer be a part of that community. So, he not only was experiencing the loss of his family but the loss of his faith community as well. Nonetheless, I suggested Andrew read some literature on the Catholic Church and its teachings on homosexuality, because many people are not aware of its position, even Catholics and apparently his own family. He could start by using the Internet to find this information, and if he wanted a comprehensive coverage of the topic there were some books he could read. We had a few conversations about the information he found online and his understanding of and reactions to the material. However, I also acknowledged my limitations in knowing about how the Church's position on homosexuality translates into actions and the experiences of gay Catholics. Consequently, we also explored the possibility of his joining a support group of gay Catholics or Christians. The support group could serve several purposes: discuss topics related to being gay and Christian/Catholic, provide feelings of belongingness relative to a faith community and the gay community, and create a sense of family to replace the loss of his "real" family.

Although Andrew's presenting problem was his not being able to practice piano and a deterioration in his academic performance, the reason for this problem was depression and anxiety resulting from the ultimatum and rejection by his family. As Andrew was able to better accept the rejection, although not fully, and decide what to do about his sexuality given the ultimatum, he became less depressed and anxious and was able to function well again academically. However, he continued to struggle with the rejection and loss, and had the fantasy that his family would come to their senses and accept him as he is. As spring break approached we talked about what he would do, given he was told not to come home. With my assistance Andrew had sought out a support group on campus. There was no group of gay Christians, but there was a group for gay and lesbian students. They would meet and have lunch or coffee and go to discussions and presentations on campus that addressed issues relevant to LGBTQ students. He decided he would not go home, rather he would connect with his friends who would also be around campus during the break. This saddened him that he could not go home. He had called his brother to ask about going home, to get a sense of whether the family had changed their position. He was told that there was no change in the family's stance.

After spring break Andrew did not return for his sessions with me. I tried contacting him but got no response. A month later he returned to the counseling center, when there was only one month left in the semester before graduation. He explained that he ended up going home for spring break and that his family rejected him again. When he returned to school he was depressed and started abusing alcohol, not attending classes, and basically was now at risk for not graduating. The same music professor who had been supportive got him to return to counseling. We processed what had happened and why, in terms of his continued need to be accepted by his family and why they continued to reject him. He expressed anger about his parents and blamed religion, whereas prior to this second rejection he only wanted to please his parents or change their mind about him. We explored his feelings for each family member, and where he felt they stood individually on his being gay and ostracized. He thought his mother was more accepting of his being gay and would likely change her mind one day about his being out of the family, but his father was adamant. The brother was also wanting him to remain with the family, but was telling him to get a girlfriend and that things would work out; basically, he told him to be "in the closet."

Given the limited amount of time left to work with Andrew, the goal became making sure that he graduated. Therefore, he needed to stop drinking, focus on making up the work he missed so that he could graduate, and gain support for his struggles. The counseling relationship, the relationship with his professor, and his relationships with his gay friends from the support group were his sources of support. His angry feelings needed to be expressed instead of drowned with alcohol. His anger at religion and his family gave vent in sessions, and we decided it would be best to stay away from both his family and the Church for the present. He had no negative feelings or conflicts about being gay; in fact, he was even more determined to be his authentic self, and to do so he now rejected both his family and his religion. Andrew was able to pull it together enough to graduate, and our sessions ended with him hopeful about his future and more realistic about his family.

This case of rather brief counseling illustrates the interaction of sexual identity conflict and religious context in terms of a young gay man and his religious family. The conflict was not so much between his sexual identity and religious identity, rather it was his sexual identity and the context of a rejecting and unsupportive religious family. The cause or source of the identity conflict can be characterized as extrinsic, "coming from outside of the individual and more dependent on acceptance by others" (Rodriguez, 2009, p. 10). The possible resolutions to the identity conflict are the rejection of a gay identity or religious identity, separation of the gay self from the religious self, or integration of one's gay and religious identities (Beagan & Hattie, 2015). Andrew ultimately rejected his family and his religion. Masculinity was not an issue for Andrew, perhaps because of his being slightly narcissistic and because within the artistic fields his manner would be viewed as rather typical. Additionally, his family did not comment on his masculinity or lack thereof, even after being outed by his brother. It is possible that with regard to his religious identity, he may eventually seek out a faith community. He was encouraged to do so if and when he felt he was ready.

References

Allport, G.W., & Ross, J.M. (1967). Personal religious orientation and prejudice. *Journal of Personality and Social Psychology, 5*(4), 432–443.

Barnes, D., & Meyer, I. (2012). Religious affiliation, internalized homophobia, and mental health in lesbians, gay men and bisexuals. *American Journal of Orthopsychiatry, 82*(4), 505–515.

Batson, D. (1982). *Religion and the individual.* New York, NY: Oxford University Press.

Bayne, H.B. (2016). Helping gay and lesbian students integrate sexual and religious identities. *Journal of College Counseling, 19*(1), 61–75.

Beagan, B.L., & Hattie, B. (2015). Religion, spirituality, and LGBTQ identity integration. *Journal of LGBT Issues in Counseling, 9*(2), 92–117.

Boswell, J. (1980). *Christianity, social tolerance, and homosexuality.* Chicago, IL: University of Chicago Press.

Bowland, S.E., Foster, K., & Vosler, A.N.R. (2013). Culturally competent and spiritually sensitive therapy with lesbian and gay Christians. *Social Work, 58*(4), 321–332.

Bozard, R.L. Jr., & Sanders, C.J. (2011). Helping Christian lesbian, gay, and bisexual clients recover religion as a source of strength: Developing a model for assessment and integration of religious identity in counseling. *Journal of LGBT Issues in Counseling, 5*(1), 47–74.

Buchanan, M., Dzelme, K., Harris, D., & Hecker, L. (2001). Challenges of being simultaneously gay or lesbian and spiritual and/or religious: A narrative perspective. *The American Journal of Family Therapy, 29*(5), 435–449.

Burdette, A.M., Ellison, C.G., & Hill, T.D. (2005). Conservative Protestantism and tolerance towards homosexuals: An examination of potential mechanisms. *Sociological Inquiry, 75*(2), 177–196.

Christman, S.T. (2012). Coping with homonegative experiences among gay men: Impacts on mental health, psychological well-being, and identity growth. *Open Access Dissertations.* Paper 775. https://scholarlyrepository.miami.edu/cgi/viewcontent.cgi?referer=https://www.google.co.id/&httpsredir=1&article=1771&context=oa_dissertations.

Dahl, A.L., & Galliher, R.V. (2009). LGBQQ young adult experiences of religious and sexual identity integration. *Journal of LGBT Issues in Counseling, 3*(2), 92–112.

Dahl, A.L., & Galliher, R.V. (2012). LGBTQ adolescents and young adults raised within a Christian religious context: Positive and negative outcomes. *Journal of Adolescence, 35*(6), 1611–1618.

Equality Network. (n.d.). *Intersectionality.* Retrieved from www.equality-network.org/our-work/intersectional/.

Festinger, L. (1957). *A theory of cognitive dissonance.* Evanstone, IL: Row, Peterson.

Foster, M., Arnold, E., Rebchook, G., & Kegeles, S. (2011). "It's my inner strength": Spirituality, religion and HIV in the lives of young African American men who have sex with men. *Culture, Health & Sexuality, 13*(9), 1103–1117.

Garcia, J.D. (2017). Intersectionality. *Research Starters: Sociology*. Retrieved from http://eds.a.ebscohost.com.liverpool.idm.oclc.org/eds/detail/detail?sid=fed0be7d-d1fd-4827-9736-447aa3c1718d%40sessionmgr4008&vid=10&hid=4113&bdata=JnNpdGU9ZWRzLWxpdmUmc2NvcGU9c2l0ZQ%3d%3d#AN=108690556&db=ers.

Gelfer, J. (2009). *Numen, old men: Contemporary masculine spiritualities and the problem of patriarchy*. New York, NY: Routledge.

Haldeman, D.C. (1996). Spirituality and religion in the lives of lesbians and gay men. In R.P. Cabaj & T.S. Stein (Eds.), *Textbook of homosexuality and mental health* (pp. 881–896). Washington, DC: American Psychiatric Press.

Halkitis, P.N., Mattis, J.S., Sahadath, J.K., Massie, D., Ladyzhenskaya, L., Pitrelli, K., . . . & Cowie, S.E. (2009). The meanings and manifestations of religion and spirituality among lesbian, gay, bisexual, and transgender adults. *Journal of Adult Development, 16*(4), 250–262.

Harari, E., Glenwick, D.S., & Cecero, J. . (2014). The relationship between religiosity/spirituality and well-being in gay and heterosexual Orthodox Jews. *Mental Health, Religion, & Culture, 17*(9), 886–897.

Helminiak, D.A. (1994). *What the Bible really says about homosexuality*. Estancia, NM: Alamo Square Press.

Hudson, W.W., & Ricketts, W.A. (1980). A strategy for the measurement of homophobia. *Journal of Homosexuality, 5*(4), 357–372.

Jäckle, S., & Wenzelburger, G. (2015). Religion, religiosity, and the attitudes toward homosexuality: A multilevel analysis of 79 countries. *Journal of Homosexuality, 62*(2), 207–241.

Jamal, A. (2001). The story of Lot and the Quran's perception of the morality of same-sex sexuality. *Journal of Homosexuality, 41*(1), 1-88.

Jeffries, W.L., Dodge, B., & Sandfort, T.G.M. (2008). Religion and spirituality among bisexual Black men in the USA. *Culture, Health, & Sexuality, 10*(5), 463-477.

Karten, E.Y., & Wade, J.C. (2010). Sexual orientation change efforts in men: A client perspective. *Journal of Men's Studies, 18*(1), 84–102.

Kocet, M.M., Sanabria, A., & Smith, M.R. (2011). Finding the spirit within: Religion, spirituality, and faith development in lesbian, gay, and bisexual individuals. *Journal of LGBT Issues in Counseling, 5*(3–4), 163–179.

Kubicek, K., McDavitt, B., Carpineto, J., Weiss, G., Iverson, E.F., & Kipke, M.D. (2009). "God made me gay for a reason": Young men who have sex with men's resiliency in resolving internalized homophobia from religious sources. *Journal of Adolescent Research, 24*(5), 601–633.

Lassiter, J.M. (2014). Extracting dirt from water: A strengths-based approach to religion for African American same-gender-loving men. *Journal of Religion and Health, 53*(1), 178–189.

Lassiter, J.M., Grov, C., Ventuneac, A., Starks, T., & Parsons, J.T. (2015, November 2). *Spirituality and multiple dimensions of religion are associated with mental health in gay and bisexual men: Results from the one thousand strong panel*. Paper presented at the annual meeting of the American Public Health Association, Chicago, IL.

Lease, S.H., Horne, S.G., & Noffsinger-Frazier, N. (2005). Affirming faith experiences and psychological health for Caucasian lesbian, gay, and bisexual individuals. *Journal of Counseling Psychology, 52*(3), 378–388.

Mayfield, W. (2001). The development of an internalized homonegativity inventory for gay men. *Journal of Homosexuality, 41*(2), 53–76.
McGlasson, T.D., & Rubel, D.J. (2015). My soul to take: A phenomenology of the struggle for an authentic gay spirituality. *Counseling and Values, 60*(1), 14–31.
McNeill, J.J. (2015). *The church and the homosexual* (4th ed.). Boston, MA: Beacon Press.
Meanley, S., Pingel, E.S., & Bauermeister, J.A. (2016). Psychological well-being among religious and spiritual-identified young gay and bisexual men. *Sex Research and Social Policy, 13*(1), 35–45.
Metin, I., & Metin Camgoz, S. (2011). The advances in the history of cognitive dissonance theory. *International Journal of Humanities and Social Science, 1*(6), 131–136.
Minwalla, O., Simon Roser, B.R., Feldman, J., & Varga, C. (2005). Identity experience among progressive gay Muslims in North America: A qualitative study within Al-Fatiha. *Culture, Health & Sexuality, 7*(2), 113–128.
Nelson, J.B. (1978). *Embodiment: An approach to sexuality and Christian theology.* Minneapolis, MN: Augsburg Publishing House.
O'Brien, J. (2004). Wrestling the angel of contradiction: Queer Christian identities. *Culture and Religion, 5*(2), 179–202.
Pargament, K.I., Smith, B.W., Koenig, H.G., & Perez, L. (1998). Patterns of positive and negative religious coping with major life stressors. *Journal for the Scientific Study of Religion, 37*(4), 710–724.
Pew Research Center. (2011). *Muslim Americans: No signs of growth in alienation or support for extremism.* Retrieved from www.people-press.org/2011/08/30/muslim-americans-no-signs-of-growth-in-alienation-or-support-for-extremism/.
Piazza, M.S. (1997). *Holy homosexuals: The truth about being gay or lesbian and Christian.* Dallas, TX: Sources of Hope Publishing.
Pietkiewicz, I.J., & Kołodziejczyk-Skrzypek, M. (2016). Living in sin? How gay Catholics manage their conflicting sexual and religious identities. *Archives of Sexual Behavior, 45*(6), 1573–1585.
Pitt, R.N. (2010). Still looking for my Jonathan: Black gay men's management of religious and sexual identity conflicts. *Journal of Homosexuality, 57*(1), 39–53.
Quinn, K., Dickson-Gomez, J., & Kelly, J.A. (2016). The role of the Black Church in the lives of young Black men who have sex with men. *Culture, Health, & Sexuality, 18*(5), 524–537.
Read, J.G., & Eagle, D.E. (2011). Intersecting identities as a source of religious incongruence. *Journal for the Scientific Study of Religion, 50*(1), 116–132.
Rodriguez, E.M. (2009). At the intersection of church and gay: A review of the psychological research on gay and lesbian Christians. *Journal of Homosexuality, 57*(1), 5–38.
Rosario, M., Yali, A.M., Hunter, J., & Gwadz, M.V. (2006). Religion and health among lesbian, gay and bisexual youths: An empirical investigation and theoretical explanation. In A.M. Omoto & H.S. Kurtzman (Eds.), *Sexual orientation and mental health: Examining identity and development in lesbian, gay and bisexual people* (pp. 117–140). Washington, DC: American Psychological Association.
Scanzoni, L., & Mollenkott, V.R. (1978). *Is the homosexual my neighbor?* New York, NY: Harper & Row.
Scanzoni, L.D., & Mollenkott, V.R. (1994) *Is the homosexual my neighbor? A positive Christian response* (revised and updated). New York, NY: HarperCollins Publishers.

Schuck, K.D., & Liddle, B.J. (2001). Religious conflicts experienced by lesbian, gay, and bisexual individuals. *Journal of Gay & Lesbian Psychotherapy, 5*(2), 63–82.

Seegers, D. (2007). Spiritual and religious experiences of gay men with HIV illness. *Journal of the Association of Nurses in AIDS Care, 18*(3), 5–12.

Severson, N., Munoz-Laboy, M., & Kaufman, R. (2014). "At times, I feel like I'm sinning": The paradoxical role of non-lesbian, gay, bisexual and transgender-affirming religion in the lives of behaviourally-bisexual Latino men. *Culture, Health & Sexuality, 16*(2), 136–148.

Sherkat, D. (2002). Sexuality and religious commitment in the United States: An empirical examination. *Journal for the Scientific Study of Religion, 41*(2), 313–323.

Shilo, G., Yosef, I., & Savaya, R. (2016). Religious coping strategies and mental health among religious Jewish gay and bisexual men. *Archives of Sexual Behavior, 45*, 1551–1561.

Sowe, B.J., Brown, J., & Taylor, A.J. (2014). Sex and the sinner: Comparing religious and nonreligious same-sex attracted adults on internalized homonegativity and distress. *American Journal of Orthopsychiatry, 84*(5), 530–544.

Spong, J.S. (1992). *Rescuing the Bible from fundamentalism: A bishop rethinks the meaning of scripture.* New York, NY: HarperCollins Publishers.

Sumerau, J.E. (2012). "That's what a man is supposed to do": Compensatory manhood acts in an LGBT Christian church. *Gender & Society, 26*(3), 461–487.

Tan, E.S.N., & Yarhouse, M.A. (2010). Facilitating congruence between religious beliefs and sexual identity with mindfulness. *Psychotherapy Theory, Research, Practice, Training, 47*(4), 500–511.

Tan, P.P. (2005). The importance of spirituality among gay and lesbian individuals. *Journal of Homosexuality, 49*(2), 135–144.

Throckmorton, W., & Yarhouse, M.A. (2006). Sexual identity therapy: Practice framework for managing sexual identity conflicts. Retrieved from http://sitframework.com/wp-content/uploads/2009/07/sexualidentitytherapyframeworkfinal.pdf.

Vieten, C., Scammell, S., Pilato, R., Ammondson, I., Pargament, K.I., & Lukoff, D. (2013). Spiritual and religious competencies for psychologists. *Psychology of Religion and Spirituality, 5*(3), 129–144.

Wade, J.C. (1998). Male reference group identity dependence: A theory of male identity. *The Counseling Psychologist, 26*(3), 349–383.

Wade, J.C., & Coughlin, P. (2012). Male reference group identity dependence, masculinity ideology, and relationship satisfaction in men's heterosexual romantic relationships. *Psychology of Men & Masculinity, 13*(4), 325–339.

Watkins, T.L. Jr., Simpson, C., Cofield, S.S., Davies, S., Kohler, C., & Usdan, S. (2016). The relationship of religiosity, spirituality, substance abuse, and depression among Black men who have sex with men (MSM). *Journal of Religion and Health, 55*(1), 255–268.

Williams, W.L. (1992). *Spirit and the flesh: Sexual diversity in American Indian culture.* Boston, MA: Beacon Press.

9 Religious Drifters

Demographic shifts in religious affiliation have become increasingly apparent as less people in the United States identify with a world religion and are categorized as religiously unaffiliated, atheist, or agnostic. Gender differences exist within those demographic shifts as more men have identified as atheists and religiously unaffiliated compared to women in the United States (Pew, 2014). The shifting demographic trends also highlight most people in the United States have maintained spiritual beliefs (e.g., belief in God) but have become disenchanted with religious institutions and have adhered to the increasing secularization of US culture. In this chapter we define a religious drifter and differentiate drifters from other religiously unaffiliated men. The particular focus is on those men who are not affiliated with any religion because their spiritual and religious needs have not been met. Religious drifters may lack meaning in their life and express disappointment, sadness, and discontent without a spiritual home. Therefore, this chapter will suggest to mental health professionals ways to assess the client's religious and spiritual journey to identify their narrative about drifting, investigate possible connections between their masculinity ideology and religious non-affiliation, and implement clinical techniques that explore the various possible ways of being meaningfully involved in a religious community, if the client so desires.

Religiously Unaffiliated Men

The term "religiously unaffiliated," also referred to as "religious nones," is a classification that encompasses a diverse group of people (Wilkins-Laflamme, 2015). This would include men who are atheist, agnostic, religious drifters, those who have no religious preference, and the "unchurched believer."

Although by definition an atheist is someone who does not believe in God, Speed and Fowler (2016) differentiate between lacking a belief in God (negative atheism) and declaring God does not exist (positive atheism). Further, they argued that a person can identify with a religious faith without having a belief in God. Similarly, agnostics are not a homogenous group in that it includes those who have the view that no one knows if God exists, those who say it is impossible to know that God exists, and those who have no strong or significant belief in God or are unsure about the existence of God (Benn, 1999). Here again, it is possible for a person to question the existence of God and yet identify with a religious faith.

The unchurched believer is a term coined by Hout and Fischer (2002) to describe the "new unreligious" who believe in God or a higher power but do not have a religion. They tend to have strongly negative views about organized religion and are likely to consider themselves spiritual as opposed to religious. Nichols (2009) noted that the term "unchurched" is one that neglects the new unreligious whose religion is not associated with a church (e.g., Judaism, Islam).

"Liminars," from the Latin word "limen" for threshold, is a term that Lim, MacGregor, and Putnam (2010) used to describe those who have no religious preference: "they stand halfway in and halfway out of a certain religious identity" (p. 598). While some may have a religious preference or identity at one time, it is one that is unstable. Others may be content with having no such preference and remaining so. Their religious beliefs remain the same and therefore are not persons who change religions. However, they tend to not have a strong attachment to their religious group in any consistent way.

Religious drifters are also called liminars (or liminals) in the research literature. However, religious drifters is a term that was coined by Eric Gorski (2009), an Associated Press religion writer. He called the United States a nation of religious drifters in response to the pervasive religion-changing that was identified in a Pew survey of 35,000 Americans in 2007. In a follow-up survey with a subsample of those (Catholics and Lutherans) who had left their former religion and were now unaffiliated, the primary reason was "just gradually drifted away from the religion" followed by "spiritual needs not being met" (Pew Forum on Religion & Public Life, 2009). Other reasons identified were no longer believing in the teachings of the religion and dissatisfaction with religious leaders.

The religious and spiritual beliefs and practices of men who are unaffiliated were examined in a 2014 Pew survey (Pew Research Center, 2014). First, the survey found that men who were unaffiliated were mostly under age 50, with about equal percentages in the 18–29 year old age group (34%) and 30–49 year old group (38%). The majority were White (68%) and almost equal percentages of married and never married men (37% and 40% respectively). Belief in God was similarly about equal, with 43% having belief in God that is either absolutely certain (23%) or fairly certain (20%), and 38% who stated they do not believe in God. With regard to the importance of religion in their life, most felt it was not at all important (43%), whereas a third of the men surveyed felt it was somewhat or very important (20% and 11% respectively). Although 74% of the men seldom or never attended church, 23% did so on occasion (once or twice a month to a few times a year). Most seldom or never pray (69%). About one-third (36%) reported feeling spiritual peace and wellbeing at least once a week, whereas the same percentage of men (36%) reported seldom or never feeling it.

Masculinity and Religious Non-Affiliation

As mentioned in Chapter 1, men adhering to traditional masculinity are more likely to be less religious (Miller & Hoffman, 1995; Robbins, Francis, Haley, & Kay, 2001; Sullins, 2006; Thompson, 1991), perhaps because they view religious activities as feminine or "unmasculine," and therefore do not participate in order to preserve their sense of manhood (Robertson, 2005). There are also some demographic characteristics associated with differences in religious participation and non-affiliation among men, which may be indirectly related to masculinity (e.g., age, marital status). However, it should be noted that the masculinity and gender-related differences in religious participation and affiliation is primarily with regard to Christianity and Western cultures that have been the focus of the research (Schwadel, 2018). In his book, *Why Men Hate Going to Church*, David Murrow (2011) noted that "of the planet's great religions, only Christianity has a consistent, worldwide shortage of male practitioners" (p. 14). Murrow argued that the church has been "feminized" and it is hard for the "typical" guy to fit himself into this feminine religious mold. Murrow primarily connects this feminization to the industrial revolution, such that the church became more populated by women and was remade in their image. Consequently, a good Christian meant being passive, gentle, sensitive, calm, and polite. He also gives the example of how it would be intimidating for a typical man "to hold hands in a circle, to cry in public, or to imagine falling deeply in love with another man (even if his name is Jesus)" (Church for Men, n.d., para. 6). Morrow has argued that it is the church that needs to make some changes in order to connect with men and meet their needs.

Thompson and Remmes's (2002) investigation of religiousness in a sample of older men can shed light on how masculinity may influence religious non-affiliation but also religious and spiritual involvement. Men who had more of a feminine gender role orientation were more likely to attend church regardless of their masculinity ideology, whereas men with a more masculine orientation were less likely to attend church only if their masculinity ideology was traditional. In other words, men who had a masculine gender role orientation were more likely to attend church only if they disregarded traditional masculinity ideology. However, a masculine orientation also related to involvement in one's religious organization, such as taking on leadership roles and involvement in church committees, and to religion as a quest. Religion as a quest is a religious orientation characterized by facing existential questions, having religious doubts, acceptance of other religious perspectives, and a strong belief in spiritual development (Batson, Schoenrade, & Ventis, 1993; Beck & Jessup, 2004). Thompson and Remmes found the quest orientation was negatively associated with being Catholic or evangelist and surmised that perhaps men with a quest orientation were more likely to be Jewish or unchurched.

Possible Psychological Issues

Religious non-affiliation in itself is not associated with any psychological issues. However, the literature indicates atheists may experience discrimination and therefore many will conceal their religious nonbelief from others, which can result in feelings of loneliness and psychological distress (Brewster, Hammer, Sawyer, Eklund, & Palamar, 2016). The other category of religiously unaffiliated men that may experience psychological issues are the religious drifters. Although no research has investigated the psychological issues associated with religious drifting or liminality, the research on quest as a religious orientation may be applicable.

The quest religious orientation may be a cause of psychological distress, because as an existential struggle or spiritual search for meaning there are costs to this journey, such as loneliness and anxiety (Graham, 2001). However, the end result can be a more meaningful and rewarding life. Burris, Jackson, Tarpley, and Smith (1996) showed that tragedy or conflict may be what precedes the quest and that it was related to religious disidentification. However, they pointed out that tragedy and conflict could result in the opposite; that is, the person could become more involved or identified with their religion. Nonetheless, a quest orientation has been found to be negatively related to religious wellbeing, spiritual wellbeing, and self-esteem (Genia, 1996), and positively related to depression, stress (Messay, Dixon, & Rye, 2012), religious conflict, and anxiety (Kojetin, McIntosh, Bridges, & Spilka, 1987).

In Graham's (2001) qualitative study on quest-oriented religion, some participants reported going through a period in which they felt abandoned by God, or that they felt their faith was being challenged. These feelings led to "seeking" answers or meaning so as to make sense of what they were experiencing. Additionally, consistent with Burris et al. (1996), several had gone through experiences with death, such as a severe car accident or loss of a loved one, which "shook the seeker's personal and spiritual foundations" (Graham, 2001, pp. 78–79).

Conceptualization, Assessment, and Counseling Interventions

Conceptualization

For some men, having no religious affiliation may be a result of dissatisfaction with organized religion or they may have experienced a change in their religious views. They may be experiencing a "crisis in faith" (Watson, 2016). As a result, they may be on a spiritual quest or searching for a spiritual home. The reasons for the dissatisfaction or change in views are worthy of exploration, as his reasons may be related to his masculinity ideology or a result of a recent tragedy or conflict. This may or may not be a source of psychological distress; however, assisting your client with resolving any religious issues in this regard would likely be psychologically beneficial to him, generally and perhaps with regard to his presenting problem as well.

Sahker (2016) offered two possible ways to conceptualize possible psychological issues related to the nonreligious that have relevance for the larger category of the religiously unaffiliated. *Spiritual struggle*, which was discussed in Chapter 1, is when the person is experiencing conflicting beliefs about religious matters that are causing distress and anger at God or religious institutions (Abu-Raiya, Pargament, & Krause, 2016). This struggle can result in a rejection of religion and disaffiliation. *Deconversion* is what may follow, which is the process of actually leaving a religion. For some, this process may result in no longer believing in God, while for others it will result only in disaffiliation. Nonetheless, the possible consequence of deconversion is conflict with one's family, friends, and/or romantic partner causing relationship distress.

Assessment

As suggested by the literature on the religiously unaffiliated, men who are not affiliated with any religion would be a heterogeneous group of men. When asking about his religious background and orientation, it would be important to inquire about his belief in God as well as his religious affiliation(s) in the past and currently. The goal of the assessment would be to clarify and understand his views about God *and* religion and if either or both are a source of conflict or stress, contribute to the presenting problem, or are a possible strength and protective factor.

Sahker's (2016) model provides a way to assess the client's spiritual journey and process of deconversion. He refers to Perry's (1970) stages of dualism, multiplicity, relativism, and commitment as a way to conceptualize the spiritual struggle. However, the stage of relativism is consistent with a spiritual struggle in terms of the person analyzing and evaluating their beliefs to gain deeper understanding. This can result in religious disengagement. With regard to deconversion, Sahker refers to Smith's (2011) model of atheist identity that includes the following stages: ubiquity of theism, questioning theism, rejecting theism, and coming out as atheist. The stages of questioning and rejecting theism suggest a spiritual struggle similar to the quest religious orientation in that the person is questioning their religious beliefs and religion because they are experiencing religious doubts. This can result in religious disengagement or disaffiliation. However, instead of rejecting theism some may be searching for a religion or ideology that is consistent with their religious or spiritual beliefs. As such, these models can help the therapist identify where the client is in the process of religious non-affiliation.

Sahker's (2016) model is useful in conceptualizing and assessing the process of a religious quest or religious deconversion if the person is questioning their beliefs about God and religion. However, there is no recognition of how masculinity may intersect with these issues. For some men, their disengagement from a religion or church may be because they did not find it fulfilling from the point of view of what religious involvement means to them as a man. They may not have consciously thought about why they no longer go to church or practice religion, especially from the perspective of its relevance to them as a man. We recommend that masculinity issues be included as part of the assessment when religious non-affiliation is of concern to the client or the client wants to discuss religious issues. When asking about his disengagement from religion or his religious/spiritual journey and struggles, listen for themes that may be related to his gender role orientation and masculinity ideology.

The following questions can be used as a guide to assessing the client's religious non-affiliation:

- To what extent does he believe in God, or has been questioning his belief in God?
- Does he feel there has been a change in how he views religion or religion in his life?
- When and why did he stop going to church, synagogue, or mosque?
- What (if anything) was unfulfilling about his religion or religious involvement?
- What did he like best about going to church, synagogue, or mosque?
- Would he like to be more involved in his religion, or involved in some other religion?

Counseling Interventions

Some of the questions mentioned above with regard to assessment are ones that can initiate the process of exploring the client's crisis in faith, religious struggle, or quest orientation in therapy. If your client has experienced a recent tragedy or series of negative events that "shook" his religious foundation, he may wish to explore or re-examine his feelings and beliefs about God and religion. To the extent that his masculine self-concept has been affected, perhaps challenged, his thoughts and feelings about his manhood would be important to explore. Further, the two may be related; that is, the questioning of his religious beliefs may go hand-in-hand with questioning his masculinity.

Howes (2011) has written a blog that can serve as a resource for therapists with clients of diverse religious backgrounds. Howes interviewed 12 therapists (who are also researchers/teachers) who responded to questions about psychotherapy within a spiritual context. One such question was "A new client comes to therapy reporting his main problem is feeling detached from God. How would you proceed?" Each of the therapists is a faith-based practitioner that offers a different religious-based therapy including Judaism, Native American Spirituality, Catholicism, Islam, Hinduism, Mormonism, African Spirituality, Biblical Counseling, Secular Humanism, Twelve Step Spirituality, Christian Psychology, and

Buddhism. In answering the question, most of the participants had in common the exploration of the client's religious/spiritual background to identify how, when, and why the client feels detached from God, and some offer a brief explanation of how they would conceptualize and respond to the feelings of detachment within their religious tradition.

If your client is describing disengagement from his faith community or place of worship due to such things as boredom and a lack of relevance to his life, he will need help in defining or specifying what those characteristics are, as they may be related to his masculinity. If so, he may benefit from understanding that his disengagement may have to do with his masculine orientation that is contrary to the culture of his place of worship. Consequently, with this understanding, he can consider and seek out other places of worship that meet his needs and appeal to his masculine orientation, or identify ways he can express his masculinity through involvement in his place of worship or faith community.

It would be important to address any feelings of isolation or relationship distress if present. For example, if he is from a very religious family his disengagement may affect his relationships with those in his social support system. Nevertheless, he may need help with finding opportunities to increase social support or identifying ways to increase his social network.

Case Example

This case example illustrates how a men's process group can be effective in healing spiritual struggles and wounded masculinity. I (Isacco) focus on one member of the group – Parker. I first met Parker during my intake shift at the university counseling center (UCC). Intake hours were known among the student population as "drop-in time" and usually entailed crisis situations. Parker, however, came into my office with an eager look on his face that did not convey urgency or crisis. He appeared anxious as he wrung his hands and fidgeted in his seat, but he did not seem particularly distressed or depressed at the onset of our intake session. When asked what brought him in for an intake, Parker reported that he already sees a counselor for individual counseling and that she recommended that he seek a group counseling experience. He asked if the UCC had any groups that he could join. I informed Parker that the UCC offers about 10–12 groups per term and that this was the enrollment period. I followed up by asking Parker why he thought group counseling would be beneficial to him. Parker reported that he has worked through "significant issues" in individual counseling and that he was having difficulties finding friends at the university and interacting with classmates in his program. His counselor informed him that group counseling could help with those interpersonal problems and Parker expressed motivation to join a group.

Another counselor at the UCC and I were starting a men's process group. Based on his presenting concerns and lack of elevated risk factors, I invited Parker to join that group, which started next week. Parker expressed curiosity about a "men's what kind of group?!" He seemed more at ease and excited to start the group after I told him that it was a group for men to work on issues specific to men while connecting with other men. The group was scheduled to run once a week for ten weeks. He was pensive for a few moments and finally said, "Yes, I need to work on those things for sure. My counselor will be happy about this." I gathered some additional information from Parker (e.g., major, year) and we wrapped up the intake session.

The following week, Parker was the first person to arrive at the group. He smiled broadly as he greeted me, the group co-facilitator, and the other group members that began to enter the room. He was a tall man, athletic build, and dressed casually in athletic clothing. Parker was in his late 20s and was a graduate student. He fit into the rest of the group in terms of age as eight of the other men were a mix of graduate and undergraduate students but were in their mid to late 20s as well. One group member was an outlier in terms of age, having returned to school at the age of 45 years old to pursue a second career. Despite the similarities in age, I immediately noticed that Parker seemed younger compared to the other men, less "edgy," and more child-like. I considered him to be the "younger brother" in the group. He was clearly trying to put his "best foot forward," and he exhibited a strong desire to be liked by the group's facilitators and members. My colleague and I noticed that he was practicing interpersonal skills in a deliberate manner such as expressing empathy, restating what others said, and assuring that there was space for "everyone to talk." During the first few sessions, Parker began to act like a third counselor in the room, using his experiences in individual counseling to set the tone, intervene with other group members, and position himself in alignment with my colleague and me. He did not demonstrate interpersonal skills in a natural, comfortable manner. He was genuine but clumsy and at times, robotic and ineffective. Yes, the group was a good modality for him.

Parker entered the fifth session very differently than the previous four sessions. He appeared more serious, flatter affect, and a determined look in his eyes. We started the group with our standard check-in. When it was Parker's turn, he reported that he had "something very important to tell the group" but that he was hesitant to make the disclosure because he was afraid of how the other group members would react. The other group members assured him that the group was a safe place for his self-disclosure, as they all basically said, "this is what group is for." With the encouragement of his fellow group members secured, Parker stated, "I am an atheist." Then, there was a prolonged silence. Finally, another group member spoke up and asked Parker, "Um, is that it? Is that what you wanted to tell us?" Parker explained that he had never told anyone about his current religious beliefs or lack thereof and it was very significant for him to make such a disclosure. The other group members began to ask Parker various questions about his atheist declaration, which served an assessment function. He described growing up in a devout Christian household but drifting apart from his parents' religion during his undergraduate studies, which he concluded were "a wreck." Parker's drifting from his religion was not a by-product of his masculinity. I conceptualized his narrative from a quest perspective. His spiritual needs were no longer met by the Christian faith of his childhood and he gradually deconverted from Christianity.

Parker thought that he would find a religious home as he transitioned out of undergraduate and into adulthood. Perhaps even return to Christianity. However, his quest took him further away from a religious community. He expressed loneliness, frustration, and a lack of meaning in his life. I recalled my first meeting with Parker during the intake shift. At that time, he seemed anxious. But now he seemed more depressed as the drifting away from his childhood religion created a void that had not yet been filled in his life. Tears rolled down his face and his body shook. In those moments, I remembered how Parker described working through "significant issues" in individual counseling. I hypothesized that he may have experienced an acute life stressor, crisis, or traumatic event that contributed to his crisis in faith and eventual declaration of atheism. Perhaps the issues were not totally resolved?

Parker's positive declaration that he was an atheist came at a cost. If he was not Christian anymore and did not believe in God or his parent's faith and what they taught him throughout his life, then who was he? Indeed, Parker was asking deep existential questions that revealed an insecure sense of self, which included exploring what kind of man he was in the world and what it meant for him to be an atheist man. I asked Parker how the group could help him. Parker reported that he felt supported by the group and that most importantly, he was not judged by them. The group did not react in the way that he feared. He asked me and the co-facilitator if they could spend some time in group talking about spirituality as men. We affirmed that spirituality was a good topic to discuss, but the group needed to decide if they wanted to focus their conversation on spirituality. One group member asked Parker why he wanted the rest of the group to discuss spirituality. Parker reported that he wanted to hear about other's spiritual journeys to deepen the conversation, to learn from others, and to reciprocate support. The other men all kind of shrugged in agreement and seemed willing to discuss spirituality, which they did for the remaining time of that session.

Over the next few sessions, it became clear that the group achieved a solid cohesion and that most of the members enjoyed the group and felt supported by each other. We initiated a conversation about termination since we were in week 8 of a ten-week program. Parker was the first to respond and expressed his desire to continue the group into next term. We sensed some hesitancy from others in the group while about five or six others also reported that they wanted to continue with the group. When asked why they wanted to continue, Parker responded first again. He referred to the session when he disclosed his atheism and described how impactful it was for him to be vulnerable with a group of men that did not judge or ridicule him. Although masculinity did not contribute to his initial drifting away from his religion, Parker revealed that he experienced a crisis in faith during his undergraduate years because of being bullied and traumatized by men in college. He remained emotionally wounded despite individual counseling. Parker lost trust in men, especially men who had the potential to be his friends. As a result, he kept men at a distance and his interpersonal awkwardness reflected his emotional wounds. Parker's deconversion from his religious community coincided with and was exacerbated by his loss of male friends. He wondered how a benevolent God could allow such terrible things to happen to him. Parker lost trust in God to the point of disbelief.

His spiritual struggle was intertwined with a disconnection from his masculinity from a male peer group. He was a lonely man in search of a sense of belonging and connection. The group counseling worked for him because Parker was able to be vulnerable with men without negative consequences. The void from his deconversion and spiritual struggle received some healing from the group. Parker, in his own words, expressed as much to the other group members as a rationale for why he wanted to continue the group. He found friendship within the group and a sense of connection with other men that he had not felt in a long time. Parker described the group as a spiritual experience, which helped to alleviate his spiritual struggles and his wounded masculinity. A few of the members decided not to continue with the group next term. Parker and about five or six others joined up with a few new members and the men's process group continued for two additional terms.

References

Abu-Raiya, H., Pargament, K.I., & Krause, N. (2016). Religion as problem, religion as solution: Religious buffers of the links between religious/spiritual struggles and well-being/mental health. *Quality of Life Research, 25*(5), 1265–1274.

Batson, C.D., Schoenrade, P., & Ventis, W.L. (1993). *Religion and the individual: A social- psychological perspective*. New York, NY: Oxford University Press.

Beck, R., & Jessup, R.K. (2004). The multidimensional nature of quest motivation. *Journal of Psychology and Theology, 32*(4), 283–294.

Benn, P. (1999). Some uncertainties about agnosticism. *International Journal for Philosophy of Religion, 46*(3), 171–188.

Brewster, M.E., Hammer, J., Sawyer, J.S., Eklund, A., & Palamar, J. (2016). Perceived experiences of atheist discrimination: Instrument development and evaluation. *Journal of Counseling Psychology, 63*(5), 557–570.

Burris, C.T., Jackson, L.M., Tarpley, W.R., & Smith, G.J. (1996). Religion as quest: The self-directed pursuit of meaning. *Personality and Social Psychology Bulletin, 22*(10), 1068–1076.

Church for Men. (n.d.). *The feminized church*. Retrieved from http://churchformen.com/men-and-church/why-do-men-hate-going-to-church/.

Genia, V. (1996). I, E, Quest, and fundamentalism as predictors of psychological and spiritual well-being. *Journal for the Scientific Study of Religion, 35*(1), 56–64.

Gorski, E. (2009, April 27). Survey Americans switch faiths early, often. *The Associated Press*. Retrieved from www.foxnews.com/.

Graham, M. (2001). *A phenomenological study of quest-oriented religion.* Master's thesis, Trinity Western University, Canada. Retrieved from www.twu.ca/sites/default/files/grahammatthew.pdf.

Hout, M., & Fischer, C.S. (2002). Why more Americans have no religious preference: Politics and generations. *American Sociological Review, 67*(2), 165–190.

Howes, R. (2011, September 2). The varieties of religious therapy: Introduction [Blog post]. Retrieved from www.psychologytoday.com/us/blog/in-therapy/201109/the-varieties-religious-therapy-introduction.

Kojetin, B.A., McIntosh, D.N., Bridges, R.A., & Spilka, B. (1987). Quest: Constructive search or religious conflict? *Journal for the Scientific Study of Religion, 26*(1), 111–115.

Lim, C., MacGregor, C.A., & Putnam, R.D. (2010). Secular and liminal: Discovering heterogeneity among religious nones. *Journal for the Scientific Study of Religion, 49*(4), 596–618.

Messay, B., Dixon, L.J., & Rye, M.S. (2012). The relationship between quest religious orientation, forgiveness, and mental health. *Mental Health, Religion & Culture, 15*(3), 315–333.

Miller, A., & Hoffman, J. (1995). Risk and religion: An explanation of gender differences in religiosity. *Journal from the Science, 34*(1), 63–75.

Murrow, D. (2011). *Why men hate going to church.* Nashville, TN: Thomas Nelson, Inc.

Nichols, C.M. (2009, December 15). Who has "religion"? Reconsidering the rise of "No Religionists" in America. *The Immanent Frame.* Retrieved from https://tif.ssrc.org/2009/12/15/who-has-religion/.

Perry, W.G. (1970). *Forms of intellectual and ethical development in the college years: A scheme.* New York, NY: Holt, Rinehart & Winston.

Pew Forum on Religion & Public Life. (2009). *Faith in flux: Changes in religious affiliation in the U.S.* Retrieved from www.pewforum.org/2009/04/27/faith-in-flux/.

Pew Research Center. (2014). *Religious landscape study. Men who are unaffiliated (religious "nones").* Retrieved from www.pewforum.org/religious-landscape-study/religious-tradition/unaffiliated-religious-nones/gender-composition/men/.

Robbins, M., Francis, L., Haley, J., & Kay, W. (2001). The personality characteristics of Methodist ministers: Feminine men and masculine women? *Journal for the Scientific Study of Religion, 40*(1), 123–128.

Robertson, J. (2005). Finding Joshua's soul: Working with religious men. In M. Stevens & M. Englar-Carlson (Eds.), *In the room with men: A casebook of psychotherapy with men* (pp. 109–127). Washington, DC: American Psychological Association.

Sahker, E. (2016). Therapy with the nonreligious: Ethical and clinical considerations. *Professional Psychology: Research and Practice, 47*(4), 295–302.

Schwadel, P. (2018). Cross-national variation in the social origins and religious consequences of religious non-affiliation. *Social Science Research, 70*, 254–270.

Smith, J.M. (2011). Becoming an atheist in America: Constructing identity and meaning from the rejection of theism. *Sociology of Religion, 72*(2), 215–237.

Speed, D., & Fowler, K. (2016). What's God got to do with it? How religiosity predicts atheists' health. *Journal of Religion and Health, 55*(1), 296–308.

Sullins, D.P. (2006). Gender and religion: Deconstructing universality, constructing complexity. *American Journal of Sociology, 112*(3), 838–880.

Thompson, E.H. Jr. (1991). Beneath the status characteristic: Gender variations in religiousness. *Journal for the Scientific Study of Religion, 30*(4), 381–394.

Thompson, E.H. Jr., & Remmes, K.R. (2002). Does masculinity thwart being religious? An examination of older men's religiousness. *Journal for the Scientific Study of Religion, 41*(3), 521–532.

Watson, E.D. (2016, January 18). Men and religion: A crisis in faith [Blog post]. Retrieved from www.huffingtonpost.com/elwood-d-watson/men-and-religion-a-crisis_b_9001926.html.

Wilkins-Laflamme, S. (2015). How unreligious are the religious "nones"? Religious dynamics of the unaffiliated in Canada. *Canadian Journal of Sociology, 40*(4), 477–499.

10 Creating More Positive Pathways That Improve Men's Health

In this final chapter we describe pathways that specifically draw upon religion/spirituality and masculinity as paths to positive outcomes for men's health and wellbeing. First, a conceptual model is presented. Then, variables of the model are described separately. This is followed by examples of how the model can be applied in your work with men by addressing the intersecting religious, spiritual, and masculinity issues. Lastly, we briefly summarize the "path to wellness."

Conceptual Models

The relationships between religion/spirituality, masculinity, and men's health can be conceptualized based on whether religiosity/spirituality is the basis of one's masculinity ideology or vice versa. The best way to illustrate these different relationships between the three variables is with the following Figures. In each Figure, the dependent variable is men's health. As described in the introduction to this book, we consider men's health to be a broad term that encompasses a man's overall wellbeing: physical, psychological, and spiritual. As seen in the Figures, we believe that religion/spirituality interacts with masculinity to impact men's health.

Figure 10.1 shows how the relationship between religiosity/spirituality and men's health is due to masculinity ideology. For example, this would be when a man's religiosity/spirituality causes him to have a certain masculinity ideology that brings about certain health outcomes.

Conversely, Figure 10.2 represents when a man's masculinity ideology causes him to have certain beliefs about religion and spirituality that brings about certain health outcomes.

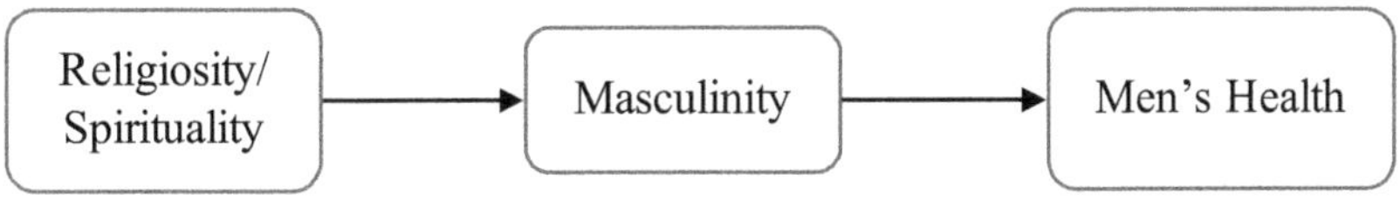

Figure 10.1 Religiosity/spirituality is related to men's health due to masculinity ideology

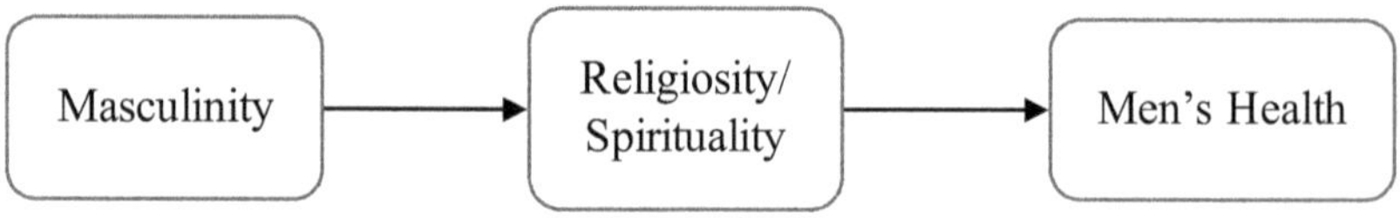

Figure 10.2 Masculinity ideology is related to men's health due to religiosity/spirituality

The relationships and influences among masculinity, religion/spirituality, and men's health are not always so clear and linear. Thus, Figure 10.3 shows how religiosity/spirituality and masculinity are both having an effect on men's health. In this model, a man's religiosity/spirituality causes him to have a certain masculinity ideology that brings about certain health outcomes, but so does his religiosity no matter what masculinity ideology he has.

Although not illustrated, conversely, a man's masculinity can cause him to have certain beliefs about religion and spirituality that bring about certain health outcomes, but so does his masculinity ideology no matter what religious or spiritual beliefs he has.

Figure 10.4 is of a slightly more complex model in which religiosity/spirituality affects both men's masculinity ideology *and* their health.

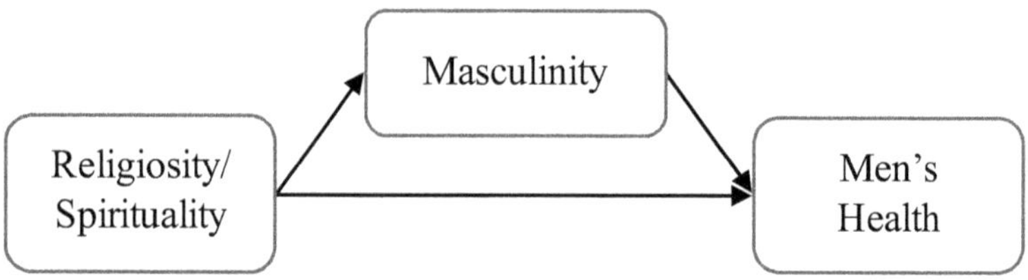

Figure 10.3 Religiosity/spirituality and masculinity ideology are related to men's health, but religiosity/spirituality is also related to men's health due to masculinity ideology

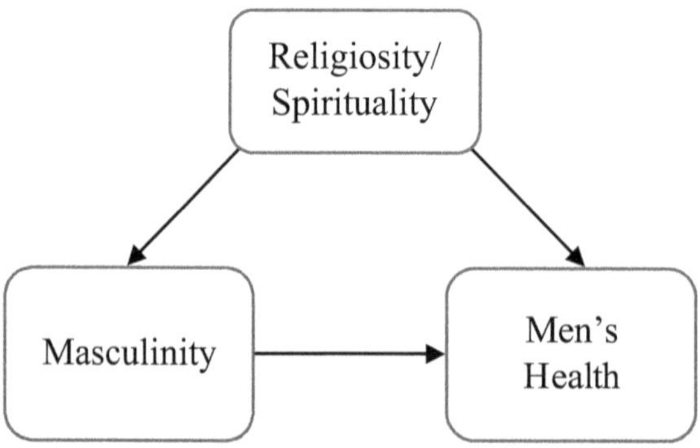

Figure 10.4 Religiosity/spirituality affects both masculinity ideology and men's health. Therefore, masculinity and men's health are related

Therefore, masculinity and health are related through their relationship to religiosity. In other words, religiosity/spirituality affects both masculinity and men's health, which indicates that a man's religiosity/spirituality is a particularly significant and salient influence in his life.

Lastly, Figures 10.5 and 10.6 depict a model in which the strength of the relationship between masculinity and men's health is due to a man's religiosity/spirituality. Religiosity/spirituality affects the relationship directly or by interacting with another variable. An example of this concept is when masculinity ideology affects men's health when men are very religious, but masculinity has no effect on men's health when men are nonreligious.

We offer these models as a foundation for conceptualizing the various pathways to men's health when considering men's religiosity/spirituality and masculinity. We recognize that men's experiences and lives do not fit exactly into these models, and that what is causative of the problems men have or present in counseling is oftentimes multidetermined and not about religious or masculinity issues. Nonetheless, how these aspects of a man's life

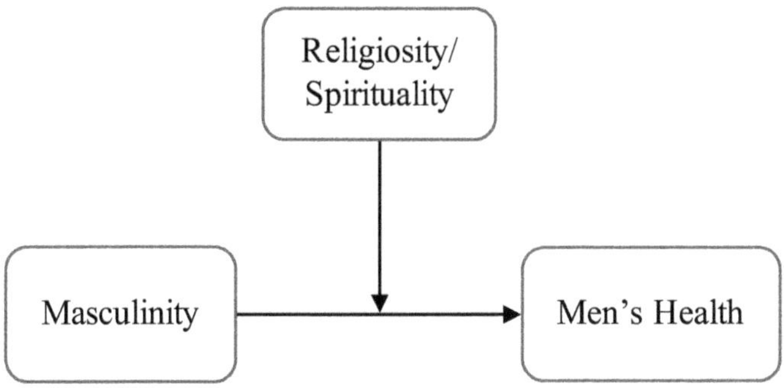

Figure 10.5 Religiosity/spirituality affects the strength of the relationship between masculinity ideology and men's health

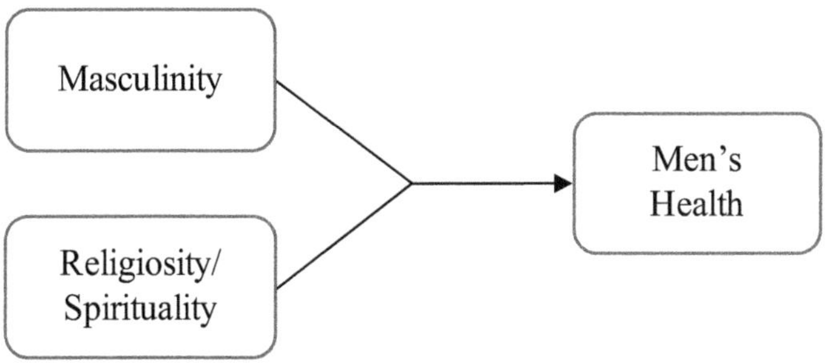

Figure 10.6 Religiosity/spirituality interacts with masculinity ideology to affect men's health

may manifest and relate to one another are important to assess, as they can inform counseling interventions.

Men's Health and Wellbeing

Although men may be less likely than women to seek treatment, it is not evident in the work that most clinicians do. Men will be your clients or patients in hospitals, day treatment programs, private practice, university counseling centers, mental health clinics, drug and alcohol treatment programs, prisons, court-mandated treatment programs, and so on. They will be diagnosed with any number of disorders. However, the most frequent issues for men who are in counseling are depression, anxiety, anger, substance abuse/addictions, or marital conflict. These issues or problems can be distinct or in combination, and they can have a deleterious effect on one's health and wellbeing. The source of men's mental health problems will vary, but we offer two avenues by which to explore men's problems and provide a way to improve men's health as a result. The expected outcomes would be improved coping skills, increased social support and sense of belonging, and greater satisfaction and meaning in life.

Some men may have more chronic conditions such that your work with them is part of an overall treatment team in which the patient receives medication, social services, psychiatric care, and rehab services. For those men who have more chronic mental illnesses it is important to remember that the patient is more than his illness; he is also a man who has beliefs about religion, spirituality, and masculinity, which can have an affect on his treatment compliance and quality of life.

Religiosity and Spirituality

Religiosity and spirituality refer to one's beliefs about God or a higher power or sacred force, and the practices or behaviors or way of life associated with those beliefs. However, one's religiosity pertains to a particular religion, whereas one's spirituality does not necessarily encompass a particular religion. Additionally, it is an aspect of identity – it is a way that people define themselves religiously or spiritually. Some people are neither religious nor spiritual, and some people are not religious but consider themselves spiritual. However, those who are religious and/or spiritual will vary in the extent to which they consider themselves to be so, from being a little religious/spiritual to very religious/spiritual.

Religious beliefs are determined by one's religion and one's faith and tend to include, but are not limited to, a belief in God, an afterlife, and sacred text as the word of God. One's belief in God is more than "I do" or "I don't," rather it is one's beliefs about God or the image of God that a person holds. Similarly, one can believe in an afterlife, but what matters more is what they believe that afterlife to be. Does he believe in heaven and hell, or certain ways one must behave now that affects his life after death? Religious behaviors include but are not limited to attendance at a place of worship, involvement in a faith community and its activities, prayer, reading scripture or religious texts, and following religious tenets. We hesitate to define what spiritual beliefs and behaviors or practices would be for those who consider themselves spiritual. The literature offers diverse perspectives on spirituality; however, given spirituality is a personal belief system about the meaning of life, it would be best to ask your client to describe what he means if he were to say he considers himself to be spiritual and does not identify with any particular religion. What is important to assess and understand about your client is how strong his religious and spiritual beliefs are, and how frequently he practices his religion or lives according to his spiritual beliefs.

Religious beliefs can have a negative effect or positive effect on men's health, often depending on one's image of God and relationship with God. However, religious behaviors, for the most part, will have a positive effect. Spirituality, or being a spiritual person, is likely to have a positive effect on wellbeing. How a person practices or lives spiritually is idiosyncratic, but it tends to involve private prayer or meditation, doing good deeds, being of service, reading literature on spirituality, and how we treat others. However, what is most important in spirituality is one's beliefs or awareness.

There is an interesting study that was done with 551 cancer survivors in which the researchers compared the quality of life of patients with low spirituality/low religiosity, high spirituality/low religiosity, low spiritually/high religiosity, and high spirituality/high religiosity (Cannon, Garcia, & Loberiza, 2015). Both mental and physical quality of life were assessed. They found that patients with high spirituality had better mental quality of life regardless of whether they were high or low in religiousness. Additionally, religious patients who had better physical quality of life were highly spiritual. The results of this research with cancer survivors has significance for the relationship between spirituality and men's health more generally, but more so the importance of exploring with clients their religious and spiritual beliefs. It suggests that heightened spiritual awareness may contribute to dealing with adversity and that religiousness alone may not be sufficient, especially if one's religious beliefs include God as a punisher.

In exploring your client's religious beliefs and behaviors there may be some that contribute to the problems he is having. He may be experiencing religious or spiritual struggles, have a negative God image, have difficulty forgiving, or use negative religious coping. On the other hand, religious and spiritual beliefs and behaviors may be client strengths that can be used to help deal with his problems, such as prayer, involvement in a faith community, positive religious coping, reading religious text or books on spirituality, and having an image of God as benevolent, forgiving, and loving.

Masculinity Ideology

Masculinity ideology refers to beliefs about how men are, or how men are supposed to be – the norms for male behavior and men's roles in society. A man's beliefs will be influenced by the culture in which he lives and the extent to which he identifies with that cultural group. Masculinity ideology also concerns beliefs about conforming to cultural standards of male behavior. As such, there are two considerations: what does your client believe about how men are and should be, and how important is it to him to live up to those beliefs? Additionally, masculinity is an aspect of male identity; it is one way that a man defines for himself what it means to be a man. What is considered traditional masculinity will be those characteristics that are widely held and enforced by one's culture, and men will vary in their masculinity ideology as well as their conformity to cultural standards of masculinity.

There is research supporting the notion that certain aspects of masculinity in US culture, as well as other cultures, have a negative effect on men's health and wellbeing. There is a direct relationship between certain masculinity beliefs and those behaviors that are harmful to oneself and one's relationships with others. However, in addition, failing to live up to cultural standards of masculinity can be a source of internal conflict for some men, just as failing to live up to moral standards of behavior is, based on one's religion. It is a matter of masculine self-image, and it has a cultural component to it. For example, if in one's culture manhood means having a good job, making good money, being married with children, and providing for and protecting one's family, and if these standards are salient for a man and he has failed to achieve them, then masculinity ideology will have a negative effect on his health. If these masculinity standards are not important to him, they likely will have no significant effect on his wellbeing. However, his not achieving or conforming to these cultural standards may negatively affect his health through how others treat him for his nonconformity (e.g., parents, family, peers, coworkers, and society in general). For some men, they may be strong enough to resist the pressure put upon them to conform, but for others it may be a source of chronic stress for which they will need to develop coping skills.

Many men do not think that what it means to be a man is based on one's culture and that there is any choice with regard to conforming or not conforming. They are not aware of gender socialization, and they believe what they think and do is the way things are and should be. For them to see and understand how their ideas about manhood may be contributing to the problems they are having is enlightening. However, it is important to let men know that what they think about manhood and how they enact masculinity is normal given their culture even though it is contributing to the problems they are having. Counseling can address how to think about and enact masculinity differently, so that it would benefit them. For example, in Chapter 7 about pornography use among men, we described how the "Centerfold Syndrome" leads to sexual objectification of women and detailed ways that counselors can identify and alter harmful masculinity scripts that contributed to problematic pornography use. Masculinity is not always problematic, but it can be, and counselors are well positioned to help men develop more positive masculinities.

Addressing the Intersecting Religious, Spiritual, and Masculinity Issues

Research on the relationships between religiosity/spirituality, masculinity, and men's psychosocial functioning within a religious cultural context can shed light on what may be important to address in counseling. Wade and colleagues (Wade, Suryani, & Lesmana, 2018; Wade & Wiloso, 2016) investigated religiosity, masculinity, and marital and life satisfaction in Indonesian men in Java and Bali. Both Javanese and Balinese cultures are highly religious; Javanese culture and most of Indonesia is Muslim, while Balinese culture is Hindu. The researchers found similarities in the way the men defined masculinity in the two cultures, but also some slight differences. Balinese manhood places importance on human relationships and the happiness of others, especially within the family and community. Harmonious relationships is a central value of Balinese Hindu culture, and the importance of caring for others was identified as a central characteristic of manhood. Although within Javanese culture harmony is the most important value in human relationships, responsibilities associated with being head of the family were identified as the most important characteristics of manhood. The importance of family roles is consistent with the Indonesian Marriage Law, which specifies that the husband is the head of the family and the wife is the mother of the household; the husband has the responsibility to protect his wife and support her to the best of his abilities, and the wife has the responsibility of managing the household to the best of her abilities (Salim & Azra, 2003).

In the study with Javanese men, Wade and Wiloso (2016) tested a mediation model based on the positive relationships among religiosity, masculinity, and marital satisfaction. They found that masculinity fully mediated the relationship between religiosity and marital satisfaction. In other words, men who are religious were satisfied in their marital relationship because of the importance they give to what it means to be a Javanese man. How Javanese men view manhood is intimately tied to their religion, which is the foundation of their culture and its values. Congruence between religiosity and Javanese masculinity within Javanese Islamic culture contributes to men's marital satisfaction.

In the study with Balinese men, Wade and colleagues (2018) tested a confounding variable model given the positive associations among religiosity, masculinity, and life satisfaction. They found that religiosity was a confounding variable that explained why masculinity was related to life satisfaction. How Balinese men view manhood is intimately tied to their religion, which is the foundation of their culture and its values. Congruence between religiosity and Balinese masculinity within Balinese society contributes to men's satisfaction with life.

Estrada and Arciniega (2015) examined the relationships between caballerismo, religiosity, and life satisfaction in a sample of primarily Mexican/Mexican-American men. Caballerismo "comprises attributes related to family centeredness, social responsibility, and emotional connectedness" (p. 192) and are considered positive aspects of masculinity in Latino culture. Their results showed that religious involvement moderated the positive relationship between caballerismo and satisfaction with life, such that only at high levels of religious involvement was caballerismo a predictor of satisfaction with life. The authors reasoned that religious values may be supportive of the values of caballerismo.

The above studies point to the importance of addressing masculinity and religious involvement with men in counseling, especially when religion is a salient aspect of his identity. It would be important to do so because his beliefs about manhood may be intimately tied to his religious beliefs and thereby how satisfied he is with his life. While a man's religion or religious culture may be the basis for his beliefs about manhood, it is also possible that a man's beliefs about manhood may contribute to his religious beliefs and practices. It is unlikely that for US men there will be the belief that "real men go to church," or "real men pray," or "real men believe in God." However, addressing your client's beliefs about religion based on his masculinity ideology will get at what may be an obstacle to involvement in religion or spirituality. This would be an important avenue to explore, but it need not be one the client must take. The question for the counselor is, "Is his masculinity getting in the way of his being able to benefit from religion or spirituality?" For example, some men feel that to ask for help is unmanly and may feel that way with regard to the counseling they are getting. So, asking for God's help or praying to Jesus is unmanly. Gently challenging such beliefs and offering alternative perspectives may result in a change in his ideas about what it means to be self-reliant, allowing him to use religious coping and spirituality to deal with his problems. Here, the counselor is creating a pathway in Which increasing positive masculinity → religious/spiritual → behaviors → improved health and wellbeing. Increasing positive masculinity involves reframing masculinity beliefs, deconstructing negative aspects of masculinity, and reinforcing aspects of masculinity that support religious or spiritual behaviors.

When religion is the basis of one's masculinity ideology, addressing religious beliefs would be the focus. For example, the head of the family role as important to manhood and men's marital satisfaction may be particular to religious cultural contexts: for example, Muslims that base marital roles on the Qur'an (Siraj, 2010), Evangelical Christians that base marital roles on the Bible (Coltrane, 2001), and Mormon theology in which men are designated to be the spiritual leaders and heads of Mormon households (Heaton, 1988). When addressing religious beliefs, often it is about making sure the client is interpreting the religious tenets correctly, and evaluating the reality of his fears/anxieties about not being able to follow or uphold religious tenets related to manhood. Chapter 8 on gay men and religion provides examples of how religious beliefs about manhood can have an effect on men's psychological functioning. However, fulfilling expectations of manhood based on one's religious beliefs can manifest in heterosexual men's experiences of marital conflict, divorce, parenting, and being a provider. Here, the counselor is creating a pathway in which changing religious beliefs → positive masculine self-image → improved health and wellbeing. Ultimately, his religious beliefs must be in sync with his masculinity beliefs and behaviors.

The Path to Wellness

The path to wellness will sometimes involve clearing the path of obstacles, or it may involve creating a new path that was not there before. Religion and masculinity are obstacles when one's beliefs about God and what it means to be a man are getting in the way of a fulfilling life – when they are a source of stress and conflict. Counseling can help men identify and remove these obstacles, such as anger toward God, spiritual emptiness, spiritual struggles, gender role conflict, masculine gender role stress, and gender role conformity. Creating a new path that leads to health and wellbeing may consist of becoming involved (or more involved) in a faith community, developing a supportive peer network, using positive religious coping, having a new relationship with God, being able to forgive oneself and others, and changing one's masculinity ideology to one that is positive and constructive.

References

Cannon, A.J., Garcia, J., & Loberiza, F.R. (2015, May). *Interplay between spirituality and religiosity on the physical and mental well-being of cancer survivors post-treatment.* Program and abstracts of the 168th American Psychiatric Association Annual Meeting, Toronto, Ontario, Canada. Abstract 63.

Coltrane, S. (2001). Marketing the marriage "solution": Misplaced simplicity in the politics of fatherhood. *Sociological Perspectives, 44*(4), 387–418.

Estrada, F., & Arciniega, G.M. (2015). Positive masculinity among Latino men and the direct and indirect effects on well-being. *Journal of Multicultural Counseling and Development, 43*(3), 191–205.

Heaton, T.B. (1988). Four C's of the Mormon family: Chastity, conjugality, children, and chauvinism. In D.L. Thomas (ed.), *The religion and family connection: Social science perspectives* (pp. 107–124). Provo, UT: Religious Studies Center, Brigham Young University. Retrieved from https://rsc.byu.edu/archived/religion-and-family-connection-social-science-perspectives/chapter-6-four-c-s-mormon-family.

Salim, A., & Azra, A. (Eds.) (2003). *Shari'a and politics in modern Indonesia.* Singapore: Institute of Southeast Asian Studies.

Siraj, A. (2010). "Because I'm the man! I'm the head": British married Muslims and the patriarchal family structure. *Contemporary Islam, 4*(2), 195–214.

Wade, J.C., Suryani, L.K., & Lesmana, C.B.J. (2018). Religiosity, masculinity, and marital and life satisfaction among Balinese Hindu men. *International Journal of Research Studies in Psychology,* 7(1), 99–114.

Wade, J.C., & Wiloso, P.G. (2016). Religiosity, masculinity, and marital satisfaction among Javanese Muslim men. *International Journal of Research Studies in Psychology, 5*(3), 37–52.

Index